The PaTriarch

a Sicilian Tale

By

Anna Mione

authorHOUSE

1663 LIBERTY DRIVE, SUITE 200
BLOOMINGTON, INDIANA 47403
(800) 839-8640
www.authorhouse.com

First published by AuthorHouse 09/28/04

ISBN: 1-4184-4272-0 (sc)

Printed in the United States of America
Bloomington, Indiana

This book is printed on acid-free paper.

DEDICATION

This book is dedicated to Poppa..

Giovanni Battista Mione, born in Castellammare del Golfo in 1888, emigrated to America as a young man. He was illiterate, because he was the eldest and the strongest, was needed to tend the sheep, therefore was never educated like his brothers. Education in Sicily at the turn of the twentieth century was not compulsory.

When he came home from his job on the Staten Island Ferry boat, he brought home newspapers which had been discarded by the passengers. I found that to be strange since he couldn't read or write. When I asked, he smiled and said, "I look at the print, and I wonder what stories it's telling."

The history of the Sicilian immigration is also for my ten grandchildren, in chronological order: John Wesley Flagello, Dezi and Annie Sienty, Clifford Flagello, Kyle Petty, Nicolas Sienty, Sarah and Samantha Brittain, Gabriella and Dante Fekete.

EDITOR: Angela Vaccaro Darling

Angela has edited my first book and this, my fourth book. She is a talented writer and puts out her own journal. It was at her suggestion that I took the venue of electronic publishing.

TABLE OF CONTENTS

ACKNOWLEDGEMENT

Writing is a 'solo' activity, but as you plod ahead, you are no longer alone, because what follows is that the characters take over. Then the writer becomes the reporter who tells their stories.

Enter: The venue of verification of background facts, for which: the Staff of the East Fishkill Library , Catherine, Carol, Christine, Dee and others who occupied the reference desk, helped me research the history of New York in those years. .

East Harlem is where I grew up. The Sicilian experience then had to be authenticated by people who grew up there too. For that, my thanks to: Chris and Wanda Scalisi, Fritzi Mione Pietromonico; Rose Mione Maltese, and big cudos to one who wishes to remain anonymous, without whom I could not have written about Sean Quinn, Justin Deeks and the newspaper business of foreign correspondents and crime reporters.

My next ingredient was to collect willing participants to come aboard my "reading ship" while work was in progress.

They are:: Gene Flagello, Josine Fekete, Dante Flagello, Lillian Martino, Chris and Wanda Scalisi, Tess and Bernie Russo, Marge Bovino, Dianne Flagello Eileen and Aldo Di Tullio, Beth

Kennedy Umana and John Umana, Ann Kennedy, Bob and Carol Ernest, Elizabeth Mullee, Ralph Umana, Michael and Phyllis Donn..

In the research of subsequent facts for the rest of the trilogy, on jurisdiction on kidnapping cases, I thank my nephew, Brian Mullee, Federal Marshall, New York City.

My deep gratitude for the religious Catholic references to Father Mathew Ernest, ordained priest at St. Patrick's Church in New York, May, 2004.

The cover of the book, as well as my photograph on the back cover are from one of the best photographers in Dutchess County, Paul Stokes from the Hudson Valley Photo Studio.

The sketches of Mary and Vito Petracca were created by Dezi Sienty, soon to graduate from the school of Visual Arts in New York. He captured a subtle sense of their story in their expressions, I am well pleased.

Having spent most of my life without a computer, it was imperative that I learn how to use one in the writing of a book. I resisted for two months, but encouraged by my daughters and granddaughter Annie Sienty, I forged ahead and bought one.

I took a course in Microsoft Word and then as a support system once I was out on my own to record my story on a computer,

I was transported to the speed and efficacy of this medium. It is now, the only way I would write.

From my neighbors across the street, Ted Pennebaker a program expert for I.B.M. ran over any time I needed help. He was the Superman of cyber space for me, and no matter how late it was, he and Linda his wife came over and helped teach my computer to behave.

After Ted and Linda moved away, I frequently prevailed upon my granddaughter Annie Sienty to help me with the computer's capabilities. She was always there for me, and though she's away, she still helps me on the telephone.

Did I have the audacity to say that writing was a solo sport? Not so..

Cast of Characters:

Vito Petracca

Mary Gallo Petracca

CHILDREN:

Marco

Maggie

Philip

Tess

Sean Quinn: Mary's second husband

Grace Quinn: Sean and Mary's daughter

Dr. Mauro Gioia: Maggie's husband

Lorenzo and Gilda Gioia, Mauro's parents

Lorenzo and Vito Gioia: Mauro and Maggie's sons

Annina Petracca di Filipo: Vito's sister

Carlo di Filipo: Annina's husband

Piddu Vidannu: Vito's first cousin

Carmela Vidannu: Piddu's wife

Pina: Piddu and Carmela's daughter

Gaetano: Pina's husband

Petracca grandchildren:

Dr. Vito Petracca: Philip & Inchon's son

Luke Crespino: Marco and Vivian Petra's son.

Lorenzo & Vito: Mauro and Maggie's sons

Sean: son of Grace Quinn and Victor

Chapter I

The Wake: June 3, 1950

Mary Petracca looked out the kitchen window. The basil plants on the fire escape were sprouting. She touched the dirt and it was dry. The basil was wilted. Mary took the watering can out from under the sink and filled it. She watered the six small basil plants and watched them perk up as the water saturated their roots. At least she could see life in a plant.

The phone rang. It was Victor Cinque, the funeral director.

"Mary, it's me, Victor. Vito's ready."

Mary's husband, Vito, and Victor had been friends. They had socialized at the saloon on 107th Street and at the midtown gym, where Vito had boxed. Vito's sudden death had shaken Victor badly.

"The public viewing is from 2:00 to 4:00. You and the kids can come in at 1:30 for private time. Can I pick you up?" he asked sadly. His voice was raspy.

"No, thank you," Mary answered, "I'll be there with my children."

"I'll be outside my office waiting."

* * *

Marco and Philip had a light lunch of fresh mozzarella and tomatoes. Tess, the youngest, wept intermittently. Maggie, eighteen, was detached, as though she weren't part of the scene. Mary hadn't cried since she learned of Vito's dying the day before. Cause of death? The coroner had said "heart attack." Vito had been the picture of health, physically fit, a man who, at fifty, was in the prime of his life.

The only manifestation of Mary's intense depression was that she couldn't focus on what had happened. She busied herself with menial tasks, doing some twice, fussing over her plants on the fire escape, washing a pot over and over. She was in shock. She had prepared chicken soup with ditalini pasta for the family. Tess came into the kitchen, composed and wearing the camouflage of makeup. She sat at the table and sipped the soup. Maggie couldn't meet anyone's eyes. They ate lunch in silence. Philip, the nineteen year old, struggled to put his tie on. His hands shook, exposing his inner turmoil. His older brother, Marco, helped him. Philip looked even more slender than usual in his black suit. Marco, the classical violinist of the family, was used to black suits which he wore in his work on the concert stage.

Maggie, the rebel, was wearing a brown dress with a white collar.

"That's not an appropriate color, Maggie," Mary said.

"Your father died," Marco snapped, "put the damned black dress on." Maggie refused, and Mary intercepted "Let it go, son."

Marco's face was red with rage. Even at this tragic moment she had to buck the traditions? He wanted to slap her face, but Mary's hand on his arm calmed him down.

At 1:30, the family left the building on 107th Street and walked around the block to the funeral parlor on 106th Street. Victor was waiting outside and escorted Mary while her children paired off in twos as they approached the casket.

Mary hyperventilated with suppressed sobs. Marco urged his mother to let it out. "Cry, Momma. Don't hold it in."

Mary knelt. She touched Vito's cold hands that were holding rosary beads. "Vito," she whispered. He looked as though he were asleep. Mary stood up and Marco knelt, said a prayer, and then sat down in the first row of chairs facing the casket. Then Maggie and Tess knelt down. Tess wept as Maggie put her arm around her sister. Maggie couldn't cry.

Philip wouldn't look at his father. He had never seen a dead person before. As a child he was terrified by wakes. So when the family had to attend them, Philip remained in the lobby with a book. Mary's biggest concern was how he would deal with his own father's wake. Mary sat down next to her sons. She held Philip's hand. His eyes looked towards the floor. Maggie looked at her watch. It was almost time for the doors to open for the public viewing.

Maggie hated public displays of emotion. "Get a hold of yourself, Tess," she said. Tess wiped her eyes and put her sunglasses on. Maggie helped her to the chair next to where their mother was sitting.

"Maggie, how can you be so controlled?" Tess commented.

Maggie turned slowly toward her. "You deal with it as you wish. I hate these barbaric three day wakes, okay? Crying isn't going to bring Poppa back. There'll be neighbors here to take score on our sorrow. You'll win first prize, you know."

Tess smiled. "Oh, God, Maggie, you're so predictable."

Mary told them not to talk, she could hear the mourners coming in. People entered in single file. They knelt at the casket, greeted the widow, expressed their condolences, then sat and socialized with all the *paesani* in the group. Floral displays filled the room within an hour.

Joe Marra, vice president of Vito's construction union, walked in with his wife, Gina, and their two children, Joey and Dee Dee. Joe wept profusely as he and his wife knelt at the casket. When he turned to face Mary, he enveloped her in his arms and wept again.

"I'm so sorry, Mary, I'm so sorry."

Mary felt for Joe. He had been Vito's shadow.

Maggie raised her eyebrow and whispered to Tess, "How's that for an act? Totally befitting the second in command at the union. Wow! Joe Marra gets an A plus."

Tess stifled a smile. She mused that this was Maggie's way of coping, putting her sorry on hold while she commented sarcastically on the Sicilian drama unfolding before them.

Maggie recalled how family members talked aloud to the cadaver, telling him to say hello to other deceased members of the family. She shared her observations with Tess who welcomed the levity of Maggie's point of view.

Philip diffused his sorrow by observing how the mourners dressed. He made mental notes of people who came in black with brown shoes. A real fashion no-no. He almost laughed at the sight of a ripped hem on a dress or crooked seams on stockings. He even spotted a safety pin on a torn hem. He covered his mouth so that he wouldn't laugh aloud.

On the third night, the mourners paid their last respects. As they lined up to say a final short prayer before the casket, Mary shook, as a chill came over her. Fans circulated the stagnant sweet air of flowers in the funeral parlor, which made the crowded room a tad cooler. Two hundred people had come to pay their respects to Vito.

During the first two days of the wake, Vito Petracca had looked as though he were asleep, but on the third day he wore the pallor of death.

"Momma," Philip whispered, "I gotta get out of here. I'm sick of this."

"Philip we're burying him tomorrow," Mary whispered, "There'll be talk."

"I need fresh air," he said and then quickly walked out. The mourners took note of his hurried exit.

Philip took a run around the block, and returned just as it was time for the rosary by St. Ann's parish priest.

Just before Father Pistella came to the casket, the hum of conversation in the room diminished. A young woman, tall, blonde, probably in her thirties, and not Sicilian, rushed in, stood for a moment by the coffin, then turned and left.

She did not acknowledge the Petracca family. Her brief appearance left questions in the minds of the neighbors. Who was she? Had Vito had someone on the side? Had Mary known? The questions bounced off the minds of the assemblage of mourners as fast as a ball in a ping pong game. The back of Mary's neck tingled. She heard her daughters.

"Who is she?" Tess whispered to Maggie.

Maggie snapped, "Probably the bitch who kept Poppa busy on weekends."

Mary was appalled. She didn't want Vito's secret life to be discussed in front of the casket with people all around.

"His obituary was in the *Daily News*," she whispered firmly. "Your father knew many people."

Her daughters, intuitively obeying Mary's unspoken request for *omerta* (silence), said nothing more.

Philip had returned to his seat and Mary put her hand in his. He gave his mother a weary look as though he could not bear it any longer.

"Soon it will be over, Philip," Mary reassured him. Philip grimaced as he faced the coffin again. "I know, I know," he said and pulled his hand away. Marco gave him a reassuring pat on the back. "You're doing good, Philip," he said. "I know that inside your gut you're screaming, but for Momma you hid it."

"Want my observation?" Philip answered. "Most of these people respected Poppa by showing up, wearing black. But a couple of *cafoni* came in torn hems and crooked seams. So much for proper decorum."

Marco was relieved to see that Philip was able to distract himself. Marco smiled. "And that's what kept you grounded, the hems and the seams?"

Philip nodded and Marco whispered, "Good for you, Philip. Momma was worried."

Philip muttered, "I know."

The final ritual was Father Pistella's recitation of the rosary, and the words of comfort to Mary and the family. After Father left, Victor announced that it was time to pay their final respects to VIto. People shuffled out of their chairs and quietly lined up for the final goodbye to Vito Petracca. The procession lasted close to 45 minutes. It was past closing time, but Victor did not hurry the mourners. After the last mourner left, Mary and her children walked up to the casket, bowed their heads in prayer, and Mary looked at her husband and said, "Vito, I **did** love you."

Maggie gasped as she heard her mother's words. "Dear God!" she whispered to Tess. "Now she tells him." Tess pulled away and felt a chill sweep over her body. She ran back to the coffin, and Maggie joined her. "Tess, let's go home." They did not speak further but went out together and joined Philip, Marco, and Mary.

At their eight room tenement apartment on 107th Street near the Third Avenue El, the children said goodnight and went to their respective bedrooms. Mary sat alone at the table in the kitchen, dimly lit by the small lamp on the china closet, and stared outside the window at the basil plants on the iron fire escape. She was pleased that the watering had brought them back to life. "Vito," she uttered, "I'm so sorry."

Mary's tears fell slowly, then continued for some time. Marco entered the darkened kitchen and, watching his mother, felt relieved to see her cry. Private, stoic, and genteel, Mary hid her emotions from everyone. Mary had hidden her feelings for years, and now that she broke down in her sorrow, it was a healing for Marco to see how deeply his mother loved his father.

She stood by the window seemingly staring at the lights streaming out of the kitchen windows facing the back yard. She could see movement in the kitchens facing her back yard from 108th Street. In the silence of the night through the open windows, she could even hear the neighbors' conversations. Even though she could not understand every word, she heard her name mentioned several times. Numb from the turmoil within her, she shut her eyes and gripped the window frame to regain her balance. She felt as though she was standing on a peninsula that had suddenly broken away from the mainland. She was alone, a state of mind she had felt for most of her life. Now he was gone. She could not depend on the children, not when they were planning to flee the nest, and their father not even buried yet. She felt Marco's hands on her shoulders.

"Momma, do you want company?" he asked as he steadied her swaying body.

"No, I'm alright. Please go to bed, Marco," she said without turning around.

He kissed her cheek, and murmured that he wasn't sleepy. He made a small pot of tea for the two of them, and they sipped it in the glow of the backyard lights casting shadows in their kitchen.

Marco was deeply concerned about leaving his mother. His siblings talked about leaving right after the burial, but Marco asked them to hold off for a few days. They clearly had made a choice fifteen years ago, when Vito and Mary had made an emotional split in their marriage.

"Momma, I worry about you," he said as he kissed her hand.

"Don't! Sicilian women are made of mortar and brick." She barely looked at him as they faced the back yard sipping their chamomile tea.

"Momma, I need to know something. When did you and my father end your marriage?" He studied her stoic expression and noticed a twinge in her cheek.

She stared at him for a while, her expression blank as a slate. The Sicilian tradition of covering up husband and wife's intimate relationships from the children controlled what they wanted their children to believe.

"Your father and I slept in the same room, in twin beds. Your question is an intrusion and an insult to his memory."

She pulled away from Marco, and went to her bedroom. He followed her, and tried to put his arms around her, but she was stiff, unbending, as though she had been ironed and starched like a shirt. Marco could only imagine what his mother was feeling.

"Momma, Poppa loved you. When we went out he'd say, 'Your mother would love this panorama.' I just want you to know that. Look, I didn't mean to intrude in your lives," he added.

"Marco, we judge a book by the cover. We don't know what's between the pages. I don't have to explain my life to my children. Ever!" Her comment precluded further discourse. He said good night and retired to his bedroom.

The eight room apartment in East Harlem on 107th Street had been custom-made for them by the men in the construction union on 104th Street. Each child had his own room. Vito had a den with a couch and a large desk with a reading lamp which is where he worked on his papers and speeches for the construction union. Often, Vito worked past midnight, then slept on the couch. Both Vito and Mary had tried to keep their sleeping arrangements from the children.

Vito had owned the building on 107th Street and several buildings in the neighborhood. Now everything was in Mary's name. Mary was well taken care of financially. He had set it up so that she would never be dependent on her children. Like many Sicilians, Vito had trusted no one with his affairs, so he had worked into the night taking care of his own rent receipts and keeping his own books. He had been meticulous, and though Mary was not troubled about finances while he was alive, he wanted her to take over after his death. It was as though he had had a premonition.

Mary had difficulty going to sleep after the wake. Her mind raced back to her son's question: "When did you and Poppa separate?" How tired she was in those early days. Married at 15 years old to a man twice her age, she had known nothing.

Her father, an illiterate, ignorant peasant from Sicily, had had a mean streak in him. He had married late in life, and when Mary was born, he had been furious. Therefore he solicited prospective husbands for his daughter when she was fifteen. After two meetings he had arranged a marriage for Mary with Vito Petracca, an older widower from Castellamare Del Golfo.

Mary and Vito had spent their wedding night at a hotel in Palermo. They had dined at the posh hotel restaurant. He had bought her a diamond ring as well as a matching wedding ring. Vito had taken her to a *sarta* who had a few ready made sample dresses, which he had purchased for her. Their wedding vows had been exchanged in Corleone, in a crude simple setting.

Before Vito came into her life Mary had never experienced kindness or love from any human being. For both of them, it was love at first sight On their wedding night, Mary had shed not only her virginal veil, but her emotional one culminating in a rapture they could only have imagined.

* * *

The next morning, the family arose early and got ready for the final event in the ritual: the last goodbye to the Patriarch before burial.

As they walked to the funeral parlor, the neighbors filed in behind Mary. The last blessing was given by the priest, while the limousines waited outside for the family and close friends to take them to the church. The lead limo passed slowly in front of the construction union headquarters on 104th Street and then drove in front of the tenement building on 107th Street near the corner of Third Avenue.

Everyone took his place in church and Mary, whose face was well- hidden by the thick black lace veil, sat on the left, flanked by Marco on her left, Philip on her right, and Tess and Maggie next to Philip.

Visibly moved, Father Pistella spoke about Vito Petracca with warmth, fond memories, and anecdotes of memorable exchanges they had had. Father spoke of the altruistic parishioner who came to Mass early, who was generous, and often volunteered to do repair work on St. Ann's school and the rectory.

"Vito Petracca will not easily be forgotten. He often spoke of his family with pride and joy and always with tears shining in his eyes. Vito loved children and was generous at Christmas with needy neighborhood kids.. At the union, he collected boxes of gloves and mufflers for them.

This man has left an impact on all of us as an example of a good soul, a loving father, and a loyal husband. I, for one, will miss him. But we rejoice and celebrate his life and thank God that we have had him in our lives. Let us pray..."

At communion, Mary lifted her veil and her face reflected the anguish she felt. No amount of facial powder and rouge could hide her sorrow. Her children were taken aback by seeing their mother so vulnerable.

After the final benediction, and in paradism, they filed out quietly after the casket. The caravan of cars followed the hearse to Calvary Cemetery in Queens.

The group of about one hundred mourners gathered around the grave site as Father Pistella gave his final commendation for the soul of Vito Petracca. The casket was lowered into mother earth as each person dropped a flower into the grave. Mary could hardly stand up as she watched the grave digger shovel earth on top of the casket. She slid down between her sons, who pulled her up. This vulnerability did not go unnoticed by the mourners, for all eyes were on Mary.

They drove back to the union headquarters where a reception was held for Mary, her family, and friends, a final closure to Vito's life.

After the meal, everyone went to Mary and told her that she was not alone, and that she should feel free to ask for anything from them. In particular, Vito's replacement, Joe Marra, a man in his fifties, reassured the children that Mary would be taken care of by him and his wife.

Mary was grateful for the neighbors' kind words and Joe Marra's offer to help, but she knew that they all would go back to their own lives as soon as they got home. The cycle of life, death, and mourning, would pass and by tomorrow each one would resume his life as though nothing had ever happened. Vito's life would be buried, like his body, and he would only be a memory to everyone, but to Mary he had left a gaping hole in her heart. She looked back at the mistakes she and Vito had made, she'd re-live the past in the next few months.

Chapter II

Mary Has Flashbacks

On Thursday, after the funeral, Mary was alone in her husband's den. As she went through the neat pile of books, she was astounded at the meticulous way he had organized every receipt and entry, accompanied by notes attached with paper clips. Had he known something? Was he sick? He had never complained to her, but then, they had not been close in any way. With intimacy between them gone, they had become like strangers sharing living quarters. Vito wrote:

"Mary, our five family house in Throgs Neck is being taken care of by Carlo Mendez. He lives in the basement and does maintenance on the apartments. He also gets a small salary. Schlomo Schwarz makes out the checks. Ask him to take you to the property. Deal directly with Carlo. The personal touch is best. Don't worry, you'll be fine."

It was strange to see his handwritten notes to her, because it was as though he was reaching out from the grave, helping her. Mary shut her eyes, and visualized Vito sitting opposite her at his desk gently explaining the process of stepping into his shoes.

She felt the salty tears stream down her face and into her lips. Mary took her handkerchief out of her housedress pocket, and wiped her face, recalling the deep feelings she once had for Vito, a man who had rescued her from her abusive home.

Mary recalled the exact moment of the emotional schism. It was right after Tess was born and she was feeling the stress of having a fourth child. The thought of going through another pregnancy frightened her. Birth control was out of the question according to Vito. These thoughts filled her mind one day as she exposed her breast to feed the baby and Vito walked into the bedroom, his eyes filled with adoration at the tenderest of scenes of a mother nursing her child. He had knelt next to Mary, kissed her face and caressed the baby's head. "Madonna and child," he had whispered lovingly. Mary had told him never to touch her again. "No more intimacy," she had said.

Vito stood up slowly as though he was in a dream-like state as he heard his wife's directive. He grew pale with shock, and ran out of the house. When he returned at midnight, he packed a bag, and as Mary tried to stop him from leaving, he pushed her aside, and walked out. After a sleepless night of anguish, Mary's immediate intent was to lash out at him in the most hurtful way: the bedroom.

The next morning Mary was up at 6:00. The children were sleeping and she felt like a caged tiger wanting to strike out. Her new tenants, a family just arrived from Sicily, had recently moved into their building, and because they had no funds, they slept on the floor of the apartment. Mary ran downstairs to the first floor, knocked on the door, and when the lady of the house answered, she offered to give them her bedroom set immediately.

Within an hour, they had cleared out every stick of furniture from Mary's bedroom and brought it to their apartment downstairs. When they wanted to repay her, Mary asked them to watch her children while she went shopping. On Third Avenue under the El, she walked into a furniture store, purchased twin beds and two end tables which they delivered within the hour.

On Sunday night, Vito returned. He had done a good deal of soul searching. He could not accept Mary's directive not to touch her again. He was still in love with her, and he was ready to negotiate how they could live together and not procreate. This time, he was ready to comply with her request for birth control. Mary was putting the children to bed. He walked in quietly and waited for her in the kitchen. Mary had never expected Vito to come home. She couldn't even look at him.

"So, you're back," she said flatly, and looked away.

"Mary, for heaven's sake, look at me. I had time to think." Feigning exhaustion, she yawned, covering her mouth with the back of her hand. She started to walk away, but he held her arm. "Let go, Vito. I'm exhausted." Vito was suspicious of her icy reception.

He took off his shoes, left them under the table, and followed his wife to the bedroom. Tonight he would make love to her, and their passion would soothe their wounded pride.

He froze as he walked into the dimly lit bedroom and saw his wife lying on a twin bed.

"Where's the furniture?" he asked, looking around the room. "What have you done with our bedroom set?"

"I gave it away," she answered. "You can sleep in the other twin bed near the wall." Vito was incredulous. This was a nightmare. Was he mad to allow her to reject him twice? He was determined that he would not give her the satisfaction of falling apart in front of her.

"I see." Vito's voice was husky. "This is your bedroom from now on. You can give away the other bed, I won't step foot in here again. I'll sleep in the den. There's no marriage. This was your choice." He pulled his clothes out of the closet and threw them to the floor. He saw his socks and underwear packed in cardboard boxes in the corner of the room and emptied them all over the floor. Mary was aghast and turned her back so she wouldn't see his frenetic actions of spite.

"Tomorrow take my things to the den," Vito said. "I want my clothes neatly in a drawer. I shall never step in here again." Mary was devastated as her impulsive act of retaliation boomeranged against her.

"Vito?" Mary sat at the edge of the bed, "Are you leaving me?"

"My four kids are here," he responded. He took his handkerchief out of his back pocket, wiped his nervous sweat, and with a very controlled tone of voice, he said, "Tonight, Mary Gallo, you castrated me." Mary winced at his choice of words, and she knew in her heart that their marriage was over.

Vito Petracca moved to a tenement building on Mulberry street where he spent weekends. Through his friends at the Sicilian club he met and co-habitated with a young divorced woman named Martha Pederson. She became pregnant, and asked him to divorce his wife and marry her. He refused. "I'm Catholic. I believe in one marriage, but for appearances and to save face in this neighborhood, you can tell everyone that we're married, and I'll get you a wedding ring." Martha grew resentful at this arrangement, was consoled by the fact that at least he was there financially and on weekends.

After their baby girl, Vivian, was born, Vito wheeled the baby carriage through the Village every weekend with his "wife" hanging on his arm

* * *

Martha knew about Mary, but Mary didn't know about Martha. Yet Mary suspected that Vito had set up a domestic arrangement somewhere else. He seemed smug when he came home. Even without the legal termination of their marriage, they were emotionally divorced.

Martha and Vito's arrangement ended two years after its inception. Vito was torn over the situation. He had never stopped loving Mary and missed their relationship. He tried to approach Mary through their mutual love of family, but she remained distant. With generations of an unforgiving Sicilian mentality, the word vendetta was a part of his belief system. Vito was torn apart by his desire to make amends and opposing his tradition. Forgiveness was not an option.

On Sunday nights, he'd return to his home on 107th Street. Often, after the family slept, he'd go to Mary's bedroom, look in at her, and sometimes, if she had kicked off the covers, he'd pick up the blanket and cover her again, and slip back into his den. He thought about her soul once more wrapped in a cocoon of survival. He missed the woman he had married. More and more, Vito began to see his plight as impenetrable. He looked to the past for answers to the enigma which his wife had become.

He remembered her frequent nightmares, and her abusive childhood, which she'd rarely talk about. He recognized Mary's survival techniques of withdrawal, and a deadly affect when she felt threatened. As a child, Mary witnessed a rooster who had chased a 300 pound pig squealing and grunting down the hill of Corleone. She had burst out laughing until her mother ran out and twisted her arm to stop her laughter.

"Get in the house! Your father is not home. You're acting like a *puttana*. What will the neighbors think?"

After that incident Mary covered her mouth when she laughed so that she wouldn't look like a *puttana*.

When Mary married Vito, and left her parents in Corleone, she had buried them long before they were dead.

* * *

After the funeral, Mary's daily routine was a busy one. She looked to Joe Marra for advice and friendship. His presence became a daily part of her life. He called, he stopped by for coffee and talk. He fixed things around the house on his way home from work. He schooled Mary on the number of tenants who paid her rent, and the composition of the family numbers in each apartment. All of this was written in Vito's log.

The girls were invited by Gina and Joe Marra for a two week vacation in Cape Cod, along with their son, Joe, and their daughter, Dee Dee, who was Maggie's friend.

Mary called the telephone company to put in an additional phone in her bedroom, as well as in the kitchen. Marco came back from his tour, delighted to see more phones in the sprawling apartment.

The girls came home from Cape Cod and Mary welcomed them.

"You have a beautiful tan," she said, embracing her daughters. "I'm glad that you had a good time, but I'm also happy that you're home."

"Momma, thanks," Maggie said.

Tess just wrapped her arms around her mother and whispered, "I missed you."

Mary had saved the picture post cards they had sent her from Cape Cod. One postcard had a recipe for clam chowder on it. Mary had never heard of this particular fish soup. It was a New England soup. Mary asked about the food they had eaten.

"Fish, Momma, everybody eats fish there," Maggie said. "and it's ten times better than New York fish. We ate it every day. That's why I sent you the recipe. Please make it, Momma."

Maggie said that Cape Cod smelled differently. The ocean was so beautiful that they had taken a ride on a small ferry boat close to the coast line. Sailboats dotted the seascape. Maggie brought her mother a painting of a fishing boat on the Cape. Tess gave her mother a set of coffee cups from Cape Cod. It was good to see her daughters in such good spirits again. The change of scenery had done them good.

Philip now took over part of the den as his office. His purchase of a dress factory, which Vito Petracca had talked about buying for his son, was about to go into contract and he was nervous about it. He would have felt more secure if Poppa had been alive. Joe Marra accompanied him to the dress factory, but when they returned, Philip seemed upset. The idea of running and owning a dress factory was more than he could handle. He was only nineteen years old. Even though most dress operators were Italian immigrants, would they respect a boss who was young enough to be their own kid?

Mary let him vent his feelings after he visited the prospective business. "You don't have to do this," she said. Philip was relieved. "I think, Momma, that it was Poppa's idea, and not mine. I tried so hard to please him." Mary caressed Philip's face, "No Philip, follow your heart." Philip laughed sardonically, "How could I, mom? I wanted to be a ballet dancer, but he said only sissies do that." Mary frowned, "Oh Philip, how sad."

Pieces of recent scenes in her family played like a trailer in a movie in Mary's mind, and as they played she saw layers of Vito she had never seen before because they had been too close to her.

* * *

The next day, Maggie had a rare private moment with her mother. It was a novelty because Maggie had always been closest to Vito. Mary seemed more relaxed and certainly less tense than when Vito was alive. It was noticed by her children, particularly, Maggie.

"Momma, you've changed, haven't you?" Maggie said. "Yes, I have Maggie. I'm trying to step into Poppa's shoes, and it's not easy, but come to me, okay?" Mary studied Maggie's face. Her daughter peered at Mary as though she was trying to figure her out.

"I want to live in the city," Maggie said.

"Sure. Poppa would have agreed to that," Mary answered.

"Do you miss him Momma?" Maggie asked.

"Yes," Mary answered. Maggie was surprised.

"Mom, you told him you loved him at the funeral parlor. I was shocked." "We drifted apart Maggie," Mary explained, "but we loved each other."

"And you waited until he was dead to tell him? Damn!" Maggie's eyes flooded with tears and Mary was touched to see emotion from her stoic child.

"We couldn't fix it," Mary said. At least Mary wasn't hiding behind that thick Sicilian wall of silence any more.

"Was he sick, Momma?' she asked.

"No, I don't think so. He worked out at the gym and boxed with other men." She paused. Revealing intimate details of her life with Vito was difficult for her. "We didn't share the same bedroom after Tess was born." Mary looked down on her lap, wringing her handkerchief into a tight twisted form. Maggie reached over and held her mother's hand.

"Momma, we weren't stupid. We knew Poppa slept in the den."

Mary was embarrassed. It was seldom that Maggie engaged her mother in any kind of dialogue, and she felt that discussing her problematic marriage with Maggie was a beginning. Though uncomfortable with it, at least they were communicating.

Maggie had a burning question, one she had to ask so that she could put her parents fractured relationship to rest.

"Momma," Maggie pressed on, "if you had to do it over again, would you have tried to make up with Poppa?" Mary said "Yes."

Maggie sighed "God, I needed to hear that."

In view of Mary's answer, Maggie felt that now was the time to repeat a confidence which her father had asked her never to reveal.

She described a private moment in her father's life when at midnight she had come into the kitchen for a glass of milk.

"I heard footsteps and I got scared. I saw Poppa in your bedroom, tucking the bed covers around you. When he saw me, he swore me to secrecy, then explained that when you had nightmares you kicked the blankets off."

"I'm glad you told me. I, too, needed to hear that." Mary said.

* * *

The following week, Joe Marra picked up Mary and they took their daughters Dee Dee Marra and Maggie to a real estate agent who found the girls an apartment near Columbia University on 124th Street. It was small, but adequate for the two girls. During the summer, Dee Dee, swept along by Maggie's enthusiasm about a glamorous exciting career as a reporter, had decided to major in journalism also.

The one child whose ambivalence worried Mary was Philip. He wanted to become a women's fashion designer. He was young, but he had his dreams thwarted so many times that Mary was amenable to anything he wanted to pursue, as long as it was his own wish.

Philip spoke about the field of women's fashion being wide open now. Since World War II, America had spawned its own designers and fashions and he wanted a piece of that pie of creativity. Mary was pleased. Philip wanted to go to school for fashion. He moved to an apartment on West 12th Street near his school so that he could tumble out of bed and go to classes. Philip's enthusiasm for fashion was infectious. By Christmas, Mary was wearing makeup and when she got dressed, she looked fashionable.

Mary went into Vito's den, and searched through his frequently used reference books, one of which was an American dictionary. She took it off the shelf and flipped the pages to see if another letter might be there. Towards the back, she found one, and kicked off her shoes, put her feet on the desk as Vito used to do, and hungered for the 'voice' of her late husband.

"Mary! I don't know how to begin this letter. We talk, and we say nothing. We look, and we don't touch, we want each other, and we deny ourselves.

But the memory of how it was in the beginning was so joyful, that I wanted it back. After you told me not to touch you again, I ran off, and I cried like hell as I ran along the East River. When I came back I had a splitting headache, and I didn't know what to do, but I couldn't stay home. So I packed, took a cab and went to a hotel. I spent the weekend in New York, went to a bar, and spent most of my time in the gym, beating the hell out of my boxing bag.

When I came back, I had gotten rid of most of my anger, and I was ready to make up. I wanted you, and I was ready to use birth control to give you the peace you needed, even though I didn't like to. I walked in the bedroom, and in one weekend, you told me no more intimacies, and you got rid of our furniture, a gift I had given you when we first came to America. You made it very clear that you didn't want me any more. I had needs. I'm a man, and so I made another life for myself on weekends. I wish I hadn't. It wasn't good.I wanted you back, but I didn't want to grovel at your feet. I had my pride, so I did nothing.

If anything happens to me Mary, I want you to know that you were the love of my life. Once we were the envy of all who knew us. I regret we never gave it a second chance. *T'amo sempre*, Vito."

After Mary read the letter, she went to her bedroom, lay down and shut her eyes. There had been so many signs through the years, and she saw them and repelled them, only because her pride was hurt. She knew he was occupied on weekends with someone else, and it hurt like a knife in her heart. She would not be his wife as long as he had a concubine on the side. Their pride created an impasse in their lives, one that neither one was culturally equipped to circumvent.

Chapter III

An Aborted Affair

Dec. 1950

It was close to Christmas. The children were all away and Mary had grown comfortable in the role of overseer to her properties. Vito had purchased a large apartment house in Eastchester the year before he died. The fifty apartments were the bulk of the Petracca estate. The building was one of the most prestigious in the town, attracting young married couples. Most were war veterans who were seeking to upscale their living quarters.

Every Saturday Joe Marra took Mary to Eastchester so that each tenant could meet his landlady. In the two bedroom apartments there were young children and sometimes older, childless couples. It was a good mix of tenants, all of whom worked and were productive. They kept their quarters clean, and Vito had contracted to have the hallways and stairs washed every Saturday morning from 3:00 a.m. until 6:00 a.m.

One Saturday, Joe was nervous and Mary sensed it.

"Joe, something bothering you?" she asked as they drove uptown to the Willis Avenue Bridge.

"No. How do you like my new Chrysler?" he asked. It was a large, comfortable car with a radio.

"Beautiful!" she said. Indeed, the seats felt like a sofa, plush and very comfortable. "When did you get it?" she asked.

"Last week. I was sick and tired of the bomb I was driving, and I figured, hey, the hell with this, let me get the new Chrysler. I swear to God, everybody in the neighborhood whistles when I pass by. Nice color green, wouldn't you say?" he asked as he caressed the dashboard.

"What did Gina say?" Mary asked.

"She asked me who I was going to take in it?"

He squirmed as he blurted out a cleaned up version of what she had really said.

"She's right," Mary said. "You spend far too much time with me. I'm ready to fly solo here, and I think we should make this the last time we meet." She felt her face grow hot. Funny how she had thought of appearances just this morning when Joe had called to verify their date. She also sensed that Joe was very interested in her. He managed to constantly touch or caress her and he made it look casual, but Mary's sixth sense was working.

"Mary, when I walk out of the house, she's accusing me of sleeping with every *puttana* from here to Mulberry street. How the hell-sorry, I don't mean to use bad words in front of you, Mary. I have to live with her, so we'll meet somewhere else outside of the block. Okay? I promised Vito I'd take care of you, and no wife's gonna tell me how I should conduct my business."

"Pay attention to your wife's needs. Marriages sour that way, Joe. It's not worth it."

"Is that what happened to you?" he asked. But Mary looked out the window and didn't answer. He was mortified.

"I was out of line, wasn't I?"

She answered, "Yes, Joe."

Joe explained to Mary that he, too, was on the payroll. Schlomo the accountant, made out a monthly check. "The week before Vito died, he left written instructions for me to help you. He loved you, Mary, it's too bad you didn't..." Joe realized that he had said too much. "God!" he uttered, "I have a big mouth."

"Joe, you keep doing it. We loved each other, Joe. I don't ask about your marriage, do I?" She was uncomfortable and she realized she was becoming more so each time they were together.

They got to the Eastchester building and visited designated tenants who were expecting Mary. One tenant verbalized his surprise at her youth. Graciously, they showed Mary their rental units so that she knew the physical outlay of the building. She was impressed with the condition of the building and how well it was maintained.

After six tenants had been visited briefly, they left Eastchester through the scenic route of the Bronx River Parkway. It was glorious. The trees were heavy with snow, and the embankments on the side of the road looked like billowing white pillows. Where the snow had turned to ice, it reflected the bright light of the sun creating a blue-white sash across the landscape.

Joe took the Tuckahoe exit to Garofolo's Italian Restaurant for a hot luncheon. Mike and Lena Garofolo had been *paesani* from Corleone, and Lena was Gina Marra's second cousin.

Mary and Joe walked in at noon. Mike came over and embraced Mary and kissed her on both cheeks. He brought over a bottle of dry white wine imported from Italy to be served with antipasto--a huge platter of fish arranged on the rim of the plate and the hot fried fish in the center. Mary told Joe she could not eat anything else after the antipasto, but Joe was hungry. He ordered several courses for himself.

When the spaghetti with clam sauce came, Joe rolled some up on his fork and offered it to Mary, feeding her himself. The proprietor didn't take his eyes off her. She was beautiful, gracious, and genteel. She looked better than when he had seen her in the funeral parlor.

Lena Garofolo was told that Joe Marra and Vito's widow were in the restaurant. "Oh, my God! I'll be right out. Joe's losing no time, is he?" she added.

Lena had grown up with Joe Marra in Corleone, and they even had mutual relatives through marriage. She wiped her hands on her apron and walked to the table. Joe got up and gave Lena a big bear hug. He picked her up like a child and lifted her above his head. She giggled and screeched.

"When the hell are you gonna stop growing?" she teased as he lowered her slowly.

"When you guys stop feeding me this good," he retorted.

Lena swatted him with her white towel. Joe introduced Lena to Mary. Lena bent across the table and Mary stood up as they embraced.

"I'm so sorry about Vito, Mary. We couldn't both come, so Mike came. You come here any time, even without this big lug. Don't feel that you're alone, okay?"

Mary smiled warmly. "How nice of you, Lena. Thank you so much." Joe's arm went around Mary's shoulder, and Lena told them to sit. She called to her waiter "Petru, get the Sambucca, oh, and don't forget two shot glasses." The waiter did as he was asked.

Joe kissed Lena's hand. "Thank you, Lena."

She turned to Joe and beckoned him with her finger. Joe got up and Lena whispered, "Next time, bring Gina, too. I haven't seen her in years. You two okay?" she asked.

Joe got flustered once more as she stared at him with a disapproving look.

"Jesus, Lena. A guy takes a friend out for lunch, and he's having an affair? Come on, gimme a break," he retorted.

"Listen, you big lug, if the shoe fits wear it. You can't pull the wool over my eyes. You got the hots for her. Go, get the hell outta here. She looks needy. Don't take advantage, okay, you *shimunitu*!" He tapped her on her rear end and she swatted him with the towel laughing as she walked away. Lena gave Mike the high sign, the kind of look between husband and wife which needed no dialogue. He took care of some business out front and then went into the kitchen.

"What?" he asked Lena. "No," she retorted, "You what? Where the hell is Gina? Did they split?" she asked.

"What are you nuts? Joe's taking care of Mary's business. He's on Vito's payroll."

"You sure it's not funny business?" She gave him a sideways glance. Mike laughed out loud.

"You read too many romance novels, Lena. Nothing's going on." "You bet your ass it is," she said.

He shook his head in disbelief. "Watch your mouth." "Screw that. Watch him." She nudged her husband as they walked to the kitchen door with the glass inset. "See? He's sitting close to her, he just wiped the corner of her mouth, and he looks like a bull in heat. Mike, you know what you're full of?" Mike put his hand on her mouth.

"Don't say it." He laughed and walked away. At 4:00, lunch was over for Joe and Mary. He asked for the check, and Mike only charged him for the food. The wine and liquor were on the house out of respect for Vito Petracca.

Joe had his arm around Mary as they walked to the car. He staggered to the car.

"Drunk!" Lena said to Mike. "He drank a bottle of wine by himself. Damn it! Mike, Mary's scared. Did you see her face?"

Lena and Mike ran to the door to see if the body language suggested anything other than a friendship. Mike didn't see the subtle signals which, to Lena, were as clear as a sunny day for Lena.

"Look! Look! She tugged at his arm. See his hand rub her back and drop down to her cute ass as though his arm was too heavy and it fell down? Oh, Mike, *quando mossi* (what an act!)"

Mike threw his hands up in despair. "Lena, you're hopeless. Remember the night you told me about the happiest couple in the neighborhood? The next week the wife came in crying because her husband had walked out after that beautiful romantic dinner where he bought her flowers and the most expensive wine in the house. Think of something else, wouldja? You listen to all those operas and you begin to believe them. You can't go by appearances. *Madonna mia,* what an imagination," he said as he walked away.

"Bullshit!" Lena said as she watched the big Chrysler drive away, "Sure!" she said to herself "he's been driving a bomb all this time, and now he's in this expensive car, and who's the first woman he puts in it? Petracca's widow. Hey, Mike!" she called as she went back to the kitchen to grab a bite to eat now that there were no more customers.

Mike set the table for the two of them and told her to eat. But she went on and on about Joe, and Mike had no recourse but to block her out.

Joe and Mary drove back to East Harlem, and Mary brought up the subject of Vito's mistress. Joe was astounded. He wanted to know how she knew, and Mary answered, "a wife knows." How right she was, Joe thought. Mary told Joe that she wanted to meet Vito's mistress.

"Why, Mary?" he asked. "I have my reasons, Joe," Mary answered cagily. Joe grimaced, "What good could come of it?"

Mary didn't answer him. "Okay," he sighed with resignation, "Consider it done." he said.

What was it about women who knew exactly what their husbands did? They seemed to sense things in a way that men couldn't. When he dreamt about seducing Mary, Gina shook him, and bellowed, "What the hell is going on with you?" It was scary, and it drove Joe crazy to know that his wife could get inside his head.

Mary knew about Vito's mistress because Vito took off on weekends. Joe wanted what Vito had: charisma, charm, and

Mary. Even the boys in the saloon found Mary desirable. As he refocused his thoughts on Mary, he was aroused. "You're too far away," he said.

He motioned for her to sit closer to him. She said she was comfortable where she was. The front of the car easily seated three, and Mary had positioned herself at the far end, near the window.

Joe reached over and pulled her towards him. The car swerved and Mary let out a cry. Frightened that he would have an accident, she obliged his request and moved closer to him. Now their shoulders were touching.

"I want you next to me," he said meaningfully. Mary felt sick to her stomach. Joe was aroused by her closeness. What she had suspected from the first moment he had walked into her house had become a reality. He brushed the back of his hand against her cold face, and she jerked away from him. "I'd like to warm you up, Mary. All over."

Mary started to hyperventilate.

"Joe, I can't breathe. You're scaring me." He had a weird smile on his face as he turned the car in a sharp swerve to a side street and parked. With a sudden move, he pulled open her coat popping the second button off. He immobilized her by pulling the coat over her arms. Mary squirmed until she was able to free her right arm. She raised her right hand to her mouth, and with her teeth, pulled her glove off and dug her nails into his face. He screamed with pain as blood gushed down his face. "Wildcat!" He jerked away and pressed his handkerchief against his cheek.

Mary swiftly opened the door and ran from the car slipping and falling on the freshly fallen snow. She buttoned the top button of her coat as she ran. Mary ran to the corner and turned up the next block.

Joe was shocked. The scratches burned. One was at the edge of his eye. He could have been blinded. Joe got out of the car and made a snowball which he pressed on his cheek. It felt soothing. The trauma of Mary's reaction sobered him up. Mary was gone. If anything happened to her, he'd never forgive himself. He staggered in the direction she had gone. His gait was erratic and he stumbled from side to side and fell several times. He turned the corner, and Mary was leaning against a tree. Joe caught up with her. Mary screamed.

"Mary, don't be scared. It must've been the wine." He approached her, but she moved away.

"Don't touch me," she said as she extended her arms to keep him away. As she glanced at him, she realized that Joe was badly wounded. Blood was trickling under the handkerchief on to his beige colored coat.

"Oh my God!" Mary cried, "What have I done to you?"

"You defended yourself, Mary. Hurry! I gotta get to a doctor." Joe walked ahead of her. When they got to the car, he opened the back door and Mary got in. They drove back to East Harlem in silence. Mary started to shake as the impact of what had happened settled in. She wasn't cold, only in shock.

When Joe got to her building, he looked at her in the rear view mirror. Mary got out, ran into the building and up the flight of stairs to her home. She headed for the bathroom, disrobed, and took a hot bath. She tried to scrub the memory of his hands from her body with Ivory Soap. As she sat back with her eyes closed, the thought of Joe Marra coming home scratched as badly would probably have horrific consequences. Mary didn't know what those consequences would be, but she shuddered to think of Gina's volatile and jealous nature. How easily she could hurt Mary.

As Mary reflected, she realized she had to move out of 107th Street, and soon.

Joe Marra drove directly to the emergency room at the hospital, and as he suspected, he needed stitches. The doctor asked him how it had happened, and he said that his friend's wife was gesticulating and talking at a party, when he walked by and got scratched as her arm came swooping down. The Doctor was incredulous, and Joe waited to see his reaction, because he had to make up something for Gina. He was afraid to go home.

After he got his stitches, Joe Marra's cheek was bandaged, his left eye bloodshot, and he didn't want to go home or to the saloon to be ridiculed by the boys. A better story had to be concocted. Ah! He remembered a sage woman who's mothering instincts were wonderful. He drove to 109th Street and Second Avenue, and parked in front of Signora Laura's pastry shop.

He walked in and when Signora Laura saw him, immediately she went up to him and asked what had happened. Joe told her the story. He trusted her. He told her he needed an alibi for Gina, for the boys, even for himself.

"You act like a kid, Joe. Mary's a recent widow, you're supposed to help her. What the hell were you thinking?" She frowned.

"*Signora*, please, no preaching. This is different. I love Mary. I've always loved her. You know what I mean?" What was he saying?

47

"Joe, spare me, for heaven's sake. You want an alibi," she sighed. "Suppose, you took Mary for lunch, you brought her home early, you had to run an errand up to Westchester where there are trees, to deliver a package. As you were walking up the brick steps of this house in Rye, a wild cat flew out of the tree, you screamed, the cat got scared and she dug her nails into your face."

Joe applauded "Perfect!" he said. "You're incredible Signora Laura. Should I call Mary and let her know the alibi in case Gina calls her?"

"Yeah, but focus on the alibi. Knowing Gina, Mary will be relieved about it. Trust me. Your wife's got a reputation, Joe. She scares the hell out of even the Mafiosi on 107th Street. Gimpy, the numbers runner even said that Gina should work for them. She's like a bull dozer."

Joe laughed weakly. "Sure, they know what I live with," he said. Signora Laura was flattered that Joe had asked for her help, so she felt that she could be blunt. "Joe, you're not dealing with a full deck either okay? Why do you hunt Mary down like an animal?"

Joe shrugged, then hung his head in shame. She poured him a cup of coffee then she told him a story of a couple who had lived in the neighborhood many years ago.

The Cascio family came from Corleone to 107th. They had two young daughters. Paula, seventeen years old was a beautiful, bright girl. She went to college, began Italian-American clubs, and paved the way for other Italians to be proud of their heritage. Sam Montana, in his forties, a Mafioso, and a private person, met Paula Cascio and fell in love--a forbidden love. He lived in the shadows of the law and avoided serious entanglements with women. Paula lived in the light, she was always involved in changing the world. She even made the newspapers. An impossible situation for them. Why am I telling you this Joe? He adored her, but he **honored** her. I don't think they ever slept together."

Donna Laura explained that though Paula loved Sam, she also loved a handsome Irish cop from the 23rd precinct more. The Irish cops were enemies with the Sicilians, but Paula did not defy her father. She married Brian Mulligan only when she had her father's blessing. Right after the wedding, Sam Montana quit the mob and disappeared. *Disonorato* is one of the worst names

49

a Sicilian man can be called. Don't you see what I'm saying to you, Joe?"

Joe felt small. He lowered his head, shut his eyes, and Donna Laura saw a tear trickling down his face. He reached over to Donna Laura, held her in his arms for a moment, and whispered, "You've been like a mother to me. How do I pay you back?"

She pulled away, caressed his face and mouthed the words: "Be a man of honor." He nodded, stood up, got in his car, and drove home.

When Joe got home, he gave Gina the scenario of his alibi. She listened, and was suspicious of his story.

"Who gave you the package?" Gina asked.

"A friend of Louie the Lip. I don't even know the guy's name, but I owe Louie, so I did it. I had to."

Gina looked at him and thought that Joe was so unimaginative that the cat attack might just be the truth.

"I swear to God," Joe said as he crossed himself. That satisfied her. Gina didn't call Mary. Joe and Gina went to bed and he pretended to sleep. When Gina began to snore, he slipped out of the house and went to the bar on 107th Street to use the phone to call Mary. She wasn't sleeping yet.

"Mary, it's me, Joe." He told her what had transpired after he had left her off. Mary listened quietly and Joe explained that she had to know what he told Gina to avoid World War III.

"Okay," Mary said softly. It was a relief to hear that Gina wasn't aware of the incident. Mary felt she had to ask, "How's your face?"

"I'll live. I'll have a scar," he answered, and he hung on to the phone with both his hands, cupping his hand over the speaker so that none of the boys would hear his conversation. He wanted to tell her he loved her, he wanted to apologize, but at this point he was grateful that she was talking to him.

"I'm sorry. Good night Joe."

She was ready to hang up, when he said "Wait, Mary. Just hear me out. I acted like a *disonorato*. It was the wine, it wasn't me. It'll never happen again. I swear to God."

"Joe, leave me alone."

"I can't. I love you," he said huskily.

Mary sighed and hung up. He was hopeless. She was convinced that he would try it again. Joe was stupid, and he repulsed her sensibilities. There had to be a major change in her life, and as soon as possible.

As the thought of a move began to germinate, Mary pictured her new home. She climbed in bed, put her arm over her eyes, and visualized the new house. It would be a fortress, a stone house, located on a high hill overlooking a landscape. It had to be large and luxurious. She could afford it easily. The thought had taken hold in her, and she sat up, lit a candle to the Statue of the Sacred Heart of Jesus, and knew that it would soon be a reality.

Chapter IV

Memories of Christmas 1949

Mary's anxieties about Christmas accelerated as the holiday grew closer. Mary shuddered at the memory of last year's Christmas. Plans and rituals had been like other years, and no one anticipated anything different. The Christmas of 1949 began as any other. The Petracca family celebrated their Christmas Eve as they always had when they were back in Castellamare del Golfo. Mary began the vigil of the holiday by preparing the traditional Sicilian meal of seven fishes for the evening dinner, which according to their yearly tradition, was served at 6:00 p.m.

The custom of the fishes varied from town to town. Some villages celebrated by preparing three fishes, others by thirteen. Corleone celebrated seven fishes. Each number represented the ritual of fasting before Christ's birth. Three fishes represented the Holy Trinity, thirteen represented Christ and his twelve apostles. The seven fishes represented the days of the week before Christ's birthday.

Christmas Eve was special for Vito and his children. He would take them ice skating from the morning until 5:30 when they'd come home, famished, happy, and tired. They were now grown up. Marco was twenty years old, Philip nineteen, Maggie eighteen, and Tess seventeen.

None of them wanted to go ice skating in Central Park, but Vito wouldn't change the tradition they had honored every year since childhood. Vito needed these rituals to feel as though he still belonged to his children. Lately his loneliness was so painful that he wept frequently. Marco grumbled to Philip, and Maggie complained to Tess about having to "play the happy family" annually with these outings. Mary remained at home to prepare the Christmas Eve dinner. It was a tradition that none of them challenged because they wouldn't defy their father.

Mary took pride in preparing this feast. She had spent the entire day and late afternoon cleaning the fish and baking some, frying others, and pickling the calamari rings. At least when they came home, they'd eat ravenously, and always compliment her. All the hours of preparation were worth it for her. The neighbors met at the market and chatted about the various fishes they'd be putting on the table.

Donna Binna asked Mary where Vito was taking the family this year, and Mary answered, "the usual, they go ice skating in the park."

Rituals kept them grounded. Though family secrets were not spoken about openly, the neighbors and the Petracca children knew that Vito's and Mary's marriage was a charade. However, they remained steadfast about the public image they portrayed. It was convincing if one didn't know them.

It could have been different for Vito and Mary. However, his refusal to use birth control had been the catalyst which precipitated the termination of his conjugal rights as a husband. As time passed, Mary withdrew into her own world. Vito was no longer privy to Mary's thoughts or opinions, and he missed that part of her intensely.

Her earlier defense mechanisms, learned when her father had brutally abused her as a child in their battles of will, returned now for her own survival. Vito had been cast out of her life on every level. And so a marriage which once was loving, supportive, and the envy of all who knew them, drowned into the murky waters of Sicilian pride.

* * *

When Mary came back from the market laden with two shopping bags of fishes, she met Donna Rosalia outside.

"Ah, Maria, don't tell me that Vito has dragged your children to Central Park again."

Mary said, "Yes, he has."

Donna Rosalia shrugged, "Philip complained that they have to entertain their father."

Mary snapped angrily, "Don't concern yourself about my son, he loves these outings with his father."

Donna Rosalia muttered, "Yeah, just to make him happy."

Mary added, "Signora, it's not your business, is it?"

Donna Rosalia was miffed. She ran upstairs to her own apartment.

Mary went up, and put her bags on the table. Philip had breached the silent oath of *omerta*. Mary was upset. She poured herself a glass of wine, took a sheet of paper and busied herself with the menu. So much had to be done. She was hungry, but she had no time for lunch.

Mary's menu was: Antipasto consisting of shrimp salad, and pickled calamari salad with chopped celery and Sicilian olives, which she had bought from the olive barrel on the corner of 106th Street and Second Avenue: the *baccala* or salted codfish which had to soak in the tub for three days to get the salt out, be reconstituted with the cold water soaking. It was then made with red sauce and Sicilian black olives, together with potatoes. Second course was the pasta with fish sauce. Sometimes Mary varied that choice of pasta with red clam sauce, or white clam sauce or *calamari* in sauce. The third course was blue fish baked in the oven; stuffed fillet of flounder with spinach drizzled with extra virgin olive oil, bought from the vendor on the truck who brought it to East Harlem right from the docks of the Fulton fish market.

Following the third course was a small platter of little fish fried in deep oil in a batter. At the end of this feast of seven fishes, roasted nuts were placed on the table, as well as roasted chestnuts. The next course was fresh seasonal fruit. Dessert was purchased from Stroncone's pastry shop on 106th Street, or Donna Laura's pastry shop on 109th Street. Mary had no time to make desserts and would make them the week after Christmas Eve.

Although Mary celebrated the secular holiday of Santa Claus, as did the immigrants in the neighborhood, Mary also repeated the Italian legend of the witch, *La Befana's* story.

Legend had it that *La Befana* swept her house, and her sidewalk down to the road every day. One night, when the light of a star shone through her tightly shut shutters keeping her awake, she went out to see where it was coming from. She saw the three wise men who told her that the star was part of a prophecy announcing that a king would be born. She, too, wanted to visit the king. But she had nothing, so she baked cookies and placed them in her basket to take to the newborn King. She ran and ran, taking her broom, and she never did catch up with the others. Every year on January 6th, *La Befana* can be seen sitting on her broom as she swoops across the sky looking for the newborn King in Bethlehem. Using the legend the Italian tradition was to give the children gifts on the feast of *La Befana*, January 6th.

Mary took out the book with the legend of *La Befana*, and placed it on the floor under the Christmas tree so that after dinner, she would read it to her children in Italian. Mary kept the Italian legend alive in her children's minds as well as the Italian language. Now that they were young adults, they still enjoyed the story of *La Befana*.

Maggie, however, would make editorial comments on the story after Mary finished reading it, which sent Philip, Marco and Tess into gales of laughter. Last year, Maggie made a comment that *La Befana* was the Italian version of the wicked witch of the west from the *Wizard of Oz,* "but, they shopped in different stores for their outfits."

Mary got a late start in preparing the meal of the seven fishes. Concerned that she didn't have time to prepare all the fishes, she skipped breakfast and lunch. Her only intake of food was espresso coffee, and occasionally a glass of wine. At 5:00 o'clock, she panicked because she hadn't put the baking fish in the oven yet. Vito expected to dine at 6:00, and she was running late. She drank another glass of wine to calm her nerves.

The room spun all around, and she fell to the floor. She could hardly breathe as panic set in. Was she dying? All she wanted was to go to bed, but she couldn't walk. She crawled to the bathroom and threw up in the toilet bowl. She still couldn't get on her feet, so she crawled again to the bedroom, pulled herself into her bed and passed out.

Vito and the family walked in at 7:00 o'clock instead of 6:00. He called Mary but there was no answer. He went to the bedroom and found her passed out. He shook her, he called her, he slapped her face, but she couldn't wake up. He smelled the wine on her breath, as he listened for vital signs. She wasn't dead, but drunk. He cursed her, then joined his family while they finished baking the fish. The usual bubbling interchange at the table did not take place. One by one, each child pretended to go to the bathroom, but went instead to check on their mother. Vito said, "She probably didn't want to be with us, so she got herself drunk." They sat quietly not knowing what was going to happen. Philip's twitching cheek gave him away. Marco bit his lip in anger. He whispered to Philip, "Momma killed herself putting this meal on the table. We were so damned late, and I mentioned it to Poppa, but he dragged his heels on purpose. I don't wanna eat."

Philip whispered back, "You better eat. Poppa will explode. Momma's better off sleeping."

After dinner, the girls cleaned up, put the leftover food away, and converged in the living room underneath the huge tree which touched the ceiling.

"Who's gonna read *La Befana?*" Maggie asked quietly. Vito was sullen, and suddenly he shot her a look and hissed. "That's your mother's job. She's not here. Nobody reads that, okay?" He was seething over every comment the children made, reading into them a hidden agenda. They remained quiet until all the gifts had been given out. They thanked their father, and Vito nodded, then stood up, and took a small box out of his pocket.

"Marco," he said, "as the eldest, I want you to give this to your mother. She doesn't open any gifts of mine. They accumulate in the closet year after year. This can't wait. You must give it to her, and wait until she opens it, there's a note for her." Marco's eyes opened wide. He stood up next to his father, who was just a few inches taller than Marco.

"Consider it done." Marco held the box as though it was a precious thing and Vito walked out of the parlor to his den, and shut the door.

"Dear God, how sad," Marco said to himself, "he can't even give her a gift. What pain they inflict on each other." Philip scowled, "and us too."

The boys went to Marco's room to listen to classical music, and the girls went to Tess's room to listen to recordings of Dick Haymes and Jo Stafford. Philip and Marco checked on their mother before they went to bed. She was still sleeping. They went back to their room and talked quietly about the worst Christmas of their lives. The girls slept together in Tess's room, and Philip and Marco slept in the same room that night. Marco left the bedroom door open, in case there was a scene between their parents. They fell asleep, tired and worried. In the silence of the night, they awoke to the sounds of Vito sobbing, so deep in

61

his gut that he sounded as though he was being strangled. Then as soon as it stopped, they heard Vito go into the kitchen. It sounded as though Vito was getting himself a glass of water. They went back to sleep, all was quiet.

At midnight, the children woke up to the shouts and screams of their father. They couldn't hear their mother's voice, for she kept it *sotto voce.*

"Puttana!" Vito screamed, "you've got to have something on the side, you whore. How could you do this to me?"

She had struggled out of his grip, and had snarled, "and what do they call a man who's a whore? No one's ever invented such a word, have they?"

Vito had pushed her on the bed and had stood above her with his hands on his hips in a menacing stance livid with rage. She wasn't even afraid, and that icy stare enraged him. There was nothing in her demeanor which even hinted that she was a human being.

Vito wanted her to fight him; instead she was like a statue watching him in his frenetic behavior. She got out of bed, and quietly said, "I'll leave. My job here is to cook. You can hire one, and one who isn't a *puttana*. We're not a family, we're a bad play on a stage. I'll leave, you stay."

Frustrated by the fact that Mary didn't react the way he wanted her to, he punched the small glass pane of the French door shattering it to the floor while blood oozed out of his hand. Vito cried in pain.

Quietly Mary said, "Shut up, Vito. What'll the neighbors think?" That possibility silenced him. He muffled his sobs as he followed her into the bathroom. He was humiliated. Mary medicated his bloody hand and poured peroxide on the wound. He watched her in amazement.

"If you think you're in prison, so am I," he cried, sobbing and gasping for breath. "You move out of here, as Jesus Christ is my witness, I'll find you and drag you back in chains."

She shut the bathroom door.

"Chains? Too noisy Vito," she said coldly, "A knife is quieter, though sloppier. But you're the Patriarch and you can hire people to wipe up my blood." Her voice was controlled.

"You bitch!" he cried, "I don't even know you any more."

"Oh, but I recognize you," she hissed, "You've become my father."

Vito felt as though he had been punched in the gut. Vito felt his chest tighten up. He clutched it and bowed his head in pain.

Vito hissed, *"Strega!"* he pushed her away and walked out. "You're killing me!"

Mary followed him into the hallway. "Aren't you confused Vito? You're the one who wants to kill me."

He had run out in his shirt sleeves to Joe Marra's apartment. It was snowing, and Vito slipped and fell as he stumbled towards Second Avenue around the block to 106th Street.

At 5:00 a.m., after not sleeping all night and crying into his pillow like a wounded animal, Vito had returned to his home, in Joe Marra's overcoat.

In this abusive domestic situation, Mary had wanted to leave her family and run back to her home in Sicily. On second thought, Corleone? Who would she have there now? Her parents surely must have died, and relatives were many but none of them had been close. Sicily had been the theater of the D-Day invasion, and so much had been destroyed. Without funds, where would she have gone? She was trapped.

Eight months later, Vito Petracca died. Everything changed. Masks were gone, and each member of the Petracca family was free to be.

"La tragedia e finita!" (The tragedy is finished.) Maggie commented sadly, after Vito's funeral.

As time passed, each one of his children took a second long look at his father, and realized how very human he had been, not the icon of perfection he had wanted them to believe he was. No posturing on Vito's part had been necessary. Vito had made an indelible impression on each of them, and even more so on the angriest son, Philip.

* * *

A week before Christmas of 1950, the first year of the holiday without the Patriarch, the children rallied around their mother, as family dynamics changed. Tess called and asked what the holiday plans were, if any.

"I'm cooking a two course meal. I'd like to have you all come," Mary said carefully as she struggled to maintain the most unhappy of all rituals, the Christmas Eve fish dinner.

"Is everyone coming?" Tess asked.

"I imagine so. You're the first one who called." Mary qualified her answer carefully. She didn't know whether her children would honor the holiday or even want to spend it with her.

"Momma I don't know what to get you," Tess said.

"Your presence at the table is enough of a gift," Mary responded.

"Momma, I'll get something," Tess promised. Mary sounded as though she'd be alright. After last year, they dreaded the Christmas Eve festivities.

Marco called and said he was flying in for Christmas Eve's fish dinner but that he had to fly out on Christmas Day because he was conducting the *Messiah* at a church in Washington D.C.

"Don't come home," Mary said. "Get us three rooms. I'll drive the family to Washington D.C."

Marco shrieked, "Really, Momma? I swear to God, I was so worried about you. But this is great, you being here? Perfect! You'll enjoy the *Messiah.*"

"Okay, son. I'm looking forward to seeing you conduct," Mary said.

"Thanks, Mom." Marco was pleased. "I'll get three rooms at the Willard Hotel. Abe Lincoln slept there, Momma, you'll enjoy it."

They hung up, and Mary called Philip. Philip was excited. He was dreading the holiday for the same reasons Mary had. It was time for Momma to turn a new page in her life.

* * *

Philip wanted to "redo" Mary's appearance. First on the agenda was the latest haircut done by beauticians at the Astor hotel. The rage now was the Italian style made famous by Gina Lollobrigida. Mary said, "Okay, what time?" Philip gasped, "Oh, my God, Momma, you'll do it?"

"Yes. When, Philip?"

Philip's enthusiasm was contagious. "Ten in the morning, okay? After that, we're going to a dress factory to get you a new wardrobe of tight fitting sexy dresses."

Mary gasped. "Oh, *Dio,* Philip."

He laughed and kissed the phone many times before he hung up repeating quickly, "I love you, Momma, I love you."

Mary made a cup of demi-tasse coffee. She sipped it and looked at her bed sheets swinging like aluminum sheets in the frozen wind. The phone rang and it was Maggie.

"Are we doing Christmas Eve, Momma?" she asked.

"Yes," Mary sounded sure of herself. "I'm making a two course dinner, and at 7:00 in the morning on Christmas Day we're leaving for Washington. Marco's conducting the Messiah, okay?" she said.

"Momma, that sounds wonderful. Only thing is, I've invited a famous journalist. He's alone. Can I take him home for Christmas Eve?" Maggie asked.

"Oh? I guess so." Mary answered, and though she didn't want a guest, maybe it might be a welcome change in the family dynamic. No family history would be discussed. After all, Vito had been buried four months ago.

She would survive the holiday; in fact it would be okay. Who knows, a guest in the house might be a new tradition they could initiate. They'd begin to collect new memories without residue of Christmases past.

Within four months after the death of the Patriarch, Mary learned the "walk of her life," each step making her stronger and more resolute.

Earlier in the week, Mary had taken out Vito's accumulated Christmas gifts. She opened them up and put them in two piles, one for Maggie and one for Tess. The girls would love to have something which their father had shopped for. Mary remembered the small box Marco had handed her last year which she hadn't opened. She had said, "You're intruding on my privacy." Marco had backed off, and she had slipped the box in the back of the right hand drawer of the desk, having no interest in its contents. Now, there was no reason not to open it. Mary rummaged around the drawer, and found it in the back. She tore the golden wrap paper off and opened it. In the box was a solitaire two karat diamond ring and a note.

She read: "Mary, I'm dying without you. I miss the heart and mind of the woman who's soul was tuned to mine. I want her back. You're my life line, and I await your answer. Hopefully, Vito." Mary folded her arms on the desk and placed her head on them. The iron chains of resentment had melted away, replaced by a deep remorse, and dream of what might have been. Last year, had she opened the box, she might have considered his request. Mary slipped the ring on her finger. As she did, a chill came over her, as though Vito was in the room. She would wear the ring to her grave. She folded the note, put it in the box, and placed it at the base of the statue of the Sacred Heart of Jesus, in her bedroom.

"Tell him," she said to the beautiful image of Christ, "that I still love him with all my heart." She lay on the bed, shut her eyes and went back on the highway of her past, revisiting the early joyful years of her marriage.

Chapter V

Mary's Family

Flashback: Corleone: 1930

In Castellamare, Marco Petracca struggled with the sorrow his family had incurred. His daughter-in-law Margherita, daughter of a local *paesano*, had died giving birth to a stillborn baby boy in Palermo. His son Vito, devastated by the loss, had become a shadow of his former self. He stopped speaking, laughing, and interacting with the family. Surely it had been a mortal blow. Marco knew that Vito felt guilty over the death on multiple levels. He had had no love for the girl and had married her because it had been arranged. Secondly, he had impregnated her immediately so that a baby would provide a familial dynamic.

No matter how many times Marco had engaged his son in private talk at the vineyards, Vito had nothing to say. Finally, one day, Marco's relentless questioning touched Vito and he broke down. Marco learned that Vito had not liked Margherita at all. He learned that his son was unhappy living in Castellamare and wanted to emigrate to America. This was not a shock for Marco, because life was hard in Sicily, even though they had enough money to put bread on the table.

Months after their tragedy, Marco received a letter from his sister's son in Corleone. "Caro Zio," it began, "my father is in the hospital in Palermo, dying. His appendix burst and he's not doing well at all. We are struggling here, and your sister cries all the time. We're asking for your help until my father either dies or gets well. I am capable of managing our properties and surviving, but I drive my mother to Palermo and pick her up every two days. I'm asking for a financial loan to hire more *contadini* to work the land while I'm taking care of transporting my mother three times a week. Can you help? *Con Amore,* Your godson and nephew, Piddu Vidannu." Marco read the letter to his wife, who had squirreled emergency money in the sugar canister.

"I have forty thousand *lire.*"

She opened the jar and took the money out. Marco was astounded. He thanked his wife for being so frugal, and told her to wrap it in a jar together with other jars containing tomato preserves in a box so that if bandits intercepted, they would not find the money.

Marco drove to the mountain he owned, where Vito was supervising his crew of *contadini* picking grapes. Marco approached his son, read him the letter and told him to go home, pack a bag, and go to Corleone.

* * *

It took eighteen hours to drive over the mountains and valleys to get to Corleone. Piddu practically flung himself in Vito's arms. He had a pot of chicken soup waiting, and broccoli *rape* with sausage and homemade bread he had bought from the neighbor, since his mother had no time to bake.

"Vituzzu! *Beddu!* You saved our lives. Your father shall be paid back as soon as this nightmare is over. My mother begged me not to write him, but I'm desperate."

Vito assured him that he needn't concern himself with paying it back right away. The important thing was the family's survival.

They had the big midday meal, then took a walk down the road to the outskirts of Corleone. Piddu was engaged to be married to Carmela, the daughter of his father's *compare*, best man at his wedding. He liked her, and when things settled down, he would marry her and she'd move in to his parents' home with him.

As they walked down the road, two women came up with baskets of fruit on their heads. One woman was in her forties, the other one was fifteen years old, tall, beautiful, with a full figure reminiscent of a Botticelli painting. "Jesu!" Vito exclaimed. "Who is she?"

Piddu told him that Mary Gallo was the most beautiful and the most unfortunate young woman in Corleone. Vito's interest was piqued.

"Her father is the meanest bastard alive. She's an only child, and the word going around is that he wants her married off. She wants to become a nun, and he refuses her."

Vito was shocked. "With a body like that, she wants to become a nun?"

They moved to the side of the road as Mary and her mother passed by, looking ahead, pretending not to see them.

"Poor peasants," Piddu said. "Giacomo works hard, but he doesn't own much land, so the dowry for his daughter isn't enough to attract a man of means, you see. He's also fighting his daughter's strong will to join the church. Giacomo's trying to stage a Sicilian seduction to get rid of her. Vituzzu, interested? Believe me, with your money, Gallo would jump at it. We're all so poor, or spoken for because of contracts our parents made when we were kids, not too many of us are available."

Vito took a deep breath. He turned as did Piddu, and followed the two women as close as they could without being noticed.

"Jesu," Vito said as he watched her sway and balance the basket of peaches, "she excites me. I must be going crazy, Piddu."

"Nah! It's normal. She excites me, too, and half the guys in Corleone want to jump her, but he'd kill us. He always carries a *lupara* (short shot gun) with him."

The next morning Vito was supposed to leave, but he didn't. He took a walk by himself to the Gallo house on the outskirts of Corleone. He knocked on the door, and Giacomo opened it.

"Yes, what can I do for you?" Giacomo said to the stranger, good looking, well dressed, and handsome. Vito asked if he could come in and inquire about his daughter Mary. Immediately Giacomo summoned his wife to get the wine. Mary walked in, saw Vito, and froze. Her father waved at her to get back into the kitchen. She lingered for a moment in defiance and stared at the stranger whom she, too, had noticed at the bottom of the road.

Vito stated his intentions. Giacomo explained that he seemed like a man of means.

"The dowry is so pitifully small, a dozen chickens, a rooster, a strip of land to build a small house at the end of my property. I have little."

Vito told him that it didn't matter.

"There's one other thing. She refuses suitors to spite me. No matter how hard I beat her, she'd rather die than do anything I ask her to. She is killing me, unless I kill her first. I married late in life. All I wanted was a woman to cook my meals, clean my house, and darn my socks. Instead, she had a child. It took her attention away from me. I want Mary married off." Vito was appalled. Giacomo continued his soliloquy filling Vito's glass so that he would feel welcome.

"You've heard, of course, that she envisions herself as a nun, and those *puttani* in the convent encourage her," he whispered. "I'm ready to stage a seduction. I want this ended. When I die, you'll get this house and my farm."

Vito got cold feet. What in God's name was he being asked to do? Rape? He would have none of that.

"Signor Gallo, I'm going to leave. I shall be back tomorrow before I go home to Castellamare. You speak to your daughter.

If she agrees, we marry; if not, then I'm gone. I won't be party to this staged seduction." He turned away, "Get somebody else."

Vito bowed, took his cap, and walked out the door. Mary heard every word.

Giacomo banged his fist on the table. *"Mariuccia!"* he shouted, *"Veni ca."* He called her inside his dining room. Mary obliged. They talked. She refused Vito Petracca's proposal of marriage. Giacomo took his belt off, and whipped her across the back, until his wife pleaded for mercy. His curses were heard across the road.

Mary went to her room and her mother came and dressed her bleeding gashes with gauze dipped in cornstarch and milk.

Vito went to his cousin's house and told him what had transpired.

"The *disgraziato'll* probably kill her," Piddu said sadly. "What a waste." Vito paced the floor. He could hear the blows from the screen door as he walked away. It was 9:00 o'clock, bedtime for a peasant. Vito had been thinking about the beautiful young maiden who didn't cry out when her father beat her.
Vito was furious. He strode back to the Gallo home, knocked on the door, and Giacomo answered it. Vito was most welcomed, even though a peasant's day began at 4:30 a.m. Giacomo banged

on the table, sending the metal dishes flying to the wooden floor.

"I wanna kill her," he said to Vito.

"Signor Gallo, let me speak to Mary directly."

Giacomo summoned his wife and told her to get Mary down in two minutes or he'd come up and beat the hell out of her.

Mary prayed the rosary and begged God to take her now. She lay prostrate on the floor in the humblest of prayer positions.

Her mother walked in, and in a drone-like monotone said, "You're wanted by your father."

Mary didn't move. Her mother kicked her. "Get up! When you don't move fast enough, he beats me too. Go down."

Mary took her time getting to her feet. She smoothed her dress and went down two flights of stairs to the dining room. She was shocked to see her father and Vito Petracca sitting at the table. She could hardly contain her happiness. Giacomo told Mary to sit down. He walked out of the room, something no Sicilian father ever would have done. But Giacomo was desperate. He walked outside and lit his pipe, leaving the dining room door ajar, so that there would not be total privacy. He told his wife to stand as a sentinel in the kitchen.

Vito bowed to Mary who stared at him directly. He was older than she. He was concise. He'd lost his wife in childbirth, and he'd lost the will to live the rest of his days in Castellamare. His plan? Emigration to America. He needed a wife. She had to make up her mind quickly, because he was leaving tomorrow to go back to Castellamare. He stood up, bowed again, and asked for her answer.

"America? I won't ever have to see my jailors again. But Signor Petracca, you're twice my age. I'm fifteen. I can't give you an answer."

"Then I leave. I can't wait for one. Good luck, *signorina.*"

Vito admired her spunk. She had everything to lose, including her life, by not accepting his proposal. It astounded him. He bowed. She stared at him, acknowledging him with a slight nod, and waited until he had left.

As Vito walked out, Giacomo walked back in. Vito paused and listened as screams erupted and the sound of a strap as Giacomo beat her once more. Mary did not scream. Her mother did.

* * *

The next day at dawn, Piddu loaded up Vito's truck with a bushel of peaches from their grove and two gallons of extra virgin olive oil. Piddu was sad that Vito had failed to capture the beautiful spirited Mary Gallo.

Vito drove out of the town from the northern exit. He had gone ten kilometers, made a couple of maneuvers, and turned the truck around towards Corleone again. At noon, he drove through, and as he approached the Gallo home he honked his horn twice. Giacomo came running out, knowing that Vito represented his last hope for his daughter to marry. He waved Vito down.

"At least dine with me before you leave. My wife's made home-made fettuccini with asparagus and marinara sauce. Please, Signor Petracca." Vito didn't hesitate. He parked his truck in front of the Gallo home. As he walked in, Mary gasped. Surprised to see him, there was a glimmer of a smile on her face.

Giacomo and Vito sat in the dining room, while Mary and her mother served the meal. The women did not dine with Giacomo. After they had served the men, they dined on the wooden table in the kitchen.

Giacomo again talked to Vito about a staged seduction. Vito wouldn't do it, but all night he had thought about circumventing this barbaric practice.

"You'll be the house guest. We'll dine. During the *siesta,* you sleep in the next room. Wait a half hour, then go to her room and take her."

After the afternoon *pranzo,* Giacomo showed Vito to his room on the third floor.

It was time for the *siesta.* The Gallos slept on mats on the first floor this time. Mary carried the wine flask and put it outside Vito's door.

She knelt at her bed, bowed her head and said, "Thank you for bringing him back, Lord."

In the quiet of the Sicilian sun's relentless heat, she heard the creaking of the loose wooden planks. Vito was walking towards her room.

"*Signorina,* let's talk." He sat on a chair and pulled it close to the bedroom door, but not approaching her kneeling form by the bed.

"*Signor* Petracca, should you not be here with me?" She sat down at the edge of her bed, and avoided his gaze, as she slowly undid the buttons of her bodice.

"What are you doing, Mary?" Vito snapped, "I'm not here for this sadistic ritual. It's your father who insists upon staging a Sicilian seduction."

The words didn't sink in at first, but as he finished speaking, she gave a side glance without moving, and saw that he was still sitting in the chair by the door. Mary buttoned her bodice again, and stood up slowly facing him. She was attracted to this elegant older man who in a moment had endeared him to her even further.

"Signor Petracca, I'm sorry for your trouble. When you asked for my hand, out of spite to my father, I said no. I prayed for you to come back. When Piddu's neighbor ran over to tell us that you had left, I was devastated."

Vito felt sorry for this beautiful young woman who had been terrorized by an illiterate peasant, who's only wish in life was to be served like a king, dine by himself, and not be put out by the love for a child.

"So, you're not here to seduce me?" she asked.

"No, I'm here as **planned** to seduce you, but I won't. I want to make love to you, but not here, not like this. I'll wait until our wedding night."

She was incredulous. "My God!" she uttered.

Vito saluted her with his hand to his heart, bowed, and walked out of her room and shut the door behind him. Mary was overcome. No seduction? A man of honor? "Thank you, Lord," she said joyfully. Yes. She smiled and took her hair pins out of her bun allowing her beautiful black tresses to cascade around her shoulders. She walked to his room, knocked on the door. He opened it, smiling slightly.

"Yes, Mary?" he asked.

"By this time," she said, "my father thinks that you have seduced me, right?" Vito nodded yes, and he was taken by her style.

"Will you marry me?" he asked her.

"Yes, Vito. I want to come to America, and I want to be your wife, but let's have fun with it. One last laugh on him. Please. I don't want my father to think we haven't slept together."

Vito couldn't believe what she was saying.

"And so?" he asked.

"He's been calling me *puttana* for years. Dishevel my hair, and kiss me. I shall unbutton my dress to reveal my undershirt. Pretend the seduction took place."

He had a dark brooding look, as he slowly approached her.

"I want you, Mary. One kiss only, because once I start, I won't stop."

He swept her in his arms, touched her mouth with his finger, tracing her lips. She quivered, as the depths of a desire which had been dormant, surfaced. The kiss was tender at first, and then erupted into a mutual passion leaving them breathless. She put her hands under his shirt. Vito pushed her away as though her hands had burnt his skin.

"Mary, not like this," he said huskily.

He turned his back trying to control his emotions. Mary stood behind him and wrapped her arms around him, pressing her body against his.

"Vito, I shall make you a good wife," she whispered. She let go of him and ran back to her room.

He knocked on her door, she opened it, and he extended his hand to her. "Come Mary, come share my life with me, you won't regret it. Let's go downstairs." She gave him her hand and he kissed it.

The priest was sent for, the marriage performed. They would leave for a honeymoon in Palermo, but first Vito drove back to Piddu's house. Vito asked Piddu to contact his father to let him know that he had gotten married and was on his way to a honeymoon in Palermo. Piddu kissed Vito on both cheeks, "God bless you, dear cousin. You've saved her life."

* * *

Their first intimacy was like nothing Vito had ever experienced. Mary shed the peels of feminine modesty and opened up to Vito like a morning glory flower to the sun. Every moment together was a treasure of discovery of each other and themselves. It was truly a fantasy come true. Mary became pregnant with Marco on their wedding night.

Two months after Marco's birth, the Petraccas emigrated to America and settled in New York's Sicilian neighborhood in East Harlem on 107th Street. Vito purchased a ten family tenement building and converted two four room flats into one large flat.

The children came, one every year. Mary was tired all the time, and she felt trapped by the never ending daily routine. When Mary's repeated requests to use birth control were refused, Mary terminated her husband's conjugal rights. Vito's Sicilian pride hammered the last nail into the coffin of the Petracca marriage.

Chapter VI

Christmas 1950

Maggie Petracca ran up one flight of stairs of her tenement building and moaned as the delicious smell of fried fish permeated the hallway. Her love interest, Sean Quinn, followed behind.

"Smells great, Maggie," he said.

"Mom used to make seven fishes. Since my father died, she won't do it any more," she answered.

"For me, even one fish is a treat."

Maggie opened the door, took Sean's coat and hers and hung them up. She heard her siblings in the parlor and walked in to greet them, thinking he'd follow. However, Sean was attracted to the exquisite smells from the dining room table. The table was set with a lace tablecloth, Lenox china and ornate silverware from Sicily. Mary walked in and set the large platter of fried *calamari* in the middle of the table as Sean walked in.

"Mrs. Petracca?" he asked as their eyes met, "I'm Sean Quinn."

"Welcome, Mr. Quinn and Merry Christmas." Sean extended his hand and Mary was struck by the looks of the handsome blue eyed stranger.

He was enthralled with her gracious demeanor. "Thanks for having me," Sean said as he caressed her hand. Mary eased her hand away.

"Do you like fish?" she asked.

"My favorite food, Mrs. Petracca."

"Call me Mary," she said quietly.

"Wonderful, Mary. I'm Sean." His eyes perused her face as well as her body. "Beautiful!" he commented.

"What is?" she asked as she stepped back.

"All of it," he answered meaningfully.

Mary was about to go back into the kitchen when Maggie came in and hugged her. Philip and Tess finished putting the Christmas packages in individual piles and came in as Mary rang her silver dinner bell.

Philip sat at the head of the table where Vito used to sit, the girls on either side, and Sean to her left. Mary did the sign of the cross and asked Sean to say grace. He folded his hands, bowed his head, and prayed.

"Thank you, Lord, for the gifts You have given us, and, in particular, for Mary Petracca for preparing this meal. *Buon appetito.*" They answered in unison, "Amen."

Sean and the Petracca offspring enjoyed lively conversation during dinner. Sean asked a provocative: "What does Christmas mean to you personally?" It certainly evoked some revealing thoughts.

"After last year, I wanted to skip Christmas Eve forever," Philip answered.

"Holidays are a nuisance," Maggie quipped, "an unwelcome interruption in one's life."

Tess raised her eyebrow critically. "I think they're necessary," she said, looking at Sean as she offered her opinion, "to celebrate Christ's birth, and to reflect."

"Mary?" Sean asked as he waited for her answer. Mary swallowed her food, and wiped her mouth with the linen napkin. "I agree with Tess. It's a time for us to stop and think about why we're here."

"Wow!" Sean exclaimed.

Mary stared into his eyes, and Sean looked away, sensing that it was his turn next.

"Sean?" Mary asked.

"No comment, Mary," he answered, "Each of you reflected my thoughts."

"All of them?" Mary asked curiously.

"All of them." Sean answered.

After the calamari salad, Tess cleared the dishes, and Maggie went into the kitchen to help serve the pasta with white clam sauce. Philip instead had linguini with marinara sauce.

Sean was amazed at the organization of Mary's culinary feast. Mary's clam sauce was not made in a pot. It was made with fresh clams, scooped out and mixed with garlic, parsley, bread crumbs and olive oil, broiled until golden. Each plate had six half clams around the periphery of the pasta dish which was made with a base of garlic and oil first. Mary added a small pat of butter to the pasta, and toasted breadcrumbs in olive oil in a huge iron frying pan as a topping. It was like nothing Sean had ever had before in any restaurant.

"This is incredible, Mary," he said as he added the toasted breadcrumbs on his linguini. "Mary, how come you don't use cheese?"

Mary smiled. "Traditionally Italians don't use cheese on clam sauce. Toasted crumbs on pasta originally was a peasant dish."

The pasta with clam sauce had a variety of color on it: golden crumbs, fresh green parsley, and broiled half clams.

"Your cuisine appeals to all the senses, Mary," he commented, and Mary smiled. For a confirmed thirty six year old bachelor, who's housekeeping skills were wanting, this indeed was an eclectic venture into the art of home making.

The baked blue fish came out, and Mary cut up the portions in the platter and passed it to Sean first. As they dined, Sean asked Philip what Marco was like.

"He's a real long-haired musician. From the age of seven, my brother Marco was on another planet. He studied violin over an hour a day, and as he got older, much more. Marco always knew what he was going to be. Nobody knew what I wanted to be, not even me, and my father asked every day. He quit asking me once when I gave the right answer." The girls laughed, because it was so true.

"What was the right answer, Philip?" Sean asked.

"When I was twelve, I told my mom that I'd better come up with a good answer because I was sick of being asked what did I want to be? Next night, same question but this time I said: 'Rich! I want to be rich!'" Everyone laughed, and Sean was amused, "So that was the right answer?"

Mary entered into the conversation, "Vito told me that he'd better put aside money for Philip so that he could go into business." Sean was impressed. The man sounded like a caring father, but something was strange. Normally a woman refers to her husband as 'my husband,' but Sean observed that Mary called him by name.

After fresh fruit, roasted chestnuts, and demi tasse coffee and pastries, the girls cleared the table, and they all went into the parlor for gift giving.

"Momma," Maggie said to her mother, "don't do the story of '*La Befana*' this Christmas, please?"

Before they got up from the table, Mary had something to say about the Italian tradition of gift-giving. Maggie seemed annoyed, that her mother had circumvented her request for no legends, but Mary was adamant.

She said that Christmas had become a secular holiday and had been so for many years as far back as she could remember. Maggie started to get up and Mary asked her to sit down.

"The feast of the Epiphany means more than *la Befana,* the witch who flies on her broom looking for the place where the Messiah was born." Sean leaned forward to listen to Mary's soliloquy.

"The Feast of the Magi, the three Kings brought meaningful gifts to the Lord. The first was gold, because a King had been born; the second was frankincense, which was incense used on holy days in the temple; and the third was myrrh, the anointing oils used upon a person's death. At His birth, Christ had been given the oil for his final moments on earth. Let's bow our heads and pray silently."

At the end of the prayer, Sean looked at Mary who seemed to be deep in thought. At the final "Amen" said by all, Maggie got up and said, "Let's go, our gifts are waiting." Sean thought that was insensitive of her, but Mary didn't seem to be affected. They went to the parlor, sat in a semi-circle close to the tree, and Maggie and Tess distributed the gifts.

Each one opened two gifts from their mother, and Sean Quinn also got two gifts, one from Maggie and one from Mary. He was embarrassed. He had brought nothing at all, not expecting Christmas gifts to be exchanged. In America, people gave their gifts to one another on Christmas morning.

He opened Maggie's gift to him, a jewelry box with a handsome hand-etched silver identification bracelet inscribed, "To Sean-Love, Maggie."

"Maggie, thanks," Sean said self consciously, "it's beautiful and I--I brought nothing,." he said apologetically.

"I know, Sean. Did you read the inscription?" She bent closer to him to show him.

"I don't deserve it," he whispered.

"You're right, you don't," Maggie quipped, and she handed him another small box from her mother. "This is from Mom."

He opened it, and it was an elegant cashmere wool scarf in black on one side and gray on the other, from Saks Fifth Avenue.

"Mary?" he said huskily, "I don't know what to say."

"Merry Christmas, Sean. Hope you like it." She answered. All he could think about was had he become so inured to the give and take of the niceties of life, that all he brought was himself? He caught Mary's eye for a moment and mouthed the words, "thank you" and blew her a kiss. She blushed and looked away, but not before Maggie saw the whole thing.

Maggie leaned closer to Sean's ear so that no one could hear.

"Sean, you son of a bitch, you're flirting with my mother. Stop it!"

As the gifts were opened and admired, they were folded and put back in the box and in separate piles. Maggie got up to start washing dishes in the kitchen, and Philip listened to jazz recordings of Louis Armstrong, one of his favorites. Philip turned up the volume on the record player.

"Can't play this stuff when Marco's around, it drives him nuts." Philip explained.

At 7:30, all the dishes were washed, dried and put away, Mary finished the Murano glass stemware herself never trusting anyone to wash them. The girls went back to the parlor to bring their gifts in their bedrooms. Philip suggested they all go out dancing at a club on 86th street which was featuring a jazz trio, and the girls went to their rooms to change into evening dresses for the occasion. Philip went out with his boots to shovel the snow banks away from the car parked across the street. Sean helped Mary in the kitchen.

"Mary, come with us, please," he asked.

"Sean, I don't socialize with my children. Vito did."

"You mean your husband?" He wanted to test his theory.

"Vito, yes," she said, as she took the broom away from him. "You're my guest, Sean, I'm mortified to see you sweep."

He took the broom back and his hands covered hers as they each held the handle. "Mary, I know nothing about protocol in a Sicilian home, but I've just experienced the best Christmas Eve of my life. Let me at least feel part of this feast by sweeping. I'd love to be *La Befana.*"

Mary laughed and let go of the broom.

"Mary," Sean asked, "I notice that you don't say 'my husband,' you call him Vito."

Mary put the towel down, "Sean, that was his name. Why do you notice?" He shoveled the crumbs in the dustpan and took his time answering, but Mary waited.

"Well?" she asked.

"I'm a journalist, words are my business. I see beyond appearances." As the words tumbled out of his mouth, he sounded so trite to himself, so arrogant.

"You're a guest in my house, Sean, I had no idea that we were being observed and analyzed. Remember, you're not working tonight."

Mary's voice took on a tone of outrage. He was stunned by the concise appraisal of his arrogance.

"As your hostess, I want you to put the broom away, and get yourself ready to leave."

Sean blushed. He had been told off. "Mary, I meant no offense."

He put the broom in the closet, then came over and took her hand in his. She pulled away quickly.

"I'm sorry," he said. "What can I do to make it up to you?"

"Respect my privacy." Mary turned her back on him. He walked out of the kitchen feeling dreadful. Maggie and Tess came in, and thanked Mary for a wonderful Christmas Eve.

"Mom, this was better than other times," Tess whispered. "There was no tension this time."

Immediately Tess wanted to take back her words. "Oh God, I didn't mean that," she said. " I wish he were here."

"I know that, Tess," Mary answered, "I do too. Remember, come home early. We're leaving for Washington at 7:00 in the morning, okay?"

Once more, Mary repeated her request to Maggie to get home early. They left in a flurry of chatter, and Mary shut and locked the door.

Mary felt dreadfully alone. She shut her eyes and tried to think of Vito, but Sean's face was in her mind's eye. Suddenly she heard footsteps coming up quickly. It must be Philip, she thought. There was a tap on the door, it wasn't Philip. Philip's knocking was always rapid with a definite rhythmic pattern. She opened the door, and it was Sean. He walked in, and he stood at the door with such a contrite expression on his face that Mary wanted to laugh.

"Don't be angry with me," he said.

"I'll get over it. Please go."

He shifted his weight from one foot to the other. Mary tried not to laugh, and Sean wondered what she found so amusing. As though she read his mind, she said, "You look like a little boy who's done something wrong, and you have so much guilt on your face, that it's amusing."

Sean blushed.

"You're right. I pried into your personal life. It was clumsy, stupid and insensitive. I apologize, forgive me, Mary."

He took her hand and kissed it and she smiled.

"Go, Sean, go enjoy yourself. I've been over sensitive too. After all, Vito, my husband -" Sean smiled as Mary was playing back his exact words. "-passed away four months ago. It's still an open wound for me."

"I can only imagine. I'll see you later."

He blew her a kiss, and she pretended not to see it. What charm he had. Mary tried to put him out of her head.

When Sean came down Maggie asked him what he forgot upstairs.

"My manners, Maggie. I hurt your mother," he said contritely.

"How?" she asked.

He snapped, "Drop it! I feel like shit!"

* * *

Mary changed into her white flannel night gown and went into Vito's den. In the waste paper basket she had the real estate section of the *New York Times*. She read about public housing called projects which were soon to be built in East Harlem. Prices on the tenement homes would be minimal.

She looked in the real estate section of Westchester County, and saw a listing for a beautiful large six or seven bedroom stone, two-story home in Warburton Avenue in Yonkers. She circled it, pulled her scissor out of the drawer and cut it out. She placed the ad in her wallet, but first she copied the phone number on a separate piece of paper so that she wouldn't lose it. Before she went to bed, she taped it on the inside mirror of her medicine cabinet.

At 11:00 p.m. Mary turned in. She set the alarm for 6:00, and went to sleep within moments. Her last thoughts before she passed out was the last encounter with Sean Quinn. It wasn't an act. The man was obviously out of touch with family life. He seemed to be too old for Maggie, too set in his ways. Hopefully Maggie would see it.

When the alarm went off, Mary attempted to wake up her family. It was difficult. Maggie told her that they had gotten in at 4:00 a.m. Mary had much to do. She woke Philip up and gave him the assignment of getting them up and ready.

Mary made a pot of coffee, put some fruit and cookies on the table and set it for the five of them. Reluctantly, they got up, and according to Mary's time table, they left at 7:00 a.m. sharp. Sean sat in the front with Mary and told her he'd share the driving. The others fell asleep. Tess brought her bed pillow and she and Philip put it between them and went back to sleep. Maggie curled up and passed out. Sean made a few futile attempts at small talk, but Mary didn't participate, which precluded further discourse.

After driving for three hours, Mary pulled over. She shook Sean, and asked him if he would drive for an hour. He rubbed his eyes, got out and stretched, and Mary took the thermos of black coffee, poured him a cup and gave it to him. He drank it and said. "Just what I needed." Mary offered him a wet towel to wash his face.

"You think of everything, don't you?" he said. She nodded. "You're not going to talk to me, are you?" he added. Mary didn't look at him. She got back in the passenger part of the car, and fell asleep.

They arrived at the Willard Hotel at noon. They parked the car and checked into their rooms. Sean and Philip shared a room, and Maggie and Tess shared the second room, while Mary slept alone. They bathed and, feeling refreshed, went down to the dining room for brunch.

Marco came at 1:30. He walked into the dining room, looking so handsome in his black turtle neck rehearsal knit shirt. His haircut was artsy, long and full. Marco looked like Vito with a strong Roman nose, full lips large black eyes, and a dimple on the right cheek. He joined the family at brunch, and gave his mother the tickets.

"Your favorite oratorio, Momma, *The Messiah*. Remember, Poppa took us every year?" he said as he ate his salad.

While Sean ate, he listened to Mary and Marco's conversation.

"How are the soloists?" Mary asked.

"It's not Carnegie Hall, Momma."

"Oh? Adequate?" she asked.

"Yeah, adequate! You'll love the soprano, not a big voice, more of a Broadway voice, lyrical, but.."

"Couldn't they get someone with operatic training?" she asked slightly disappointed.

"She's studied opera mom, trust me, you'll love her."

Mary raised her eyebrow, and whispered, "Maybe **you** love her, son." Marco grinned.

* * *

The concert was wonderful, and performing it in the cathedral gave it a proper setting. During the "Hallelujah Chorus," the audience stood up as they did in its London debut in 1750. Sean, who sat next to Mary, asked her why everyone stood, and Mary couldn't answer, so she held his arm until it was over. When they sat she told him about the tradition which has been carried through the years. He was enthralled. Mary was emotionally lifted at the beauty of the music, the joy of seeing her son conduct, reminding her of past performances of *The Messiah* in Carnegie Hall with Vito.

After the performance, they all went back to the Willard for a late supper, and Vivian Petra, the lyric soprano, came also. Sean sat next to Mary at the oval dining room table. Mary looked at Vivian, and couldn't believe how pale the girl looked. Blonde hair, white skin, blue eyes, and facial hairs that weren't prominent, but very fair.

"Mayonaisse," Mary muttered softly without realizing that Sean, Maggie and Marco heard her. Maggie giggled. Sean asked Maggie why, and Maggie explained that Mary was referring to Vivian's coloring, and something else.

Maggie whispered in Sean's ear. "Marco's interested in Vivian. He's Mom's son." Sean whispered back, "What is that supposed to mean, Maggie, I have no clue." Maggie got very serious. "No Sicilian woman thinks any woman is good enough for her son," she said, and Sean laughed. "And what about the daughters, does she feel the same way about them?" Maggie said "Not at all. Women are expendable, even to women, but a son is a son is a son." "Got it!" Sean replied.

Going back to New York, Sean and Mary rode up front. Maggie, Tess and Philip continued to sleep in the back, and finally Sean was able to engage Mary in conversation.

Sean touched on safe subjects, and then wanted so much to ask about her utterance of mayonnaise. Mary burst out laughing, and covered her mouth. He reached for her hand, and said, "Laugh, Mary, laugh. Why do you cover your mouth?"

Mary's eyes squinted at that remark and Sean covered his mouth,

"Oh, God, did I do it again?" Sean asked and Mary smiled "Poor Sean, you're afraid to talk to me."

"Not really Mary. Now tell me about mayonnaise." He was amused as she drove and gesticulated with one hand.

"Years ago, Vito had a *nguria* for different types of people. That's a Sicilian word in slang which means an insult, or making fun of, anyway, any blonde woman who's facial hairs faded into the one bland color of her skin was mayonnaise. I thought Vito was funny. Oh, he had a list of them."

"What would my *nguria* be, Mary?"

"Sean, you'd get insulted. *Citruolu* — a cucumber. Because you're tall, and your body has no curves."

"I'm not insulted," he said.

104

"Well, if Vito were here, you'd be," Mary smirked.

"You're enjoying this, aren't you?" he asked.

"No," she said softly, "Words are weapons which leave deep scars. I was wrong to label the singer."

Mary's expression changed, then Mary tapped her fingers on the steering wheel. "I suppose, if Marco wasn't interested in her, the *ngiuria* might have remained unsaid."

Sean was impressed by her candor. He asked her if she would elaborate and she said no. He looked out the window. Clouds were thickening before them and the day looked ominous, as though snow was going to fall. He asked Mary if she had snow tires, and Mary told him they were on the car already. The gas gauge was low, so Mary pulled into the next fuel stop. Sean got out and stretched as the attendant pumped gas into the car. Mary crunched her shoulders and Sean walked over and massaged her neck. She moved away from him.

"That's fine, Sean, I'm okay."

"Did I hurt you?" she nodded, "No, actually it felt good."

"But you walked away," she looked away, embarrassed, but he understood. Putting his hands on her body was too personal.

He paid for the gas, and held the door open for Mary as she got into the passenger side of the car. Sean pulled out and picked up speed so that they'd beat the possibility of getting stuck in a snow storm. It was tense driving, and Sean didn't talk, but concentrated on driving. He tried to hold Mary's hand, but she pulled away and looked out the window. The clouds were opening up, and it was snowing, lightly at first, and then the flakes got thicker and fell in a steady slow pace which stuck to the road.

When Sean pulled into 107th Street, several inches had accumulated. He helped the family bring the bags upstairs, thanked Mary for her hospitality, and left. Maggie put her arm through his and walked him to the taxi stand on 106th street under the Third Avenue El. Sean looked weary.

"Too much family life this weekend, Sean?" Maggie asked.

"Not at all. I have no family, and being with one during a holiday is unusual. I often turn these invitations down, but not this time, and I'm glad I didn't. Your mother is a gracious hostess." Maggie thanked him.

"Maggie, did your father ever call your mother by a *nguria?* "

"Yeah, *monica.*" Sean was puzzled, "Monica? Doesn't that mean nun?" Maggie nodded. "Poppa tried to get under her skin, but Momma never reacted."

He got it! Vito and Mary didn't sleep together. That's why Mary had commented that words were weapons, even though she was guilty of doing it herself by labeling Vivian. Vito's use of *nguria* had victimized Mary. No wonder she was so sensitive.

The cab driver waited at the corner, under the 106th Street station. As Sean was getting into the cab, he kissed Maggie lightly on the lips and she drew him to her and kissed him fully. "You sure you don't want me to come with you?" she asked. "I'm bushed, Maggie. Stay with your mother." He got in the cab and the cab drove away. Maggie watched the cab until it was out of sight.

She had invited him to see how he would react to family since he had none, and didn't ever want one. Her family had made a good impression on Sean, and perhaps he'd be more sanguine to a serious relationship with Maggie. At least that was her intent when she invited him to spend the holiday with her family.

Chapter VII

Bayside Beckons

The post office workers loaded the iron dollies with mail bags from the truck crashing into the heavy swinging doors of the post office, and breaking the silence of the night. Gina Marra was jolted out of a deep sleep and almost fell out of her bed.

"Damn it to hell!" she bellowed.

Joe Marra woke up frightened. "What's wrong?" he said.

Gina sat up in bed. "Those damned post office workers. I'd like to find out where the hell they live and shoot firecrackers underneath their windows," she complained as she sat at the edge of the bed.

"After all these years, just now you gotta complain?" Joe said. Gina turned to him in disgust. "Yeah? All day long it's the busses, the fire trucks, the kids screaming in the streets, and the shootings on 107th Street. Oh, yeah, peace. You know when I'm gonna get a good night's sleep? When I'm stretched out in that box.."

Joe laughed. *"Momma mia!* Are you dramatic!"

She sighed deeply and Joe punched his pillow and attempted to get back to his wonderful dream. Gina, of course, wouldn't let him. She hit him with a provocative question: "Joe, who killed Vito Petracca?"

Once more he was jolted. Gina had a direct way with words which shocked him.

"What, are you nuts? Go read a book on Pearl Harbor. Go! I'm going back to sleep."

"Damn you, Joe! There's talk, okay? There's talk that you found him and that you know something." He was fully awake now. She continued. "I even heard Angie from 107th Street say that you were the last to see him alive."

Joe was annoyed. "Vito stepped on somebody's toes."

"Tell me," Gina said.

"Listen," Joe continued. "In 1946, right after the war, dry walls did our union in. Vito and me took a ride to Levittown. Cheap-built houses used dry walls. For seven grand, you got no basement, the first floor had the usual plus two bedrooms. On the ceiling, tiles held up by metal strips were knocked off in less than an hour. The second floor unfinished, could've been made into two more bedrooms for our kids. I almost bought one, but Vito said they would fall apart in a year. He was mad as hell, and he kept saying: 'We're dead!'"

"Why the hell are you giving me a real estate lesson?" she asked.

"You know, Gina, you don't mind your business. Vito died because he screwed up his life. Too much pressure from everywhere: the union, the bitch downtown, and his damned pride. He knew he made a mistake by walking out on Mary. He was nuts about her. Poor girl didn't even know it. Spite work all the time. He gave her presents every Christmas and she put them in the closet unopened. Two women? And all that guilt? That would kill me." Gina was incredulous. Here he was describing exactly what he was doing. "Like you weren't ready to juggle two families with Mary?" "You know, you got a wild imagination. I'm getting paid for helping her out, what the hell are you talking about 'juggle two families.' Are you nuts?"

Gina couldn't believe how deeply involved her husband had been with Vito Petracca. There wasn't a day that passed, that Joe hadn't come home with detailed reports on what went on in Vito's life. Almost every day, Joe would visit Vito after supper, even for a few minutes, just to be able to see Mary.

The next morning, Gina called Angie on 107th Street and told her she had to talk to her.

"I'll put up a pot of coffee," Angie said.

When Gina arrived at Angie's she unleashed her fears, her suspicions and her terrible sense of rejection. Angie listened, then said, "Grow up, Gina. Most of the boys at the saloon have a *comare.*" "You know Charlie Fatili's wife?" she continued. "Watch her. She's got a new fur coat. Charlie's been out of town for business-funny business."

Gina was wide-eyed. "Oh, my God," she said. "I noticed the coat at the butcher last week. I thought to myself: who the hell goes shopping for chopped meat in a fur coat? So...you think Dianne Fatili knows?"

Angie sipped her coffee and shrugged, "Of course, Gina. Nobody's stupid. But if she opens her big mouth like you do, she'd get nothing. Look in your closet. Last time you looked, did you find a fur coat?"

Gina was shocked. Angie went on. "Gina, you know how many diamond rings I got? Five! I polish them up, and when I go shopping I put one on each finger. They're like the purple heart in war. Soldiers get medals for their service, and we get diamonds for looking the other way."

Gina stood up. She got nervous and had to wash her face with cold water. She felt like a fool talking to Angie. This *comare* business of having a woman on the side was nothing new.

"I should look the other way?" Gina wiped her face and sat down opposite Angie who was lighting a Camel cigarette.

"What have you got to lose, Gina? Everything! Don't you get it? What are you trying to do, put a leash on him? You have nothing to show for his screwing around. Get something out of it, you know what I mean?"

"I don't know if I can do that," Gina said, "What about my pride?"

Angie laughed, "Proud people destroy themselves, Gina. Don't even go there. Go home. I'm gonna go buy some prime rib steaks for Rocco. My sweetheart's coming home with a new gift tonight. He called, and asked me what color did I want my expensive new bag in?"

Gina was devastated. She thanked Angie for the coffee, and went home. Angie had shocked her sensibilities. Was there nowhere she could go to vent her frustration and fear of her husband's wandering eye? Was the double standard everybody's practice? She wasn't sure. Her own father had been so devoted to her mother. All she ever wanted was the same thing from Joe.

She figured he wasn't exactly packed tight in his head, but after all, what else could she have attracted, a brain surgeon?

Angie had opened up a box of realistic marital scenarios of the boys in the block, and Gina didn't like it one bit.

Gina had no strategy to keep her marriage together. If anything happened to Joe, she wasn't even able to make a living. What could she do? Work in a laundry? Clean houses? She had to hang on to him, and that need she had for him was more than love or companionship, it was necessary for her physical survival. With no family left, Gina was alone.

But Angie had more to tell. There was talk of an investigation at the union, she said. Over forty thousand dollars in union dues were missing. Vito Petracca was being investigated, and fear and anxiety had been his constant companions. When Vito dropped dead at his desk, after sipping a cup of coffee, attention against Vito was diverted, and rumors pointed to Joe Marra, the second in command.

Gina told her husband what she had heard from Angie: that he was being suspected of having absconded with the union dues.

* * *

It was Tuesday night. Gina soaked the dirty dishes in the sink and hurried out for dish night at the movies. She joined Angie, Stella, Connie and Giovanna to the movies. It was always crowded, and they had to hurry to get the best seats in the middle of the theater. The Star movie house on Third Avenue under the El had a double feature, a weekly serial as well, and gave away a dinner dish. A number of the neighborhood wives ran to the 7:00 o'clock show for the movie and the free dish.

At 9:00 o'clock, Joe Marra was tired. He washed the dishes which would please Gina so much, and he was in turmoil over what Gina had revealed to him.

How the hell did she know about the missing funds? Would anybody be after him as vice president? It was time to move. He heard about new attached homes in Bayside, Queens. The John Scalisis from 107th Street bought one and moved out to 215th Street in Bayside. At least the houses were made of brick. Might as well get a new start. The tenements were doomed to be knocked down to make way for urban renewal projects anyway. Within a year or two, landlords would get their letters advising them that their buildings would be purchased at a fair price fixed by the government.

John had paid about fourteen grand for the house. It had three stories, a finished basement where he housed his enormous record collection, a main floor with kitchen, dining room and living room, and upstairs three bedrooms with two bathrooms. Not bad. Perfect in fact.

The local bank, Emigrant Savings Bank on 116th Street, offered a 3% interest on a 30-year mortgage. In the morning he'd go to the bank. Then he'd call John Scalisi and make a date with him and Marie so that he and Gina could see their house. Now he grew anxious. He'd rather live close to another Sicilian. The "heat" was on with women gossiping about absconded union funds and investigations starting.

He wondered if Mary knew anything. He must call her tomorrow. Joe's mind was bubbling with a cauldron of anxieties about rumors of Vito's murder, missing funds, and possible investigation into Joe's finances and joint account with Mary Petracca to implicate the Petracca name with the missing union funds. Exhausted from fear, Joe finally fell asleep.

The next day he took care of his business and got the okay from the bank for a mortgage. He called Marie Scalisi, who cordially invited him and Gina out to see their home. She asked if they would come for supper on Sunday for the ritual Italian meal of *pasta cu sucu.* Joe accepted.

Joe went to the saloon. Already the boys were booking bets on the big fight at the Garden that night. Charlie Fatili got the most expensive tickets-ringside-seats when the fight was first announced. He bought them all, then sold them individually at scalper's prices. Each ticket was a whopping twenty bucks. The men all forked over the asking price, and Charlie made out like a bandit, which he was.

* * *

Gina was enthusiastic about seeing Marie and John again, especially at dinner in their new Bayside brick home. Thank God, Joe had made this decision. Oh, he'd miss the neighborhood, the boys in the saloon, and Mary. But he was planning to keep the apartment on 106th Street in case he wanted to hang out in the neighborhood. Gina wouldn't have to know.

Gina went to First Avenue to shop for Italian cheeses and imported olives from Sicily to bring as a gift to the Scalisis. They were no longer in an Italian neighborhood where these specialties were sold. Bayside was an eclectic mix of nationalities, most of them second generation.

* * *

Joe had a bundle he was going to bet on Sugar Ray Robinson. However, out of loyalty to the Italian fighter, Jake LaMotta, middleweight champion of the world, he was also placing a bet on him. Sugar Ray was smooth, and fast. He could take it as well as dish it out. Most of the boys were betting heavily on LaMotta. However, those who bet on Robinson hid their bets from their fellow *paesani* just not to be accused of being disloyal. Sugar Ray Robinson was a welterweight champion after being undefeated in 89 previous amateur bouts. In 1946, Robinson won the welterweight title, a position he held for five years.

This match with LaMotta was different. Robinson, the welterweight, was fighting LaMotta, the middleweight champ. Once before LaMotta had broken Sugar Ray's record of forty victories. Now Sugar Ray wanted to challenge LaMotta and take his crown away from him. This was a familiar pattern for Robinson. Each time a fighter had defeated him, he sought a rematch and inevitably won. Robinson would go down in the annals of boxing as one of the best, if not the best.

It was a fight that lasted for thirteen rounds. Jake LaMotta lost in a brutal battle to the swift and tough Sugar Ray's relentless blows. The crowd of cigar-smoking men went wild, as points against LaMotta added up. The fight was broadcast and the rest of the boys in the saloon who hadn't bought tickets from Charlie were glued to the radio on the bar in the saloon. Nothing else mattered in the city on that historical night of February 14th, 1951. For all the boxing fans, this was a sweet Valentine's Day gift. Sugar Ray Robinson gave up his title and fought as a middleweight champion for the next ten years.

Joe Marra came out winning a thousand dollars, a big fortune in 1951.

"Now I can buy my house," he said to himself as the boys took cabs back to the saloon to celebrate. They sent for pizzas, and the beer flowed as the celebration got louder and louder. Nobody complained. Nobody dared to. Money was exchanged as bets were paid off to the boys, and many lost their shirts having bet heavily on their Italian hero, Jake LaMotta.

Gina waited in bed for her husband who tiptoed into the kitchen at 3:00 a.m. She knew he was coming home because the shouting all over the streets died down finally.

"Gina?" he whispered, "you awake?"

"Yeah! I heard Robinson won. What did you lose?" she asked.

"I won a grand. I bet fifty on LaMotta, 'cuz he's a wop like us, but it was brutal. Damn that guy could hit. Thirteen rounds, Gina. I mean the guy wouldn't give up. Here's the money. This is our down payment on the house in Bayside. Stash it away, okay?'

"Son of a gun! You bet on Robinson?"

Joe kicked off his shoes, dropped his pants and collapsed on his side of the bed. Gina bent over and covered him.

"Jesus, you smell like a brewery," she said, "Phew! Joe, stretch out. I'm sleeping on the couch. You got the whole bed. Glad you bet on Sugar Ray, he's a champ. I could-a told you. At the races, you find out how a horse runs and, damn it, if he's the best in the field, bet on him. You made out big time. Thank God, Joe."

By this time, Gina struggled to cover his heavy body, then took a blanket and pillow and went to sleep on the couch.

The next day, Joe had a horrible hangover. Gina was going shopping on First Avenue for the best produce at low prices from the pushcarts. Instead of Joe making his own coffee, he left the house and went to Signora Laura's pastry shop on 109th Street and Second Avenue, for a big pot of demi-tasse coffee. "No sugar," he said to Signora Laura. She laughed when she saw what lousy shape he was in, and asked him if he had gone to Madison Square Garden. He said he had and that it was the fight of the century.

"I swear to God, I screamed my head off. I think I swallowed half my cigar, I was so nervous. Blood all over the place, and still LaMotta wouldn't give up. Thirteen rounds, signora, did you hear it on the radio?"

"How could I listen to anything else with my husband, Luigi, being a big boxing fan?"

Her daughter, Immaculata, took over the counter, while Signora Laura joined Joe at the small wrought iron white table at the far end of the store.

"You know, Joe, my husband, Luigi, thought that your friend Vito Petracca was a fabulous boxer. The guy was in great shape, healthy, fast on his feet, and had a body like a man half his age. Luigi raved about his ability in the ring when he went to the gym. But what happened? How did he die?"

"Who knows?" Joe fidgeted. Why did all conversations have to start with one topic and always end up with Vito Petracca? "So, back to Sugar Ray, did Luigi place a bet on him?"

Signora Laura blushed, and covered her mouth so that the Sicilian customers who walked in wouldn't hear her.

"Yeah, he bet on LaMotta just in case, but Luigi put a bundle on Sugar Ray. He made close to two grand. You heard the neighborhood went nuts?" she said, and Joe looked at her with sheepish eyes and she laughed. "Yeah, I can see you were one of them."

Joe changed the conversation to the death of the tenement neighborhood. "It's bound to happen," he said. She retorted that if this happens within the next two to three years, they'd just retire and move to Miami, "where all the Jews live. They know how to live. They don't work like mules the way we do. We work until we drop dead. They make sure they got the best life, and we gotta copy them. I told my husband I want a full length mink coat before I move to Miami."

Now Joe burst out laughing, "Where you gonna wear it, Signora? It's hot down there."

"Ah, but when I come back, I'll need it for the New York weather. I gotta come back looking rich and spiffy."

"Who you gonna impress? Everybody will move away soon."

Signora Laura's smile disappeared. "Yeah, I'm gonna miss every face that ever came into my pastry shop."

The talk drifted towards real estate again, and Joe told Signora Laura that on Sunday he and his wife were visiting former residents of 107th Street, the Scalisis, who had bought a brick home in Bayside Queens. Signora Laura wasn't impressed.

"I want an old house with the old fashioned walls made out of wire lath and plaster. I don't want these paper houses they're smacking together for big money."

"I don't blame you," he said. "Maybe my wife and I should go to Staten Island. There's lots of land there, and I could build my own home with solid walls and ceilings."

Joe felt fully awake and thanked Signora Laura for the coffee and the conversation.

On Sunday, the Marras got in the big car and drove to Bayside, Queens. Joe told his wife that now with the power steering and easier manipulations of the mechanism, she, too, could drive a car. She had to take lessons before they moved away.

"What the hell for?" Gina responded, "You ain't going anywhere."

"Neither was Vito Petracca, but he died." Joe said quietly.

"You planning on running off with Mary?" she asked, always unsure of his intentions. Gina's jealousy was not imagined. Sometimes she fantasized that Joe was having an affair with Mary. Sometimes Gina fantasized about how many different ways she'd kill him.

"You nuts?" he answered.

Gina softened her belligerent mood, "Joe, don't leave me, okay? I'm scared you will. I'm scared that you'll plant me in a house with plaster walls and fancy ceilings and then you'll run the hell out of my life to Mary's bed." She was teary, and took out a handkerchief from her pocketbook, blew her nose and wiped her eyes.

"Damn it, you're obsessed with Mary," he snarled.

"No, Joe," Gina answered, "Aren't you confused?"

They drove over the Throg's Neck Bridge. Gina looked out the window at the boat traffic on the river, and silently cried, sensing that Joe no longer loved her. If it wasn't Mary, he'd find somebody else. This move to Bayside seemed suspicious. She was sure that Joe would keep the apartment on 106th Street, and come home once in a while.

Why couldn't they be lovers like the Scalisis? Gina couldn't help but notice the warmth between husband and wife. It was almost a holy experience to see them interact.

John adored Marie, and she, in turn, looked at him as though he were a god, and indeed he was. He laughed at his wife's sense of humor.

Marie shopped not only for food but for practical jokes which she could play on her guests. She had a little sugar spoon with a sizable hole in it, so that when they took the sugar from the bowl, it never made it into the black coffee. Of course, after many attempts at sweetening his coffee to no avail, Joe Marra burst out laughing.

"Marie, sugar spoon has a hole in it." Marie feigned great surprise as Gina uttered, "Yeah, it matches the hole in Joe's head." John and Marie looked at each other and smiled weakly. It was a nasty crack towards Joe.

* * *

Joe Marra had it all figured out: he would buy a house across the street from John and Marie. He would plant his wife in the new home, hire someone to give her driving lessons. He'd buy her a new car, and then he'd be free. He'd call her every day, and she'd attack him verbally, as usual with her vulgar mannerism of speaking, and he'd sleep in the tenement flat he had no intention of giving up. On occasion he'd come home. Gina knew his plan. There'd be no divorce. He'd live his life exactly as the Patriarch had. He'd have it all.

Gina knew why Joe was doing this. Divorce was not an option in a Sicilian family. The double standard prevailed. Angie had impressed upon her that she had to accept it, because that's the way it was. Gina knew that she would not accept this arrangement, and ultimately would have her own way.

Chapter VIII

The Letter: March 1951

Mary went downstairs, anxious to get the mail in hopes that she'd hear from Nino Caruso from Yonkers. He had promised to mail her figures and information on the house Mary wanted to buy from him. His accounts were sloppy and he was frustrated because he hadn't been able to answer any of her questions on heating bills, electric bills, and taxes. She was astounded to see that a man who owned a magnificent twelve room house on an acre of land could keep such poor records.

She shuffled through her mail and ran upstairs quickly. Mary made herself a cup of demi-tasse coffee and sat at the table facing the back yard and laid the five envelopes of mail before her. She saw a letter with her name scrawled on the envelope. There was no return address. She tore open the envelope quickly, curious about who could possibly be writing her a letter. Certainly it wasn't Mr. Caruso's uneven scrawl. Who could possibly have written her? She opened the letter with a kitchen knife and read:

"Dear Mary:

It's been a long time. I wanted to call you a half dozen times, but I was at a loss for words. Laughable, isn't it? The man of words speechless. I'll get to the point. You know about the police action we're in with Korea?

I've been assigned to cover it. That's what I do.so briefly, I need two things from you: one a photo of you, and two: I want to see you. Dinner? Dancing? Even talking. I'll be shipping out soon. I have to see you. I'll call you. Sean."

Mary's heart was beating out of her chest. His letter was like a breath of fresh air. She hadn't been able to get him out of her mind either, but what about Maggie?

The next day another letter came. This one was for Philip, but when Mary saw the return address she opened it and gasped. Philip was being drafted. Mary's heart sank. Sean's words suddenly held more significance. Police action? What was that? Were we at war or not? The Petracca boys were eligible for conscription.

It was Friday night. Philip was probably out with his friends in Greenwich Village. No, she would not call Philip tonight. She had hoped that because he was a student, he'd be exempt from the draft. But his choice of career wasn't crucial to the United States or the cause of freedom. She was deeply worried about Philip, especially because he was so fragile and frightened of everything. Oh, how could she bear her son going to war? Then there was Marco. As of now, no letter had come for him. Sean, Philip and maybe Marco?

It was a horrible time for Mary, a worrisome time. War put a shroud of fear in people's hearts. After packing Vito's books in boxes, she took a bath, then went to bed and slept fitfully, visions of war invading her mind.

On Saturday, as she was cleaning her house and packing Tess's books in boxes, she heard a knock at her door. She was alone. Mary had a chain lock installed on her door, so that she could see who was out in the hall. She opened the door with the chain lock. It was Joe Marra. She wasn't surprised to see him, he was so predictable.

"Mary? It's me. You got a new lock on the door?"

Mary ignored that. "What is it Joe?" she asked.

"Aren't you inviting me in?" he said.

Mary said, "No. You're to leave me alone."

He backed away from the door, his face dropped as though this was a surprise, "I didn't think you meant it." Mary was unnerved, "Yes, I did." She shut the door, and listened for him to walk away. She stood quietly, he was still behind the kitchen door. Her heart was beating rapidly with fear. What if he broke in? Finally she heard him muttering to himself as he went down the stairs. Mary went to the parlor window to look through the Venetian blinds at Joe Marra. He walked slowly shaking his head, then looked up at the window several times. Mary heaved a sigh of relief. She ran to the other three doors of the apartment and pushed heavy furniture against them in the event that he should attempt to break in.

She was in the tub when the phone rang. Mary looked at the little wind-up cat clock in her bathroom and got out of the tub to answer the phone. If it was Philip, she must keep his letter secret. Lately he sounded so happy, and not as frenetic as usual. The phone rang six times, before she picked it up.

"Mary?" and her heart was beating rapidly. She held her fist to her chest to quiet down the rapid pulse.

"Sean?" She grabbed a chair and sat down.

"You got my letter, yes?" he asked, and from the rhythm of his rapid speech, he seemed agitated.

"Sean, how sad, another war?"

"Yes. Will you see me?" he asked.

"Of course, Sean," she replied, "How bad is this police action? Philip's been drafted. I'll worry about both of you."

He was pleased that Mary had included him in her concern.

"Mary, can we meet Sunday night?" he asked anxiously.

"That's tomorrow. Isn't it sudden, Sean? I wasn't expecting to--"

Sean exhaled, in an erratic flow, followed by a long pause.

"Sean?" she asked, "What time?"

"Luigi's bar and grill, 41st Street and Third Avenue at 7:00. I'll be at the bar waiting. Take a cab, I'll take care of it when you get here, okay?"

"Inside the bar?" Mary asked again.

"Yes, we're going elsewhere, okay? It's my hang-out."

"Okay." She hung up and started pacing the floor. She had never been inside a bar with men all over the place. It was awful, but hopefully she would not see anyone she knew.

Day 1: The Overture:

She went to her closet and pulled out six Jonathan Logan dresses which Philip had bought for her. Each one was more

131

stunning than the next. She tried on every dress and chose a black one because she was still in mourning.

On Sunday, Mary went to the 8:00 o'clock mass, came home and cooked herself an omelet with red peppers and onions, and took a leisurely bath. Then she started getting anxious. This was crazy, she thought. It was a simple thank-you gesture for last Christmas Eve. No, she couldn't even hide it from herself. He had come into her home, three months ago, and had remained in her mind since.

It was getting late. Her stomach was grumbling. She drank an Alka Seltzer to calm her nerves.

She looked at her image as she put on her terrycloth robe. Her black hair framed her face and, even though she had wet it at the nape of her neck, the cut was perfect because it created a halo of black curly hair. She went into her bedroom, and put on clear nylon stockings, straightened her seams, put on black medium sized heels, and her simple, elegant Jonathan Logan dress. She looked in the full length mirror: Perfect. She was amazed at her appearance. She hadn't felt attractive in years, down playing her curvaceous body and her natural beauty. Once more, her inner dialogue revealed her apprehension.

Her greatest fear was that she'd make a fool of herself. She looked as though she was going to a concert instead of a simple dinner. Sean was probably dressed with a wrinkled shirt, his hair unkempt, as he was dressed last Christmas Eve, and she'd look like a fool all decked out for a casual evening which he was offering. She felt stupid. It was an ill-conceived decision to agree to meet him.

She called information, got the telephone number of Luigi's bar and grill and asked the bartender if she could speak to Sean Quinn. There was a lot of noise in the background and the bartender could hardly hear what the woman was saying. She shouted out "Quinn" several times.

"Quinn!" he bellowed, "Phone!"

Sean was surprised, "Who?" he asked.

"Some broad." Luigi said.

Sean said hello several times, but the person had hung up.

At the bar, Sean drank a beer and nursed it. He didn't want to become inebriated, not tonight. The guys at the bar all knew each other from different newspapers. They talked mainly about boxing, and many had a blow by blow description of the famous Valentine's Day win by Sugar Ray Robinson. They talked briefly about assignments, but not the war. Newspaper people reported wars, but never discussed them in public places. The World

War II slogan, "loose lips sink ships," was indelibly imbedded in their minds. One never knew just who else was at a public place, listening to pick up important information, especially from reporters.

"Damn! I bet Mary called." Sean said to his drinking buddy, Dennis.

"What time was she supposed to come?" Dennis asked, his words already slurring as he spoke.

"A half hour ago. I'm being stood up. Why am I not surprised?" he asked as he called for another beer.

Just then, in the misty, dimly lit, smoke filled saloon, the door opened, and cold air blew in as Mary walked in, looking downright fashionable. She perused the scene at the bar, and saw men at the bar, cigarettes dangling from their mouths, and smoke coming out of their nostrils. Most of the men were oblivious to her. She hesitated for just a moment, then turned around and walked out again. Sean was nowhere in sight. The cab driver was waiting at the curb for her, in the event that Sean stood her up.

"Thanks for waiting, sir. Would you take me back to 107th Street?" He said "sure," and Mary stepped into the cab. Suddenly Sean came tearing out of the bar, ran to the cab driver, banged on the window, and Mary told the driver to stop the cab. He pulled in to the curb again. Sean opened Mary's door and put his arms around her. "Where were you going? Didn't you see me?" The cab took off again. "Sean, how could you even see yourself in such dense smoke? I thought the place was on fire."

Sean laughed. He put his arm around her, "Let's go in for a minute. I want you to come back in. I want to show you off. You are knock-out beautiful!" Mary looked at him in disbelief, but it was such an endearing appeal that she went back in the bar. Most of the men were soused, but they obliged Sean by getting off their stools, and bowed in unison. Some couldn't even stand up. It looked like a routine in a vaudeville stage show. "Did they rehearse this?" she asked. Sean was surprised. "Not while I was at the bar." Most of them sat back on the stools and looked at Mary for a moment or two, then resumed their drinking.

Sean introduced her to the newspaper guys from the *Herald Tribune*, the *Daily News,* the *Daily Mirror* and two from the *New York Post.*

A correspondent from the *Tribune* asked her what in God's name was she doing with such a bum? Mary laughed and as she brought her gloved hand to her mouth, Sean intercepted it in midair, brought it to his mouth and kissed her hand. The guys applauded and some whistled. She had made a hit with his buddies.

Mary and Sean left to go to a restaurant on Second Avenue and 39th street, one which was lit by candles on each table. Reservations were for 7:30, but Sean and Mary got there at 8:00 o'clock.

Her first date was a revelation to Mary. From the moment she first met him, conversation seemed to flow like wine. He was so interested in what she had to say. Encouraged by his receptiveness towards her, and having had enough to drink to give her courage, she probed into an unanswered question: "Sean," she said. "Remember on Christmas Eve when you asked for opinions about Christmas?"

"Why, Mary," Sean was amazed that this was still on her mind.

"We each gave such different opinions and when I asked you for yours, you agreed with all of us. How could you agree with all of us?"

"Mary, I couldn't answer. I had no frame of reference to have an opinion. We celebrated nothing, not even birthdays. We were too poor," he bit his lip recalling his childhood.

"I didn't mean to probe, Sean, I'm so sorry."

His jaw tightened up. "Not as sorry as I was, but," he smiled warmly, "we always managed to have a tree. My brothers would go off in the afternoon with a hatchet, and bring one home by dusk, they'd came running up the road dragging the tree they had stolen from somebody's farm. My sister decorated it with paper napkins she had squirreled away from school. She'd make bows and lay them on the branches. Our Christmas dinner was a feast of baked potatoes."

Mary looked down as tears fell down her face.

"Mary, don't," he said. He reached out to wipe her tears. "We survived."

Sean asked for her photograph and Mary opened her purse and gave him a small photograph taken in front of St. Ann's church.

After a delicious dinner of a fillet mignon steak with a portobello mushroom, salad, bread, and several glasses of wine, Mary felt sleepy.

Sean paid the bill, and hailed a cab to his place. When they arrived, Sean walked into his building, but Mary didn't follow. Sean ran back for her, and Mary whispered, "I can't do this."

"Mary, for God's sake, you're exhausted, and so am I. I have one bedroom, and a couch that opens up into a bed.

Look," he said and let go of her hand. He put his hands on her shoulders.

"I still can't believe you agreed to see me. I won't do a damn thing to spoil it. Trust me, okay?"

"Are you asking me to sleep over, Sean?" she asked incredulously.

"Why not, Mary?"

She swayed towards him, then shook her head to clear it.

"Sean, I can't make it home. Promise me you won't try anything."

"Mary, I promise. I'll lend you pajamas, give you my bed, there's a lock on the bedroom door. Sleep wherever you want, and all I want is to sack out, too."

They walked up four flights of steps to Sean's four room flat. He had cleaned all day, and newspapers were piled into bundles in the four corners of his living room. Sean gave her a new toothbrush he had bought for her earlier in the day, and she burst out laughing again.

"You are so subtle, Sean Quinn," she said in amusement.

"You think so? Make no mistake about it, I want you, but not until you make the first move. I'm just so damned tickled to have you here under the same roof that I'm grateful for that."

She washed up, brushed her teeth, and got into his pajamas. His pajamas were tight on Mary. She wore his robe and went into his bed. He blew her a kiss and showed her where the lock on his bedroom door was.

"Mary, I don't walk in my sleep."

She was amused at Sean's constant reassurances.

Sean shut the bedroom door, then went back to the bedroom and knocked on the door. "By the way," he said. "Before you came, did you call Luigi's to cancel our date? He told me a woman was on the phone."

"Correction," Mary said. "Luigi told you that a *broad* was on the phone."

They burst out laughing.

"Then you were breaking our date?"

"Sean I was scared."

He wanted to hold her in his arms, but he held his hands behind his back. For the first time in his life, Sean Quinn was not jumping a woman. This one was opening up to him in a way that he wanted. She would come to him. It was the only way.

Mary said goodnight, and shut the door, but didn't lock it. He listened for that lock, but never heard it. Dear God, she trusts me, he thought.

Sean looked at his clock on the end table near the couch, it was 1:00 a.m. He fell asleep hugging the pillow and content that Mary was in his bed sleeping. Sean fell into a deep sleep, and mentally traveled in the nocturnal voyage of the mind to the World War in Anzio. His sleep was agitated, and he flailed, moaned and thrashed in his sofa-bed half the night.

Chapter IX

Sean and Mary

Day 2: Prelude

The next morning, Mary got up early, brushed her teeth with her new toothbrush, wet the washcloth, and washed and wiped the sink clean. She walked into the kitchen in her stockinged feet, while she carried her shoes. A pot of coffee perking on the stove would fill the small apartment with coffee aroma. Maybe she would even find bread and a toaster. Even a bachelor had to eat and drink. She opened up a cabinet, and it was empty. She went along the small row of cabinets, and found that they too were empty. Mary looked inside the refrigerator, and there was a six-pack of Rheingold bottled bear and a can of beans with rusty residue on the lid.

She sat on the stool and contemplated her next move. He had been moaning during the night, and she had woken up, opened the bedroom door, and saw Sean's face buried in his pillow with his legs folded close to his body, as the blanket lay sprawled on the floor. God knows what nightmares he must have had.

So, that's why he's slender, she thought. He doesn't even buy the bare necessities. She filled the only glass in the kitchen with cold tap water, sat on the only stool in the kitchen and waited for him to wake up. She wanted to say good bye to him before she left.

Suddenly his very loud and irritating alarm clock went off and Mary jumped with a start. "Damn you!" Sean snarled, followed by the sound of something falling on the floor. He had probably knocked it down. My God, she thought, Sean talks to his things. Maybe that's what happens when you live alone.

He crawled out of his sofa, and shuffled past the kitchen, with his eyes half shut. He went to the bathroom and didn't shut the door. She heard him gargle, spit and run the shower. He took a long shower.

Mary got up, and looked out the window. Traffic was already moving in lower Manhattan, and she stood on the precipice of a decision, or indecision, about whether to sleep with Sean. It never left her mind from the first moment they had met. She wanted him. She was fast losing the battle of conflict, that is, the *she* from Corleone, the *she* from *onore,* the *she* who had been schooled against the worst sin a female from Corleone could commit: adultery.

Sean came out of the bathroom in his T shirt and boxer shorts. He didn't call out for her, nor did he realize in his quasi-sleepy state that he was not alone. Maybe she should just go. She decided to leave. No consequences, no regrets, no sins. It would be easiest that way.

He shuffled into the kitchen for a glass of water and saw Mary slip into her heels. "Dear God, Mary. I forgot you were here. Did anything happen between us last night?" Mary laughed at her conflict. Obviously she didn't make such an indelible impression. He had forgotten her in his bed.

"Sure, Sean," she said sarcastically. He pressed his hands on his temples, and looked at her. He wasn't tuned in to her at all. She'd play the game. Why not? In a little while, she'd be back in her own world of solitude and books.

"Was it good?" he asked provocatively.

"Yes, very good," she said. "That's why I'm still here."

He put his arms around her. "Does this mean a shotgun wedding?"

"No, Mr. Quinn, no wedding is necessary, but coffee is, and all you have is beer." She relaxed now. He was so perplexed, so child-like that once again he became endearing to her. How easily she could forget who she was, and what she was, and follow him wherever his fancy took him.

Sean had been meticulous, leaving nothing out of his preparation for her visit. He had cleaned the apartment, gathered all his newspapers in neat, high piles, placing them in the four corners of his living room, and changed the sheets on his bed. But he hadn't planned the coffee the morning after. Well damn, he thought, there was no morning after.

"Mary, I don't do breakfast here, I just sleep here. Give me a minute, and we'll go out for breakfast." She smiled and he kissed the nape of her neck, and she kissed him gently on the corner of his mouth.

"Mary, don't start anything you won't finish," he warned.

"It's only a kiss, Sean, a simple kiss," she said as she looked away modestly. He cupped her face in his hands, got close to her and whispered, "Simple?" He threw his head back and laughed heartily. "Okay, one minute I'll get my shirt and tie." He added "Yep, I do own a tie, Mary. And we'll go for a big breakfast-the works."

"Coffee's fine, Sean," she responded. Mary experienced another conflict. His kiss had been passionate, and it was clear that he wanted her. That should be enough. She could run now, maybe regret it, but she'd be safe. Quickly, Mary took her bag and walked towards the door. She could still hear Sean muttering, "Where the hell did it go?" as he searched for his tie.

Mary tiptoed out the door, and quickly went down the four flights of stairs. As she got outside, Sean was leaping down the stairs like a jaguar.

"Mary! Mary!" he shouted as she raised her arm to hail a cab. "Don't leave me, for God's sake, don't walk out on me." As the cab screeched to a halt at the curb, Sean caught up with her and opened the door and got in next to her. "Plaza Hotel, please," Sean said as he slipped on his tie. Mary was pleased that he had pursued her.

"Where the hell were you going?" he said furiously.

"Home, Sean, where I belong."

"Without breakfast?" He lightened up very quickly. He must not alarm her, he thought, if he hadn't already alarmed her with his weird morning ritual.

She teased, "I thought of making beer and beans, but I couldn't find a can opener."

Sean laughed and said, "Well, not only is she beautiful, but she has a sense of humor."

He put his arm around her, and nuzzled his face to her ear, and she shut her eyes, and leaned back as Sean kissed her ear lobe, and then turned her face towards him and kissed her deeply. She returned the kiss, and they clung to each other like magnets. Mary pulled away as she sensed his level of arousement. He was shaken, and he took her hand to his face and held it there.

The cab driver stopped at the Plaza. Obviously he had been looking through the rear view mirror.

"Hey buddy, hate to interrupt you love birds, but we're here." Sean cleared his throat trying to regain his composure. "So we are." Sean groped in his back pocket for his wallet, and said, "Mary, I can't move. Here's my wallet, pay the man. See what you do to me?"

She paid the cab driver and tipped him.

As they walked into the dining room, Sean was recognized.

"Mr. Quinn, how nice to see you. For two?" Sean Quinn rarely brought a date to his breakfasts at the Plaza. This woman perhaps was special. It sure looked that way to Kevin, the waiter.

Sean replied, "Yes, for me and my lady."

Mary liked that. His lady. It pleased her.

He ordered a large American breakfast: eggs, bacon, pancakes and juice and coffee. Mary wanted only black coffee and a piece of fruit. Sean asked her to move in with him for the next four days and nights. She shrugged, "I don't think I can, Sean." But Sean persisted. "We want each other. You say no, but your body says yes. Mary, I have little time left. No games." Mary winced at the implication that he might not come back.

"Sean, I'm torn up. For you it's easy, for me it's not."

He caressed her face. "Easy? I don't think so. I tried to forget you, but I couldn't. Usually when I cover a story, I just go where I'm assigned, I have no ties, so that's easy, but now? You're in my head. **That's** not easy. I need to feel close to you."

Mary's eyes were watery. Had they fallen in love? They seemed to be so well tuned to each other. What had she to lose? He kissed her hand trying to persuade her, as he changed his sense of urgency to levity:

"Either you stay with me, or you stay with me."

Mary giggled. "That's my choice?"

He wore a serious face. "Yes, Mary."

"Okay," she said. Now what was she saying okay to? Was she humoring him? She was in conflict over this.

"Damn!" Sean thought, is this what it's like to be with a Sicilian woman? Would she come out of her self-imposed prison?

"Mary, what does okay mean?" His bright blue eyes filled with expression penetrated hers.

"It means 'yes,' Sean. I want to."

He was surprised by her answer. Unpredictable. He sensed a promise of unbridled passion in her warm look.

"Mary, you won't regret it," he said softly.

As the waiter brought breakfast, he realized that he had intruded on a tender moment. "Mr. Quinn, shall I come back with this?" the waiter asked delicately.

"No Kevin, my lady is hungry and so am I. Love does that to your appetite, you know." Sean had finally uttered a word which Mary noticed.

The platters of breakfast were on a large plate with a metal cover over each dish, even Mary's sparse breakfast. Mary shed her reserve, and began the act of love at the table. She took Sean's hand and kissed it.

"*Buon appetito, mio amore,*" she said softly and provocatively

"*Anche a te, tesoro,*" Sean responded in perfect Italian.

They dined in silence as their promise of love had been sealed. There was so much about this man she wanted to learn. Just a few days in a lifetime. Maybe she'd never see him again, but she'd have those memories. Mary's spirits were in tune with her mindset. It would be her secret love, even if they never saw each other again. There would be no consequences if they were discreet.

It was almost 11:30 a.m. when they got up from the dining room table and walked into the main lobby of the Plaza. There was a group of young people holding clothing bags breezing into the lobby with a sense of purpose. Mary thought at first that they were actors, and as she looked at each one, dressed so artsy, black clothes, outrageous jewelry and frizzy Afro hairdo's on the girls, she saw her son Philip. He was shocked to see his mother at the Plaza, especially in the morning.

"Momma, what are you doing here?" he asked surprised to see her.

"I was having breakfast with Sean Quinn." Sean was behind Mary and at first Philip didn't see him.

"This is a bad joke, isn't it, Momma?"

Mary was displeased at his choice of words so that Sean heard them. He motioned his mother to come away with him.

149

Sean remained behind. All Sean could think about was that he had tried to be discreet, taking her to a posh hotel for breakfast, and who walks in front of her, but her son. So much for being discreet, but now Sean believed that she'd probably bolt and run. He stood on the side, watching them talk. Philip was agitated, and gesticulated like an orchestral conductor. It's over, Sean thought, this is not going to happen, not after Philip saw his mother.

Philip interrogated his mother like a prosecutor. "What are you doing with him? Why him? What about Maggie, what about how crazy this is. He's a son of a bitch making out with mother and daughter;.nice momma, nice, when did you lose your marbles? Poppa's turning in his grave."

Mary let him go on like this, and turned the conversation to what *he* was doing here. He told her that they had a special showing in one of the larger rooms of the student's fashions, and he was showing his fabric designs in ascots, scarves and accessories. He asked his mother if she was staying, and she said she couldn't.

He asked her if she was involved with Sean, and Mary answered "No. We're just friends, Philip. He's shipping out to Korea, and wanted to take me to breakfast at the Plaza as a gesture of gratitude for last Christmas eve." Mary had not lied, she just gave him selective truths because he was not ready for more, and she couldn't tell him how much she cared for Sean Quinn.

Mary told Philip about the letter of conscription. He paled as she told him, and handed it to him. "Philip, I'm sick over this," she said, but he simply took the letter and put it in his pocket. Philip turned his back to his mother, tried to compose himself with the eruption of what he was feeling. In an instant, he had been given news that could kill him. He wasn't ready to die. He hadn't lived yet. The focus of his anger evaporated in view of his draft notice. Philip was like ice: cold. He admonished his mother not to destroy the family, then ran off to join his fellow students.

Sean studied Philip's body language: surprise, outrage, and finally a cold demeanor, as though he was in shock. Mary re-joined Sean, and they took a cab to the *Herald Tribune* office.

Sean put his arm around Mary and inquired if everything was alright. He was of the mindset that any moment, Mary would tell him that she had had a change of heart. He would take her home, and his dream would be shattered. He braced himself. "Mary, what's the status?" he asked. She didn't understand his question, and asked him to say it another way. "Are we to be together?" and she took his hand and kissed it. "Yes." There was no further conversation. Mary was obviously in turmoil. She shut her eyes and put her head on his shoulder. It broke his heart to think that he was causing it.

"What's troubling you Mary?" he asked finally.

"Philip." She opened her eyes and sat up. "I handed him a letter from the government. He's being called to serve."

Mary couldn't speak of it, and Sean realized that whatever was happening was not about him. Sean commented, "I saw it. One moment his face was animated, and then shocked. Mary don't beat yourself, he had to know sometime, no?"

"Not like this. I gave him a double shock, seeing me with you, and telling him that he was drafted. What rotten timing!" she shook her head.

"Look, I feel terrible. What do you want to do? I could take you home after the *Trib*. We'll cancel Plan A." Mary was moved by his ready compliance for her. "Sean, no! You're going to war. I don't know if I'll ever see you again, so, I won't go to Plan B." He held her in his arms.

They were determined now in a single mindset to make this short time perfect for them, to make every moment filled with intimacy of every kind, to make the memories to comfort them when life was frightening.

Sean took Mary to the newspaper office, and, holding her hand, brought her through the large news room. Everyone looked up in surprise to see Sean Quinn walk in with such an elegant woman.

Maybe Quinn had graduated from bimbos to ladies. Perhaps there was hope for him, the newsmen thought as he waved happily and passed by their desks. He took Mary to his editor, Patrick Mulcaney. "Pat, this is my lovely lady, Mary. Mary? Patrick Mulcaney." They shook hands. Mary was impressed at the way Sean was treated by his fellow workers. He was liked, and teased. He had a sunny nature, and yet was very realistic about life, perhaps because of the nature of his work. He caught humanity in its most destructive moments and reported those moments with his own style. However, Sean had opinions, and on occasion they slipped into his copy which sometimes got him into trouble. But he was an outstanding journalist. Everyone on the staff of the *Herald Tribune* looked up to him.

Sean walked out with an envelope he had to look over, and, even though he had the week off, he still had to come in for papers, briefings, and the latest directives from the editor-in-chief. Reporters wrote, and the written word was always more powerful than guns or political speeches. People read their newspapers as though they were reading the Bible. For most Americans, an article was truth.

After leaving the paper, Sean took Mary shopping and bought her a pair of slacks, a blouse, a jacket, and walking shoes. "Now, you're dressed like me-casual, now we look good together, and of course I look like less of a slob."

Mary laughed. "Which makes me more of a slob?" she retorted.

Sean was amused by her ability to take things literally. "Damn! I put my foot in my mouth. Don't Sicilians hold grudges?" he asked boyishly

"What'll happen if I do?" she asked, and in earnest he replied, "Then we can't make love."

Mary laughed aloud, and he applauded. "Brava, Mary! Now that's what I call a laugh." She blushed again as they walked. He kissed her ear, and held her close to his body. A sense of exhilaration came over him as he realized that what was happening was emotional intimacy. Like magnets they had meshed, everything he was feeling she was too. Her eyes sparkled, her body was receptive to his touch, and he felt like

Goliath. What was different? No, why analyze it, just go with the flow.

Mary enjoyed Sean's little eruptions of a "Damn!" or some feigned expletive, but she didn't feel that he meant it. In fact, Mary was convinced that the bluster covered up a deeply sentimental man who had withdrawn as she had, to protect himself from the games of life.

They took a cab to the battery and then got on the Staten Island Ferry. When it arrived, they took a bus to Hylan Boulevard. It was a huge road with open fields on either side. At the end of the boulevard, they got off and walked on the sand facing Perth Amboy, New Jersey. They walked, held hands, kissed frequently, and talked.

There was a sense of urgency to make every moment count.

Sean's eyes hardly left her face, and she opened up to him in a way reminiscent of the early years of her marriage to Vito.

"Sean, what does your name translate to?" she asked as they faced the murky waters of the bay.

"Gaelic for John." he answered. He slipped his long slender fingers through her hair, "You know, Mary, I don't go to church any more, but the most beloved of all God's kingdom besides Jesus was always Mary. There's a grace about Jesus' mother, which is the ideal of womanhood. When I first saw you, one word bounced in my head, "grace" and then I learned that your name was Mary. How fitting, I thought at the time. Mary, full of grace, and that's how I see you."

Alone together standing watching the waves slap the shore, they were locked in each other's arms with Mary's head resting on his chest below his chin.

After a while, they took the bus back to St. George ferry terminal. Sean asked the bus driver if he could drop them off at a good fish restaurant. The bus driver stopped in front of one on Bay Street overlooking the Hudson River.

The restaurant was decorated with fishing nets, old wheels from sailing ships and other memorabilia from the sea. Sean and Mary were starved. They ordered home made clam chowder, a salad, and fish fry with fried potatoes on the side. Mary ordered a baked potato.

They dined leisurely and talked about their childhoods. Sean came from a large family of nine children, eight of them boys. At first the stories he told of his family had a charming comedic delivery, but underneath there was a sadness, which Sean avoided.

"Sean, you didn't mention your father at all. Had he died?"

"No, Mary when I was three years old, he flew the coop. I hated my mother's life, maybe even more than she did, and I figured that she was imprisoned by the marriage trap. That scared the hell out of me."

"I know how she must have felt," Mary said, "I did, too. Surrounded by a family, I felt alone." Sean swallowed hard when he heard Mary echo his sentiments. He grew anxious that Mary would be his for a few days, and no more. He regretted having stressed no roots to her a few times. As she spoke, he felt that she too was reticent about involvement. "Damn you, Sean Quinn," he thought to himself "you have a big mouth!"

Sean wanted to know everything about Mary's youth, how she got married, who her friends were, and information on her parents and how many siblings she had.

She laughed sardonically. "That's easy and short. I had a shotgun wedding, I wasn't allowed to have friends. I had a sadistic father, a mother whose voice I seldom heard because she was afraid to speak, and no siblings. My father hated children." Her eyes opened wide and he sensed that her concise answer precluded further questions.

"And that's it, Mary?" he asked, and she shut down again. She stood up, and went to the ladies room.

Sean thought about her brief answers and what they implied. A shotgun wedding spelled only one thing: rape. How horrible. Oh, God, he thought to himself, let me have the opportunity to give this beautiful woman some joy. He felt like Goliath, like David, Romeo, Dante, and all the great lovers of history. He had a mission. He was going to make a difference in her life. Yet, what was he dealing with? How much time did he have? Would he be special for her? He wanted to be her hero. The questions bounced off the walls of his inner sanctum, and he had no answers.

Mary returned to the table. Sean paid the bill at the cash register, while Mary waited outside the restaurant.

"Great food, sir," Sean said to the proprietor. "I hope we didn't overstay our welcome."

The heavy set man, smiled. "I know a pair of lovebirds when I see them. For lovers, time stands still. It was a pleasure having you here. Come back again. Is she your girlfriend, or wife?" he asked out of curiosity.

"In my head, sir, everything." Sean shook hands with the man, who called out, "God bless you both."

Sean and Mary went to the St. George ferry terminal, and Sean called his friend Jack McCool, a fellow newspaperman, who together with his wife ran a bed and breakfast in St. George. Jack told him that the room was ready, and the cab dropped them off at the McCool home. Their room was on the third floor facing the lower Manhattan skyline. This was the setting for their rendezvous, and it afforded them the privacy they needed to make their fairy tale come true.

Chapter X

Day 2: Intermezzo

Mary and Sean checked in at the McCool bed and breakfast. Josine McCool, from a Sicilian immigrant family, was enthralled when her Irish husband Jack told her about his friend Sean, a confirmed bachelor, and his girlfriend, an immigrant from Corleone. The Italian-Irish combination in a couple was rare. Prejudices still abounded in both ethnic groups.

Josine made great efforts to prepare the honeymoon room with its built in fireplace, footstools, exquisite paintings of nudes, and a small refrigerator. She even put a needlepoint heart pillow on each sleeping pillow as a romantic touch. Josine reassured them that no one else had reserved the other three bedrooms on that floor, so they really had the whole floor to themselves.

They even had their own small ante room with a love seat, a radio and books. Josine even included a bible next to the night table on the right of the bed. The bed was a four poster, and the mattresses were feather mattresses which were very high so that one had to step on a footstool on either side of the bed, to climb on to the bed.

Sean opened the door to their room, swept her into his arms and carried her to the edge of the bed. He knelt at her feet and kissed her hands murmuring "My beloved Mary." As Sean stoked the fire, Mary stepped down to the footstool, and sat on the thick rug facing the fireplace. In front of the window was a round marble table with a cooler in which lay a bottle of champagne chilling and two stem glasses. Sean popped the cork, and poured the champagne, then sat next to Mary.

They could hear the sonorous, mournful wailing of the ferry boat's long whistle as it pulled out of the St. George slip. It was so quiet in comparison to the street noises of the city they had to endure.

"Oh, Sean, you chose such a beautiful, quiet place."

"It had to be perfect, Mary. Jack told me that his wife owned a bed and breakfast. I had no idea what it was like until now." Mary looked at the twenty foot ceilings and the scroll work of the early days of construction, and felt as though they had not only left their lives behind them but that they were stepping into the time frame of five decades ago.

Sean drank his champagne and Mary sipped hers. They talked of the room, and the moment, leaving any topic which wasn't immediate out of this time together. He put his empty glass down on the ceramic tiles in front of the fire place, and waited until Mary had finished hers. She drank slowly and over the rim of her glass, her black eyes looked into his. He wanted to make love to her, leisurely, tenderly, and he wanted Mary to make love to him.

"Sean," Mary said as he kissed every feature of her face in small tender kisses, holding her face in his hands like a rosebud. "Sean," she whispered his name again, "When did you plan this?" Sean stopped kissing her, and looked seriously into her eyes and answered, "When I hit puberty." Mary laughed. Sean got up, pulled the pillows off the bed for each of them, and stretched out his body on the soft rug. "Mary, make love to me."

Mary began the act of love. Slowly she disrobed Sean, then herself. At first he watched her and allowed her to take the lead, enticed by her every move. With each caress, she murmured a term of endearment in Sicilian. Each touch, each kiss of hers aroused him so that he could no longer watch her. In one move he enveloped her and fell into the rhythm of her body in the act of love. Sean shut his eyes and murmured Mary's name, overwhelmed with feelings he did not articulate. Mary shivered with the aftermath of passion, and Sean reached for the blanket crumbled in a heap at the edge of their feet, and wrapped it around her and cradled her in his arms.

Like a sensitive conductor who's intent was to interpret faithfully the composer's intent, Sean's sensitivities were tuned in to Mary's deepest emotions. "Incredible," he whispered as he stroked her hair, and kissed her face, looking at her as though he was memorizing every feature, every expression.

They lay on the rug until the fire had turned the logs into embers. They felt chilled as the fire died down, so they climbed onto the huge billowing bed, and sank into a cloud-like softness which embraced the curves of their bodies. Sean's fingers traced Mary's brow gently. "Mary, what are you thinking?" Mary said, *"Tesoro,* I've known you all my life." He whispered, "Mary, tonight I made **love** to a woman." Two human beings had meshed at the pinnacle of passion. They would never be the same.

"Plan B was never an option," Mary said. Sean snickered.

"I'm glad," he said, sighing deeply.

In her arms, he was home.

They lay in bed, in a euphoric state with their arms around each other, until sleep overcame them lulled by the boat whistles from the harbor. The windows were long, had no shades, and the room was filled with light of the full moon.

Day 3: Tuesday:

Mary got up first, and used the bathroom. She dressed in there, and an hour later, Sean was up. He sat at the edge of the bed and looked out the window to the peaceful scene of the harbor and the docking of the Staten Island Ferry.

His morning clock was different than Mary's. Once her eyes were open, she was up. It took Sean a few hours to acclimate his alert reflexes. Mary kissed him as he walked towards the bathroom, and he gave her a glimmer of a smile, and walked on like a sleep-walker.

She was amused. He reminded her of a **few** of the seven dwarfs: grumpy in the morning; sleepy at night; happy when he focused on her; dopey when he woke up. Out of habit, Mary pulled the covers and fixed the bed. The room was large but the bed dominated it, and Mary couldn't tolerate disorder. Sean never noticed it. He came out of the bathroom and asked her why she was fixing the bed, they were only going to get back in it tonight, or maybe even this afternoon. "Mary, that bed is reserved for making love, don't fix it."

"We operate on different wave lengths." Mary commented, and he grunted.

An hour later, they went down the creaky stairs to the main level. Josine McCool greeted them warmly. Their table was set before another long window, and in the center were real red roses. She greeted the lovers warmly and asked them what they wanted to eat. Mary asked for fruit and black coffee, which wasn't brown coffee with no milk, but double roasted coffee. "You have Medaglia D'Oro?" Mary asked. "Yes Mary, my parents came from Montagnareale in Northern Sicily. I do cater to an Italian clientele from Brooklyn." They slipped into Sicilian dialect and Sean looked from one to the other, understanding an occasional word. Many of their words were not Italian, they were words left behind by conquering armies in the past centuries. When they ended their Sicilian exchange, Josine left to make their breakfast.

"Mary, What in God's name does *mischinu* mean?"

"It means: poor thing, masculine gender." He raised his eyebrows, and said, "I suppose I'm the mischinu you're referring to." Mary said yes. She also wanted to know if Sean had studied Italian, because he seemed to understand and enunciate the Italian language well. He explained that he took a cram course in Italian during World War II. Mary was impressed. He had so many talents, and was a man of eclectic tastes. Her opinion of him based only on his appearance had totally dissipated. Mary had discovered the treasure of Sean Quinn.

Josine rolled the cart with their food on it. Mary giggled as she saw the feast being brought over. "Sean, you speak Italian and embrace the Italian culture, but you don't eat like us. You eat like an American." He agreed, "Yeah, Mary, once I go to work, lunch isn't even a thought. Sometimes I just go around the clock, and maybe I have two meals a day, so I eat breakfast like a camel who stores his food in his pouch." Mary could see that happening in a busy newspaperman's life.

Sean ate ravenously. He had juice, and tried some fruit which was not part of his morning diet, cornflakes and milk, followed by two eggs, bacon and potatoes. Mary enjoyed watching him eat. "You're so beautiful," she whispered as he ate. He looked at her in disbelief, "Mary, nobody looks beautiful when they eat." She insisted, "You do," and finished the thought in her head, "because I love you."

After breakfast they walked for an hour. When they came back to the small inn, Josine handed Sean the keys to their old Ford sedan. "Jack wants you to explore the colonial town of Richmond comfortably, instead of taking busses." Sean thanked her. The community of newspapermen and women was a family.

They looked out for each other, and often helped research a story together.

Sean asked Josine for written directions which she had ready.

They visited the intact colonial village of Richmond, and spent the entire day looking back in history during the revolution. The artifacts and museum were of great interest to Sean and Mary. They discovered that they had much more in common than they knew. Sean was surprised that Mary had a great passion for books and read voraciously.

She confessed that for years books were her only friends, and that when the family was out of the house, she'd take a train to the library on 42nd street, borrow a book and read it for several hours. She'd return home just before the children came home from school.

"Your kids didn't know where you spent the day?" he asked.

"No, Sean, nobody knew, nobody asked, and all of them were self involved, and this was my wonderful secret life where my mind could travel, experience and see, and yet I was always home on time for them."

Sean had to inquire, "Then Vito never knew?" She shook her head no.

Sean grew more and more enthralled with Mary, and wondered what life would have been like had he met her sooner.

Interestingly enough, they were going through a similar thought process as they uncovered their interests to each other. Opinions about each other were being reformulated.

They dined once more in a seafood restaurant at 5:00 in the late afternoon, eating five types of fish including fried calamari rings as an antipasto.

They drove back to the McCool inn at 8:30 p.m. Sean carried tuna fish hero sandwiches back to the room with a six-pack of Rheingold beer. They made love in the bed, and had their sandwich dinner in front of the fireplace. Sean added more logs, and the warmth of the fire was so comforting that they put the blankets and pillows on the floor and slept in front of the fire.

Their time together was filled with feeding all of their senses and sensibilities, and it was a perfect intermezzo to be memorized for a time when they needed to recall the passion, the friendship, and the sense of unity and peace they felt by opening up the private books of their lives and sharing them.

They made love at midnight, and before Sean fell asleep, he whispered to Mary, "I had no sense of time before tonight. We escaped our lives just like Peter Pan, and we went to our Never Never Land, but now my mind is polluting my euphoria with you Mary, and I'm getting a sinking feeling in the bottom of my stomach-it's going to end, isn't it? Where is Tinker Bell, Mary? Where is God, Mary?"

She shivered and put her arms around him and held him and rocked him as he burst into sobs. She wanted to comfort him with words, but all he seemed to need or want was to vent, and be held just as she was doing. She chose not to say anything. Why should she crowd his mind with her words when his fears of facing yet another war were dominating his intellect and his emotions. She was perfectly still. Finally, he stood up, went to the bathroom, washed his face, took a shower, and came back to Mary.

"Tesoro," she whispered, as he added another log to the fire, and got under the covers with her. He tucked the blanket around them both. "Sorry, Mary." She shook her head and kissed

him. He shivered and buried his face in the nape of her neck. She held him and stroked his brow until he fell asleep.

Chapter XI

Finale: Day 4: Wednesday

The next morning, Sean got up first, stoked the fire, and piled two logs on the iron cradle. Cold winds had been blowing and creeping into the room through the old window frames. Pipes of the house's old radiators banged and hissed as the heat came up.

The howling wind only made Mary want to shrink deeper into the soft mattress. She was cognizant of the morning sun as it flooded the room in the early hours, but she kept her eyes tightly shut, not quite ready to bounce out of bed. Mary reached over for Sean, but he was gone. She sat up with a start. "Sean?" she called. She heard the shower running, got up, and joined Sean in the shower. He was delighted to see her, and they scrubbed each other, and made love in the shower, something Sean had wanted to do.

His anxieties about war, and his concern that Mary and he had been only an interlude, had gotten the best of him on the last night of their rendezvous.

But this morning, Sean was in great spirits. He shut his eyes as Mary scrubbed his back and uttered endearing words in Sicilian. After their long shower, they dried themselves off, got dressed, and packed their bags to go home. Sean shut the metal-mesh curtains in the fireplace and ran down to let Josine know that the fire was still burning in their room. Josine assured him that she'd take care of it. They paid their bill, and thanked Josine for her warmth and hospitality. Jack was already at work. He worked the first edition and was at the newspaper at 3:00 in the morning while other people slept.

Josine drove them to the ferry, and invited them to return. The ferry was filling up with cars, so there was a quick last embrace and a run to get on before it pulled out.

There had been no time for breakfast.

The ferry boat was revved up, causing intensive vibrations that made the outdoor passengers hang on to the rail.

"You'd think they'd know how to drive this damn boat." Sean commented.

"Sean, the tide is strong and the captain has to shift in reverse sometimes to ease into the slip."

Sean asked Mary how she knew this, and she told him that when the children were young, she took them to Staten Island, and

Philip took off to the captain's quarters on the top level. One of the crew members stopped him, and the captain was kind enough to invite Philip in his cabin. He explained how hard it was to moor the ferryboat into the slip without the violent shaking of the boat. Sean was enthralled with the information as well as the anecdote from her life. He wanted so much to know more about her history, but Mary was reticent to do so. He had learned first hand what *omerta* meant, especially to Mary.

They knew that once the boat docked, life as they knew it would resume. Yet Sean seemed content. Mary couldn't get the vision of his outburst last night out of her head. She wished she could make his turmoil go away. "Are you okay, Sean?" she asked, "Yes, Mary. You've given me a glimpse of what Shangri La must be like." Mary didn't understand, but she knew that it must be a good place.

He wrapped his arms around her. Mary wore a shawl around her head. "You look like a Russian peasant," he said. Mary disagreed. "No, a Sicilian one, Sean. I don't remember my mother ever going out without the black shawl covering her head. Most married women did, they were always in black, because when somebody died, the time one had to wear mourning was a lifetime for a husband or parent or child, and at least a year for other relatives." He was pleased. Mary was unfolding as she articulated snippets of her history.

As the ferryboat approached the Manhattan skyline, Sean whispered in Mary's ear: "When did you know that I wanted to make love to you?" She whispered in his ear, "When I got your note saying that you needed to be with me."

"Precisely!" She faced him, and once more spoke in his ear because the wind outside the boat was howling and blowing and creating its own frenzy.

"Sean, when did you know that I wanted to make love to you?"

He grinned. "When you said you'd see me," he said.

Mary laughed. "And I thought that it didn't show."

"When we had a tug of war with the broom in your kitchen," he said. "I held your hands and you acted as though you had been burnt. There was a strong attraction and it frightened you. You know, you're transparent."

She said, "You saw through me?"

He nodded. "Of course, Mary, that's why we're here."

At 11:30 a.m. they docked in Manhattan. They ran up two flights of stairs to the Third Avenue El, paid the nickel fare and sat down. He had his arm around her and held her right hand.

When Sean got to his stop on 42nd Street, he kissed Mary deeply in a goodbye kiss. He stood on the platform and watched the train pull away.

Sean took a cab and went to the newspaper. He saw his editor, they had a short conference, and Sean was starved. There was no time to have breakfast at the Plaza, so he bought two bacon and egg sandwiches on a roll at the nearby deli, a container of orange juice, a banana and a large cup of coffee, and went home.

He found a note tacked to his door. It could only be Maggie. He recognized her handwriting. He opened the door, put the letter on the kitchen counter, and had breakfast first. After the last drop of coffee had been consumed, Sean opened the envelope:

"Sean darling:

Where are you? I've been frantic. Nobody at Luigi's knew where you were. I came to your place at 11:00 p.m., called your apartment at 3:00 a.m. Where the hell are you? Damn it! Are you sick in some hospital? Or better scenario: Are you having a role in the hay with some sexy Communist spy working for the C.I.A.? Let me hear from you or I'll scream! Maggie."

Sean called Maggie, and told her he had been away. He laughed at her caustic imaginative note, and said Mata Hari had been promoted to the 'spy in the sky' organization of the next world.

Maggie giggled. She wanted to see him, and he told her to meet for drinks at Luigi's tomorrow night. He had to say goodbye, and face her insidious interrogation, but he had no idea how disturbing that meeting would be for him, how it would open a can of guilt he had safely stored in the closet of his mind.

* * *

Mary got home at 12:30. She made herself a cup of black coffee, and ate an apple. She put the contents of her bag on her bed, hung up her dress, and felt so strange in the apartment she had called home for many years. It wasn't home any more. No one was here, and she didn't want to be here either. Soon she'd move. For now, her senses were still tingling with the memory of Sean Quinn. As she opened the windows to circulate air, the phone rang. It was Philip. He had taken a leave from school and was coming home. "Where have you been, Momma? I was worried sick." Mary said she'd tell him when he came home.

When Philip arrived, Mary told him that she and Sean Quinn had gone away for the past four days. Philip knew he had intercepted something when they had met at the Plaza. Mary wanted to be brief, but thorough in her rationale.

"Philip, I was diminished by your father's contempt. Then I met Sean Quinn and I felt beautiful. Philip, I had to be with him." Philip stared into his mother's eyes, and saw the pain in her heart, and he listened without reaction. "We needed to see each other." Mary was finished. She raised her eyebrows for Philip's reaction, and Philip's eyes were soft. The timing in this case was perfect.

"Are you marrying him?" he asked with hesitation, afraid of the answer.

"No. Marriage wasn't even mentioned." Philip sighed, "Good! Okay, it's behind you. Tell nobody, okay? No need for anyone to know."

"I know," she said, and embraced him, but Philip held back his usual affection.

There was a double standard here. No one had ever questioned Vito about his weekend escapes, but she had to answer for her indiscretion. No surprise for Mary who had come from a nation of double standards for men and women, and the beat went on with the next generation of Sicilian-American males.

* * *

Sean and Maggie met at Luigi's bar. They sat in the back of the restaurant at a table tucked away from the other clients.

"What happened, Sean?" Maggie was direct as always.

"I've met someone, Maggie."

"What about us?" she asked, wanting to storm out of there and not allow him to see how she was crumbling inside.

"We had a great six month love affair, Maggie. I'm thirty seven years old. I could be your father. You deserve better, a young man closer to your age." Maggie wanted to slap him.

"Really? Why didn't you think of your age when you fucked me? Don't tell me your Irish-Catholic conscience is bothering you." She stormed out trying to hide her tears. Sean tore out after her, grabbed her and called a cab. Maggie wished he hadn't intercepted her so that she could burst her sorrow and let it out.

He was perturbed, and his frown dominated his face.

"I'm a bastard, and I'm sorry, but don't you remember how you propositioned me? Your exact words were: 'how would you like to fuck a virgin?' Maggie frankly I thought you'd been around with an approach like that. I was amused as all hell. Who knew that you were a virgin? I didn't believe you, so I took you on. It was wrong, wrong as all hell and I'm damned sorry for it, Maggie, you have **no** idea how **sorry** I really am."

Sean raised his voice, and broke out into a sweat. There seemed to be no resolution to the matter of Maggie.

"Okay, Sean," Maggie didn't want to alienate him further. She softened her attitude, "I have no right to tell you who to sleep with or who not to sleep with. You withdrew after Christmas. I don't know what the hell happened to you. And" she loudly said, "I even entertained the **thought** that you were hot after my **mother.** Wasn't that crazy and stupid?"

Sean stared straight ahead. His blood ran cold. He was tasting the bitter poison of his actions. His innards were churning with an acid attack at the mention of Mary. Mary, who's extra curricular secret life was at the public library on 42nd Street.

The cab pulled up at Maggie's building. He told the driver to wait, while Sean walked her into the vestibule. She stood on her toes to kiss him on the mouth, but he turned away aborting her kiss.

"Wow! You're committed aren't you?" he nodded as guilt gripped him. "Okay," Maggie feigned a bravado she did not feel, "Will ya write?"

"Sure." He said, and she snapped, "Yeah, that and a nickel will get me a subway ride. Sorry Sean, take care of yourself, write me and I'll faithfully write back, give you a daily log of life at Luigi's."

Sean kissed her forehead lightly and ran off. Maggie crumbled as he drove out of sight. Her intent had always been to ensnare him to marry her. That Christmas Eve when he came to her home, it was to introduce him to her family.

Sean went back to Luigi's, and asked Dennis to go out for a walk with him. He was mortified after that encounter with Maggie. He poured his story out to Dennis, not sparing his own culpability.

At the end of Sean's soliloquy Dennis said, "What the fuck are you looking for, Sean? Absolution? You're disgusting, you know that? Go see a priest. You have no conscience." Dennis left abruptly.

Sean felt rotten. In three days he'd be leaving. He felt murky inside, and this feeling had to be addressed before he shipped out. Dennis's reaction was like a cold bucket of water on his psyche. He went home, and wanted to drink himself into a stupor, but he stopped. No! This wasn't the answer. He called Mary, and when she said hello, he hung up. God knows she had her own issues to deal with, especially now with Philip going to war. Once more he was thinking only of himself. Every encounter since he had gotten back had been a negative one, and he was suffering. He tried to read, but the words did not sink in. He was desperate for Mary. She had anchored him, given him a sense of self he never imagined he possessed. But he couldn't call her, what could he possibly say? Could he tell her that her daughter and he had been lovers? Did she even suspect it? The evening wore on, as he busied himself with chores he had to do. He even cleaned his bathroom thinking how proud Mary would have been of him. He had noticed that when she left a bathroom, it was clean. Everything about her was special to him.

* * *

Sean hadn't shut his eyes until 5:30 a.m., he called his childhood buddy, Father Peter Sullivan assigned at St. Barnabas church in Yonkers. He needed to talk, so Father Peter told him to get himself up to the Bronx by subway and he'd pick him up by car at the station.

Sean unfolded his double love affair with a mother and her daughter.

Father Peter knew that Sean was in deep trouble. "Sean," Father Peter said, "let me do my job. Come, say a prayer and make a good confession." The invitation to clean his inner house, was the logical next step to Sean's dilemma.

Father Peter picked up his book and vestments in the sacristy, and Sean followed him in to church. Father Peter put on his vestments and took his Latin prayer book inside the box. He blessed Sean, and Sean started his confession: "Bless me Father for I have sinned, it's been too many years since my last worthy confession." Sean now spoke to Father Peter about his sins leaving nothing out.

Had he been so unaware of his behavior that his conscience had been anesthetized by being ignored for so long? As he confessed his sins, a weight was lifted from his soul. When Sean asked Father Peter what to do about Mary, Father Peter felt sad for his friend's confusion about morality.

"Sean, you know what to do, you did the right thing, that's why you're here. However, I'm a priest, **and** I'm your friend, but I'm not your conscience. Making the right decision doesn't have to feel good, okay? Now say an Act of Contrition. For penance say ten Our Father's and ten Hail Mary's." Sean knelt and prayed.

Father Peter gave him holy communion. Sean was exhausted. Peter took him to the rectory and upstairs to his room so that Sean could catch up on sleep. Sean slept for five hours. When he woke up, Father Peter took Sean to an Italian restaurant in Tuckahoe off the Saw Mill River Parkway.

Peter and Sean's favorite food was fish. Both came from large Catholic Irish families, and hunger had once been their constant companion. As children, the fish they caught on a Saturday afternoon staved off starvation. It became their favorite food.

Sean retold the sumptuous feast of fishes that Mary Petracca had prepared last Christmas Eve, and Peter noticed that Sean glowed when he talked about her. He obviously had strong feelings towards the young widow.

"You care about her, don't you, Sean?' Peter asked.

"She's my soul-mate," Sean replied.

When the menu came, they ordered a plate of linguini with white clam sauce, and fried calamari with salad, and a loaf of Italian seeded bread, which they dipped in a mix of extra virgin olive oil sprinkled with oregano. They drank a bottle of wine and memories of their boyhood.

After dinner, Father Peter drove him to the subway terminal in the Bronx. They embraced, and Father Peter blessed Sean. "God bless you, Sean," Peter said. "Thank you Father," Sean answered. "Pray for us."

Two days later, he shipped out to California, then took a transport ship to Korea.

* * *

Philip was to report for duty at Fort Dix on Monday morning at 10:00 a.m. Mary made reservations for her family in a nearby hotel for Sunday night. Everyone would be on the road in the morning, and she didn't want to chance his being late. Philip was always early for everything. Maggie, Tess, and Marco had come home to say good bye to their brother.

On Sunday afternoon, Mary made meatballs with beef and pork, bracciole, spare ribs, and pork chops in the sauce. She made two kinds of pasta, the macaroni the girls liked and the linguini for Philip which was his exclusive pasta choice. "The linguini kid," Vito used to call him.

Faced with the inevitable, Philip grew up overnight. He too had managed to feign a great façade of courage about what he had to face. Only Mary knew of his fears, and she too was proud of the stoic Sicilian character Philip struggled to show. Vito had always worried about him the most. Impetuous, brilliant, a free spirit, Philip had been Vito's favorite.

After dinner, the girls washed the dishes while Mary talked to Philip in his bedroom.

"Momma, I'm sorry about Sean. For you to act as you did, it's clear that you love him. I was hard on you. You know, in Sicily, I would've killed him and gotten away with it. Mom, did you know that Maggie still sees him?" Mary controlled the urge to react. It was over, she knew that. When she agreed to the affair, she expected it to be only an interlude.

"No, I didn't know, Philip." Philip stood up and paced. Mary asked him to sit down.

"Now you do. Get him out of your head," Philip declared with assertion.

Mary was shaken. Surely Sean had to be a part of a memory she would always cherish, but she had no expectations. He made it clear that marriage was distasteful to him.

Mary asked her son to sit a while longer. She had to tell him how she and Vito met and married. His eyes opened wide as she described the staged seduction in Corleone. She spoke highly of the young Vito, and how loving their marriage had once been.

"Poppa loved you," Philip said. "What happened?" He felt honored that his mother had singled him out to talk about her past, a woman who had been bottled up for so many years. Her recent rendezvous with Sean seemed to have affected her former rigid sense of secrecy.

"I told him I wanted no more children. He packed a bag and left. I thought he'd never come back. In a panic, I gave away our beautiful bedroom set." Philip heard his mother's version of the breakup for the first time.

"Mom, he went nuts. He said you were spiteful."

"No, Philip," she explained, "I thought he abandoned us."

"What a shame! You should've screamed at each other. Instead the silence and pride destroyed our family." Mary held his hands, "I know son. It's a Sicilian tragedy. Did you ever watch a rooster walk proud with his head up? And hens walk with their heads down? And I always think, the rooster is Vito and the hen is me."

Tess tapped on the door.

"Mom, we cleaned up. It's time to leave. Are you ready?" Mary stood up. "We'll be right out," she said. She got up from the bed, and Philip smoothened out the bedspread. "Let's go, Philip," she said. He was at the door, then turned back to pick up a scrap of paper. He looked around the room as though he was memorizing it. On the bureau was an album of his favorite scat singer, Louis Armstrong leaning against a framed picture of Vito.

"Philip?" Mary called him. "Wait Mom," he said.

Mary waited in the hallway and watched him.. He put the album in his record cabinet, then put his hand on the photo-portrait of his father. "Poppa," he whispered, and walked out shutting the door behind him.

"Ready Philip?" Mary asked. "Almost." He stepped in front of his mother. "Momma, did you love my father?" Mary's lip quivered, "With all my heart, Philip." He sighed, "Now I'm ready."

As Philip came out of the building, Donna Rosa who lived down the block sat on a chair, on the stoop of the building. "*Buona fortuna, Filippo!*" she shouted, and Donna Binna pelted Philip with rice as he covered his face and ran into the car. "She's wishing you good luck," Mary explained. He groaned. "Ugh! You could-a fooled me, I thought she was shooting me with a bee bee gun."

Mary laughed. "At 80 years old, Donna Binna can choose occasions for throwing it." Philip snarled, "Don't invite her to my wedding, okay?" Mary giggled, "Okay, Philip." Philip sat back, shut his eyes and snuggled closer to his mother on the long drive to Fort Dix.

Chapter XII

After Ft. Dix

Philip fell right into the army life. Discipline, energy, focus, obedience and respect; things he had learned at home. Philip wrote.

"Dear Tess:

My drill sergeant reminds me of Poppa. He wants everything his way or no way. I feel like I never left home, except that the drill sergeant's voice sounds like a truck trying to make a hill in first gear. Why the hell does he have to holler like that? Poppa could punish you in such a soft voice and have you thinking that he was doing you a favor. I'm making a list of how to break down the will of a soldier. It's an art form here. But, it's not bad. Made a few friends, and my sense of humor keeps me afloat. When I climb up ropes to a ledge in our training, I picture that the ropes are linguini, and you should see how fast I go up. The sergeant says I'm good. He's right. Can't wait to come home. Tell Momma to stock up on linguini. Love Philip."

At boot camp where extreme neatness was taught to the recruits, Philip did well. He wrote to Tess, "Remember I told you that the sergeant reminds me of Poppa? Well, Momma could teach recruits. When I was a kid, she drew a diagram of a bed-sheet, told me if I did it right the first time, she'd give me fifty cents. I did and she did. I became an expert overnight. There's no bribes here, just terror tactics...ugh. Write me. Got lots of stories to tell. Love Philip."

There were no form fitting sheets around in the 1950's, and Mary kept a meticulous, orderly home. She trained each of her children never to leave a room unless it was neat, everything in its place. Philip went through the grueling physical training as though he had done it all his life. He moved fast, and was a natural athlete with incredible agility and speed. He earned a second nomer besides his mother's *mercury:* Eagle. A bird capable of fishing for salmon by swooping down in a nose dive.

Because Philip was olive skinned, a few of the enlisted men thought he looked like an American Indian, so they called him Eagle-foot, in the Indian tradition. Philip accepted his new title with good humor. He was well liked by his fellow servicemen and caught the notice of high ranking personnel. They found him to be a natural leader. Other soldiers emulated him. Philip looked like a soldier should, so very shortly he was being watched during the grueling basic training exercises.

Climbing mountains perpendicular was part of the difficult basic training of a soldier. Philip went up indeed on an eagle's wings. The servicemen secretly bet on his scores, or his achievements with every challenge he met. However, when Philip hit the sack, he'd pass out. The energy he had expounded was extraordinary. His ability and talent did not go unnoticed. The big brass looked for a select number of people to command the soldiers, Philip's name came up, and they waited until basic training was completed.

Philip was dating Dee Dee Marra. She was in love with him, and he loved the attention and adulation she gave him. Mary dropped negative comments about the family whenever she could. She echoed many of Vito's comments, *"cafoni"* (uncouth) and *"strazzuni"* (rag-pickers).

Philip assured his mother when he called that his relationship with Dee Dee was platonic. Mary warned him that platonic often led to a life long sentence of marriage. Philip listened to his mother, and told her not to worry, but he didn't break off with Dee Dee right away. He wanted a girlfriend so that he could receive more mail. Mary backed off from the situation.

Philip had asked his mother soon after he left, if she would let Dee Dee know when he called her, but she declined to do it. "No Philip, your conversation with me does not have to be monitored by Dee Dee." It was the last time he asked. His relationship with his mother got closer with each contact. He had time to think about Mary, and her needs, and he felt worse and worse about the directives he had issued to his mother about Sean.

* * *

Mary was ready to close on the big house in Yonkers. The topography of the land was odd. The front of the house was on a hill, and the seventy two steps leading to the front door were made of cement. The back of the house faced another street which was level to the house. Therefore, the front entrance was rarely used.

The house had four bedrooms and guest rooms on the second floor. Ceilings were high, and windows were the full length of the wall to the floor. It was European architecture at its best. Mary hired a housekeeper to help her with the house, and also to keep her company. When Philip called Mary, he asked her why she was buying such a big house.

"Why not buy big?" Mary answered. "It's an investment. Real Estate appreciates, and at the same time, I have a house big enough for each of you." Philip realized that his mother was becoming an astute business woman.

She mentioned that she was going to school to improve her skills. She bought a Smith-Corona typewriter, and took typing classes as well as English grammar and English literature. Mary loved books and Sean, and though she had no plan to be with him, her secret wish was that destiny would bring them together.

After basic training, Philip called home to inform his mother that he was coming home on furlough before being sent to Officer's Training School. He wanted to take a fellow lieutenant home with him. They had qualified for the training school, and were cited for leadership roles in the army. Philip looked indeed like a walking ad for the U.S. Army. Impeccable in his grooming, he came home looking like the star of a war movie. Mary was proud of him. He seemed very self assured and seemed to adjust to the discipline of Army life. "You look like Tyrone Power," she told him.

His friend was Lieutenant Marty Goldberg, age 25. The Army had interrupted his post graduate work as a professor of eastern history. He was well versed in the history of Asia, having taught it at Ann Arbor in Michigan, and was flattered that he had been sought out for special duty. Marty would not see action, but would be put in advisory duty with the commissioned officers in a special intelligence unit.

Mary called her family and told them that Philip was coming home on a three day leave. He had a friend with him, and she wanted them to make themselves available for their brother and his guest.

Maggie and Tess came quickly, and Marco had to fly in for one day, but Mary had insisted. They understood the urgency in the event that Philip might not come back.

Dinner was a hearty home made minestra soup for the family with the exception of Philip who had to have his linguini with garlic, oil, and toasted anchovy and breadcrumbs on top. First course was followed by meatloaf, broccoli rape, and yams, with a huge mixed salad.

Marty was enthralled to see so much food, and so well prepared. "We only eat one course, Mrs. Petracca," he said. Mary thought he looked undernourished. "But not when you're in my house, Marty," she responded.

He was over six feet tall, slender, wore glasses, had sharp features, and a short G.I. haircut. He looked like a man who was immersed in his studies.

Marty Goldberg was immediately attracted to Maggie. He could not get his eyes off her, and she turned on her charm of wit, sometimes outrageous wit, and gave him all her attention. Marty was hooked. Mary noticed, and was pleased.

At 25 years old, Marty Goldberg had become a professor of Eastern history, and his work consumed most of his day, so he had time for little else. Maggie got him to talk about himself and though he was socially reticent, she made it easy for him by hanging on to his every word.

Yet, the young people meshed. They laughed when Philip told them that he had been blessed with a new nomer of Chief Eagle foot. Maggie smiled and asked her mom, "Hey momma, what do we do with Mercury?" and Mary feigned a haughty reply, "Philip was born to have many titles. Some people belong to royalty and others don't. Philip belongs." The girls applauded and Philip took a bow. With this, Marco came in with a mane of hair longer than usual. He liked the Leopold Stokowski look, and on him the long hair looked sensational.

"My brother," Philip explained, "*literally* the long-haired musician." Everyone laughed, and Marco, not to be outdone stood up and ran his hand over Philip's short hair. "And may I present my brother," he retorted, "a direct descendant of a prehistoric porcupine." Maggie applauded, and Philip laughed the loudest. The teasing and banter continued and then Mary suggested they take Marty to New York City to see the high points of the skyscrapers, Rockefeller Center, and the Battery. They cleared the table and left all the dishes in the sink, which for Mary was a first.

Her car was parked at the curb across the street, and they toured the city that night. It was a fabulous mini vacation for Marty who almost went home to an empty house. His mother was staying with his sister in Los Angeles, and his father was dead.

Marty, Maggie and Philip sat in the back of the car, Tess and Marco sat in the front, with Mary at the wheel. Marty asked Maggie if she'd write to him, and she said yes. Encouraged by the conversation in the back of the car, Mary was pleased.

Philip had mentioned that Dee Dee might come to New York with them, but she didn't show up and Mary thought she didn't come because there was no room in the car. When they got to Little Italy for pastries and coffee, Maggie pulled her mother aside.

"Momma, did Philip tell you that he and Dee Dee had a falling out?"

Mary answered, "What happened?"

"She wanted to get engaged. Imagine? Philip's such a baby."

"Thank God," Mary whispered.

"You don't like the Marras, do you?" Maggie asked.

"Poppa said that they were *cafoni*." At the mention of Vito, Maggie stopped the inquisition. "And they are." Mary said.

Marty Goldberg had managed to steal a kiss with Maggie and she was glowing. Maggie could not resist the attention, the attraction, and his elegant good looks in the Army's uniform.

The family got home at midnight, and Mary was happy to see her children together and the new face she hoped would be added to her family.

As soon as everyone had a nightcap of hot chocolate, they retired to their rooms. Mary made up Marty's bed in Vito's den. Everything including books were packed in boxes which were lined up against the wall. The move would be smooth, and quick with everything ready to the big house on Warburton Avenue, in Yonkers.

The girls were invited to Mary's bedroom for a talk. All the cards were set on the table, and now that the girls had matured and were curious about their parents' past, Mary thought it would be a good time to tell them the family's secrets. She told them everything that Philip had been told before he left for service. The girls were quiet as their mother spoke about her childhood, her parents, and her marriage to their father.

Maggie and Tess lived in a Sicilian mentality of distrust all their lives and many secrets were kept. Mary was not one to share her feelings or her history with any one. Confidantes were non-existent. With Vito dead, Mary saw the urgency of establishing herself in the family. She felt that she had to reveal her history as well as Vito's. The girls were surprised to learn that Vito had been married before, and had lost his first wife and first son in childbirth.

Maggie realized that she and her siblings didn't know a thing about their parents, because their parents had shown them only what they wanted them to see. Much of Vito's and Mary's past had been buried in a shroud of secrecy.

"Why didn't you or Poppa ever tell us?" Maggie asked irately. "Why in heaven's name did you keep the story of your lives away from us?"

Mary shrugged. "I was brought up with a constant reminder that when you confide in someone, you subject yourself to consequences that can backfire. That's the Sicilian mentality. Secrecy, the silence of *omerta,* trusting no one, even in the family. Maggie, I didn't have the childhood you had. I would have loved to have had a father like yours for myself."

"You did, Momma," Maggie snapped incredulously, "and you got rid of him. You thought we were stupid? We were horrified that our father had to sleep in the den. We thought that one day one of you would kill the other." Mary shuddered to hear this, "Maggie, I acted as I was taught to." She looked down at her hands and said quietly, "Once we loved each other. He wrote that he loved me. Words, only words, so I was surprised, because I didn't think so."

Tess, couldn't look at her mother's anguished face as she explained the family secrets, but Tess's thoughts were in another direction. She was bothered by the sudden demise of her father.

"Momma," Tess asked, "was Poppa sick?"

"No," Mary replied quickly.

"Do you think someone did him in?" Tess asked.

"Yes." Mary was angered thinking about it. Often in the Sicilian neighborhood when there was a murder, the authorities didn't bother to investigate, and that was a reality most of the immigrants lived with.

"Jesus!" Maggie exclaimed, "Tess, how do you know something I don't know?"

"You're too busy with men, Maggie. I'm so into reading murder mysteries, for the legal angle, and the thought of my father's death came into my head, and I've been haunted by it."

"Me too," Mary said. She mentioned Joe Marra and the fact that Vito had put him on the payroll to help Mary with the real estate holdings.

"There was union money missing girls, and somebody must have threatened your father. I have my suspicions. So, when Philip leaves, I'll investigate."

Tess asked "Whom do you suspect, mom?"

"Joe Marra," Mary said with resignation.

Maggie protested vehemently. "No! He's Poppa's best friend."

"Your father always said that one's enemies are those who are closest to you."

Mary told her girls that she saw Vito working diligently on the books for the union. He never made mistakes, and there was a lot of money missing.

"Of course, the bastard!" Maggie said, "he moved away, bought a new house, a new car, and Gina's clothes have suddenly become stylish and expensive. Damn!"

"Maggie, don't curse please," Mary chided her daughter.

"Oh, Momma, that's Sean's favorite word, sorry. You pick up language from those closest to you."

Tess' curiosity was aroused. "Closest to you, Maggie?" Tess opened her hands in a shrug meaning she needed an explanation.

"Well, at least I was close to him. I don't know where the hell his head was in the past few months. He's written a few times, and for a man of words, he sure says nothing in his letters." Mary shut her eyes, afraid that the girls would see the hurt in them, and walked into the kitchen. The girls followed still talking in whispers. Marco, Philip and Marty were asleep. Tess suggested to Maggie that she look elsewhere for a beau. "He has plenty of loose wires in his head," she said. Maggie laughed, and Mary could not bear to hear him denigrated so.

"I'm going to bed," she said.

They were going to the early show at Radio City Music Hall the next day. Marty would surely be in awe over the size of the theater and its famous organ.

They said goodnight, and went to bed.

The entire weekend was filled with wonderful activities, fabulous New York spots, and the final day in Little Italy in the village. Marty and Maggie had meshed beautifully, and because of the constraint of time, Marty asked Maggie to be his girlfriend. Maggie groaned, feeling it was too soon, but he was going off to war. "Marty, let's take this a little slower, please? We don't know each other. Let's write, and see where it takes us." He agreed. The flattery was a refreshing change from the uncertainty she had had from Sean Quinn.

Mary drove Marty and Philip to Ft. Dix, after Marco flew back to Chicago to join the orchestra, and Tess returned to school. Maggie remained with her mother.

Mother and daughter grew closer than they had been. Maggie's warmth encouraged Mary to probe further into her daughter's relationship with Sean.

"Maggie, how close were you to Sean Quinn?" she asked as they drove back together from New Jersey.

"I had an affair with him, but he ended it." Mary didn't wince at that comment, which seemed very strange to Maggie. Why was her mother questioning her?

"When?" Mary asked.

"Right after Christmas Momma. I brought him home so that he could meet my family. I thought we were getting married. Instead he dumped me."

Mary took a deep breath. Oh, thank God, she thought to herself. The picture Maggie painted was different than the one she or Philip had imagined. So Sean wasn't involved with the two of them at the same time. That was the impression Philip had given Mary.

"You hated him, didn't you, Momma?" Maggie said as they stopped to pay a toll. "No, I just thought he was not for you."

"Well I thought different," Maggie sighed.

"I feel for you, Maggie." Mary said softly. Maggie shrugged her shoulders like it was no big deal.

"Momma, what are you going to do about Joe Marra?"

"I haven't figured it out yet. Say nothing to Dee Dee. Once more I ask you to observe *omerta,* okay? Say nothing about this."

"I won't Momma, don't worry." Maggie reached over and kissed her mother on the cheek, a rare show of affection. Mary held Maggie's hand. "I love you Maggie."

"Me too, Momma," Maggie said as they crossed the bridge into the city. "I'm glad you shared your story with us. Better late than never. How weird."

"I don't think so. I knew nothing about my parents either, Maggie."

It must be a Sicilian thing, Maggie thought after that remark.

Chapter XIII

Sean's Lost Letter Arrives

Philip and Marty returned to their camp to begin their studies in Officer's Training School. Philip warned Mary that there'd be no time to write, but he'd call on Saturday nights.

The move out of 107th street cost double the moving fee because Mary wanted to move at 11:00 p.m. None of the neighbors were aware of her move. She had been so careful not to let anyone in her apartment, because all of the family's belongings were packed in boxes. The chain on the kitchen door allowed a four inch opening when she talked to people. Donna Binna and Donna Rosa were suspicious. They knew everybody's business, and each one had a short visit at people's homes, then converged after supper on the stoop of the building in their metal folding chairs and exchanged gossip. It frustrated Donna Binna that Mary would not let them in. Her feeble excuse was that her house was a mess. It was a credible excuse because they knew of Mary's passion for cleanliness and neatness.

"*Ma che ci vuole a farmi una tazza di café?*" (But what does it take to make me a cup of coffee?") Donna Binna asked, but Mary, not wishing to be rude, handed Donna Binna a bag of home made cookies and sent her away. At least Mary could keep the gossip averted.

Mary came downstairs and looked for Donna Binna and Donna Rosa. They were gone on their daily rounds to the neighbors. Mary was relieved. She opened her mailbox with her small key and there was a letter from Sean.

Mary gasped, and clutched it to her breast. She grabbed the rest of the mail and ran upstairs. The letter was in bad shape. Carefully she opened it up and read:

"Beloved:

Hope you're well. Sorry for the scribbled writing but I'm not at my messy desk at the paper. I'm here. It's no picnic. The good guys and the bad guys all look alike. Where is Philip? Let me know.

This police action is no game. Troops moving about, faces with one expression, abject fear. Everyone is heavy with equipment and I chase around writing the story of the soldier, the tragedy of a nation split in half and used as an international pawn in this fear of Communist rule. In movies the good guys wear the white hats and the bad guys wear the black hats. Here, everybody looks the same, except us. I've got a tough job, I've gotta report national policy.

On a more sanguine note, those euphoric days of rapture coated my psyche with a warm blanket of memories. I've been terrified of feeling anything, and though we came from different cultures, our experience was parallel.

Mary, for God's sake, before I shut my eyes, before I get killed in a war which makes no sense to me, I have to tell you, I love you. Let me close by saying that I've never been loved before as you loved me. Coming from a culture like yours, it had to be a tough decision to make. I'll always remember Mary, the woman of grace who dared to risk her reputation, and her *onore* to meet me more than half way in a love affair which bathed my soul in light. "To Be Continued" is in your hands. Write me, I love you, Sean Q."

Mary's immediate thought was that she was glad that she reserved judgment when she hadn't heard from him. Life's hard lessons were being learned one at a time. Her life with Vito could have been different had she not reacted to his sudden departure after the directive she had given him. Oh yes, dear God, Mary thought, Sean did love her, and she hadn't been used, as she had begun to believe. She kissed the letter and said, "I love you too, Sean."

Mary was shaken. His description of the war was horrifying. Why were American men being sent there to die? For supremacy over a country? Or was it to keep the Japanese peninsula at bay? This wasn't chess, this was a game of horror by a country who had always had honor in their dealings with other countries.

Yet his last phrase, "to be continued," filled her with hope. Her house would be their house, and now she must step out of her joy and deal with the tasks to expedite this process of purchasing and moving.

It was 1:00 o'clock before Mary left for the bank. Although she was able to purchase the house in Yonkers in a cash deal, Schlomo had advised her to get a mortgage, and she did.

At the bank, Mr. Donovan smiled as Mary walked in. He came around the desk and pulled out the chair for her. He offered her a glass of water, which she accepted, and after a few minutes of niceties he reserved only for beautiful women, he settled down in his leather chair.

Mary inquired about the balance of the joint account with Joe Marra.

"You had over forty five thousand dollars here, Mrs. Petracca."

"Mr. Donovan, there must be some mistake. Joe Marra collected a small stipend from my husband which he put in this account. Where did he get forty five thousand dollars?" she asked incredulously.

He showed her the record of transactions and dates. She feigned a loss of memory because of the trauma of her husband's death. Mr. Donovan patted her hand. His hand lingered on hers. She needed him to be distracted by her presence, so she smiled and acted the part of the confused "little woman" to get exactly what she wanted from him.

"I need a cup of coffee; just trying to piece things together here." He walked into the back office to pour Mary her coffee.

Meanwhile Mary took out a pad and pencil and copied the entries of each transaction writing as fast as she could. Mr. Donovan returned with the coffee and served it to Mary. She sipped it and looked into his eyes, "You're so kind," she said, and he blushed. "It must be difficult for you. How can I help?"

"Sir, I need to have the dates of these transactions. You'd be a dear if you could just have me copy the dates of deposit and withdrawal from this joint account." Mr. Donovan showed Mary to an unused office, and provided her with what she needed.

Mary spent a half hour copying the information. After she had what she needed, she invited Mr. Donovan for a pizza and a glass of wine at Patsy's two blocks away. His face lit up. Patsy's pizza was the best in the city. Even Frank Sinatra came up to East Harlem for a pizza when he was in town. His autographed publicity picture was framed on Patsy's wall.

Vito had been respected by all the Italo-Americans in the neighborhood, and when his widow walked into Patsy's, the red carpet treatment was shown her. Patsy offered the wine gratis to his special friends. Mr. Donovan was impressed. The pizza was made with fresh tomato sauce. Patsy served them three small dishes of toppings, consisting of mushrooms, sausage and eggplant. It was a complete meal. He also brought a house salad with balsamic vinegar, and extra virgin olive oil dressing.

Mary talked to Mr. Donovan about how difficult his job must be, and as he let off steam about dealing with the immigrants, Mary listened intently. She wanted more from him. She wanted him to tell her about his dealings with Joe Marra. She was pleased that he remembered him. "A big fellow, looks like a teamster. Bigger than Mr. Petracca. Sullen, and rich I imagine." Mr. Donovan had said too much, but he was already on his second glass of wine.

At 6:00, Mary and Mr. Donovan left Patsy's. As they parted Mr. Donovan kissed Mary's hand, a custom he had picked up from his elite Italian clients. "Anything in the world I can do for you, call me." He gave her his card.

Mary went home, bathed, and called Schlomo, Vito's close buddy and accountant. She asked him about Vito's generosity towards Joe Marra in terms of paying him to help her acclimate herself in her small real estate empire.

Schlomo corrected Mary about Vito's generosity towards Joe. "Mary, he only paid him a stipend of thirty bucks a week, enough for gas and his time." She tried to be casual about what she had just learned. Where had the money come from? Why had she been so trusting, so much in a trance that she hadn't ever examined the account before? "I see, Schlomo." What if Schlomo was in on this scheme of hiding this money in an account which bore her name as well as a co-signer Joe Marra?

"Schlomo, would you check your records and let me know how many checks you've issued Joe since my husband's death, or did you start issuing checks before Vito's death?" Schlomo was surprised that so much time had passed before Mary even questioned the finances Vito had arranged. "Why now, Mary? I expected you to come forth a lot earlier. Yes, I'll get the information for you, and get back to you in a few days. Come to my office on 47th street and third avenue. I'll meet you and we'll examine everything together."

"Schlomo, you ask why now? Where were you? You were supposed to be working for my husband, and in so doing you neglected your responsibility towards me."

"Hey, Mary, Joe Marra told me he was taking care of you. Didn't he?" Mary snickered sarcastically, "Oh yeah," she said, "He tried to take care of me in every way." Schlomo never did like Marra. He hung around Vito almost like an understudy in an opera, waiting for the star to pass out, have an accident or drop dead. Joe studied Vito too closely. He was too interested in "taking care of Mary." How stupid had Vito been to trust him. This confused young woman was deeply aware of a hidden agenda. So was Schlomo. But it was her life, her husband, her family.

Mary made it clear that she wanted to deal with her own affairs without having Joe Marra breathe over her shoulder. Schlomo sensed Mary's apprehension, and he knew that he had to keep closer to this young innocent woman, caught in a web of intrigue of her husband's life. Too much was surfacing too soon, and Mary really needed protection. It sure wasn't going to come from Joe Marra. He had his own ulterior motives. Schlomo sensed the hunt of the male in heat, and Mary, by what she had not said, had made it very clear.

Mary was tired. She took a bath and put the copy of Mr. Donovan's bank statement next to her night table. She'd deal with it tomorrow. Now? She would have her hot chocolate, and sit by the table in the kitchen and write to her beloved.

"Dearest Sean:

I opened the mail box downstairs and when I saw a letter in such bad condition, my heart was thumping like crazy. I ran up the stairs, sat in my kitchen chair and tore it open. The date of your letter shows that you mailed it two months ago.

Honestly I thought it was over for both of us. I didn't hear from you and I just thought that you were ending it. It's okay, Sean, because my mind had the same thought. Let me explain.

After we parted, I got in the cab and thought 'I shall never see him again,' and I meant it. There was Philip, and then of course Maggie. My behavior shocked even me. I had defied everything I believed in.

It hurt that I got no mail, and Maggie did, then your letter came.

Sean, so many changes here in my life that I don't know where to start. I'm moving to a home upstate. I'll send you the address soon. Don't write until you hear from me. Everything's in boxes. There's no reason to be here any more. I need a drastic change.

Philip did not ship out with the battalion he was originally in. He's becoming an officer. He made many friends, one is Marty Rosenberg who's dating Maggie. He likes her a lot, but I'm not sure how it will turn out.

In closing I want you to know that I love you too. Even at the height of our passion you couldn't say those three words. I wanted to, but I held back. I ask for nothing. Permanence is scary, even to me. And if it's our destiny never to see each other again, I will have had no regrets. *Con tuttu miu amure*, Mary."

Chapter XIV

Mary Has Many Questions

Mary mailed her letter to Sean via the west coast general post office to Korea. Her beloved, the man who had given her life definition was gone, and she saw no future with Sean. If he stepped into her life again, she'd alienate Maggie and Philip. Tess wouldn't be a problem nor Marco who lived in his own world of music.

Yet how could Sean fit in? He, who was used to wings, would not be comfortable with the shoes he'd have to wear as a husband and step-father to children, who, Mary felt, would make his life miserable. In their eyes no one could possibly fill the shoes of Vito Petracca.

There were three things which she forged ahead with like a Sherman Tank: her suspicions of Vito's untimely death, the mystery of the cellar rental to the mob, and the possibility that his mistress had somehow been implicated in his death.

Mary recalled the brief visit of the blonde woman on the last night of the wake. She walked in, stared at the corpse and left.

To Mary, it seemed as though the woman was there to verify the obituary in the *Daily News*.

Another question bothering Mary was: Why did Joe Marra deposit forty five thousand dollars in their name? Was it a move to incriminate her? There was another player in this financial puzzle, Vito's accountant and friend, Schlomo Schwartz. Could he be part of a plot?

Mary's head was spinning with another question: what had Vito's life been like towards the end?

She called Schlomo and arranged to meet him in his office.

Schlomo's office looked like a tornado had hit it. Papers were all over the place in piles, none of them neat piles.

"Mary?" he stood up momentarily as she walked in the office door.

"Hello Schlomo." There were newspaper sections on every chair, and all of them were from the *New York Times*.

"Sit down, Mary. Grab a chair," he said as he waved across the four chairs opposite his desk. "Where? They're covered with newspapers."

He stood up with great difficulty. Schlomo looked pale; he had a huge stomach. He ate an unbalanced diet: pastries, apple pies, ice cream, candy bars and occasionally a steak sandwich. He drank no water, but he drank beer. He loved Hershey almond chocolate bars with beer as a chaser. He grew more obese each time she saw him.

On the side of his cluttered desk was a tall table with a record player on it. He listened to opera, *Carmen* in the morning, and *Otello* in the afternoon. If he worked late, it was *Aida.* He shuffled to Mary's side, looked around for the chair with the real estate pile, picked it up carefully and placed it on another chair in another direction so that the two piles would not get mixed up.

The articles on each chair pertained to four different subjects. One chair held the financial page of the *New York Times,* the second chair was piled up with opera reviews from the Metropolitan Opera Company; the third chair contained articles about art exhibits and auctions; the fourth chair had a shorter pile of articles from the real estate section of the New York Times. Schlomo lived alone. He had no family in this country, most of them had died in the holocaust in Germany during World War II.

Mary sat down with hesitation.

"Schlomo, how could you find anything in this office?" she asked.

"I know where everything is."

"Really?" Mary couldn't imagine being in this room much longer. It was stuffy, and the windows were so filthy that you couldn't see anything outside.

She asked Schlomo for clarification of the funds in the bank which were in both her name and Joe Marra's. Schlomo listened with concern.

"Mary, there were missing dues. Joe Marra? I don't wanna jump to conclusions, but where the hell did he get that money? Holy Crow!"

Her heart was beating rapidly and suddenly she felt dizzy. Schlomo offered her a glass of water, but his windows were dirty and tightly shut, and what Mary needed was air. It was stifling in his office and nothing smelled good.

"Schlomo, let's go eat. I'm not feeling well." Mary looked pale. Schlomo picked his jacket up from the floor which had fallen there that morning when he first came in. He locked the office door, and held Mary's arm. They came out of the building, and Schlomo asked where she wanted to go. She suggested Luigi's where the reporters hung out.

It was early, and most of the reporters were not around. The past few months only one or two of Sean's buddies were still here. The next wave was due to be sent overseas in a month or so.

Luigi recognized Mary. She was dressed in a black silk suit with a silk checkered ascot at her neck, a creation her son had made specifically for her. He noticed her with a man, but it didn't seem like a love interest, it couldn't possibly be, Luigi thought, not after Sean Quinn. He greeted her and brought them to a table in the back of the restaurant where there was more privacy.

"How's Sean? What do you hear from him?" Luigi asked, and Mary was embarrassed, "I guess he's okay," she answered, and Luigi wasn't surprised. Why would she talk? She was Sicilian.

Mary ordered a bowl of soup with bread and a glass of white zinfandel. Schlomo was embarrassed because his eating habits were atrocious. Vito had always ordered food for him. He'd say, "When you're with me, you're eating real food." Schlomo always deferred to Vito in these matters. He loved the guy. It was easy to understand. Vito had a generous nature.

"Order for me, Mary. I'll eat anything you order, except salad, greens, or sauces." She smiled. "Okay," she said, "grilled breast of chicken with potatoes." Schlomo said, "But please no side orders. Bring bread and plenty of butter." Mary asked for a dish of extra virgin olive oil to dip the bread in. Schlomo muttered. "No butter please." Mary said to the waiter, then she looked at the pained expression on Schlomo's face, "Waiter! Please, change that to two pats of butter, okay?" The waiter obliged. Schlomo suggested that Mary eat more than soup, and she grimaced and touched her stomach, "I can't. I haven't been feeling well."

Lunch was long and leisurely. Schlomo cut up his chicken and ate a few bites and pushed the others on the edge of his plate.

Schlomo talked. "Vito worried that plaster walls would become obsolete. He was right, because dry walls were put up in Levit-town, Long Island. He was also agitated about his personal life."

"What are you telling me, Schlomo?" Mary was suspicious that Schlomo was intimating that Vito had died of a heart attack due to stress.

"Mary, union funds were missing. Vito knew the combination, so he was being investigated on top of everything else this poor guy was going through. I think it was a set-up. Your husband was wealthy. He didn't have to steal. He doubled his life insurance policy with you as beneficiary."

"Oh my God, then it meant that he was afraid for his life, and he made sure that our family would be provided for." With each bit of information Schlomo was revealing, Mary felt more and more culpable.

"Mary, I wonder about another possibility. Perhaps Vito felt cornered and took his own life. He was this big, capable intelligent man who's world was crumbling under his feet. Did you know any of this?"

Mary nodded her head in disbelief. That had to be the worst horror.

"God no. I should have, my poor Vito. Our conversations were limited to the children and food, and little else. I knew nothing about Vito," she said sadly. "He was very private."

"Oh Mary, I said too much." Schlomo was contrite.

"No, you didn't. I have to know. Tell me everything." Mary kept her emotions in control, because if she broke down, he'd stop talking, so she kept a stoic façade, even though her body was tense.

"A few months before he died. Vito got calls in the middle of the night, the phone would ring, and nobody spoke. Didn't you hear it Mary? You lived there. This happened under your own nose."

"No! Vito slept on the other end of the apartment. He was so alone. I wish I had known." Mary had deep remorse, and thought how inconsequential the differences between them had been. Had she known, she would have stepped into his life and be his support system as she had been in the early years of her marriage. Maybe he'd still be alive.

"Mary, your marriage was an enigma," Schlomo commented. Mary agreed, and she wondered why Vito insisted on keeping up appearances for the neighbors, the children, and his colleagues that he had a good marriage. Did Vito think that people didn't know that their marriage was a sham? The crumbling walls continued to fall in the wake of a lifetime of deception.

Schlomo told Mary that Vito had invited him to his Mulberry Street apartment years ago. "How much information can you take without getting upset?" he asked before he continued. She sighed, "Schlomo, I'm beyond hurt. Talk!" she lied. She had stomach pains.

Schlomo continued. "He had a child with this woman Martha Pederson. It was not a good union, but he wouldn't leave his kid." Mary gasped. "A child?" she asked. "Yes, Mary, a daughter," he answered. "She's an opera singer, studied voice

at Manhattan School of Music, two blocks from where you live."
Mary was shocked. "How old is she?" Mary asked. "In her late
teens," he answered. "Very mature for her age."

"Schlomo, would you contact this Martha person for a
meeting?" Schlomo squirmed in his seat. It was bizarre, but
Mary must have her reasons. He felt sorry for her. She seemed
overwhelmed.

"Okay. Mary, he wasn't happy with her. Martha married
this Mafioso and he and Vito had a fist fight. He's Sicilian too.
The worst part is that Vito beat the hell out of him. The other guy
threatened Vito, but Vito didn't care. Vito kept the apartment and
the kid moved in with him. Are you sure you wanna meet Martha
after everything I told you?" he asked.

"Yes, Schlomo, I'm very sure," Mary said with assurance.
She needed to unearth the mystery of the life Vito led away from
home.

"I suspected that your marriage was in trouble. Once I
asked how you were, and he said 'if you wanna find out how
Mary is, why the hell don't you ask her?' I swear, I never brought
your name up again. I knew then that you had a bad marriage."

The bill came, and Mary and Schlomo reached for it at the same time, but Schlomo was quicker. "Next time," he said as he took the bill from Mary.

They parted, and Mary took a cab home. She was heavy-hearted over the unfolding narrative of Vito's miserable life. The anger she had felt melted away. He had paid dearly for his indiscretion, paid for it with his life. Now the possibilities included suicide too. But Vito was a staunch Catholic, and that was the worst of sins according to the church's teachings. As Mary continued to digest all the points Schlomo had made, she refused to believe that suicide was a possibility in Vito's death. Had this been true, Mary would have felt guilty.

Early in their marriage Vito had bragged to the people he worked with and those he socialized with that his wife was the light of his life. Not only was she a beautiful young woman, but astute and interesting. Their early years had been so mutually fulfilling, because they had enjoyed intimacy on every level, especially communicating. Vito's supreme compliment towards his wife was that she was his best friend.

That night, Mary had a nightmare about Vito. He was disheveled, and his clothes were torn. His mouth was open wide and he seemed to be screaming though no sound came out of him.

She cried out to him asking him to come to her, but he looked at her with disgust, and then dissipated into a haze of sunlight.

Mary awoke in turmoil. Her covers were on the floor in the bare room filled with boxes. She looked at the clock and slowly got up. It was 6:00 o'clock in the morning. Mary picked her robe up from the floor. She had been horrified by the dream. Why had Vito looked in such terrible shape, as though he had been beaten? Mary shook her head to clear it. She staggered towards the kitchen. The sun shone in through the kitchen window with tiny dust particles dancing on the beams of sunlight. "Vito," she cried, "Haunt me. Tell me that you didn't kill yourself."

Suddenly Mary felt food and wine come up her esophagus. She ran to the bathroom and threw up in the toilet bowl. She clutched her stomach to ease the discomfort of spasms. She went back to bed for an hour, then got dressed and went out.

She left the apartment, bought the *Daily News,* and walked to the 109th Street pastry shop for a cup of demi tasse coffee with lemon to settle her stomach. Donna Laura asked about Philip, and Mary opened the newspaper. "This is where my son is," she said sadly. The headlines read that the U.N. troops fought their way back to the 38th parallel. "Mary, pray for him," Donna Laura said. Mary finished her coffee. "Yes!" she said. "That's exactly what I'm going to do."

Mary went to St. Ann's church, around the corner of 110th Street, and smelled the pungent stench of gas from the two huge gas tanks which were across the street from the church. She walked to the front of the church where the large statue of Mary stood in an alcove to the right of the Altar. She lit a candle and prayed, "Oh Blessed Mother, forgive my sins against my husband. Protect my Philip and Sean. Amen." Mary said a rosary. Though she wanted to confess her sins, she couldn't, because Father Pistella would know who she was, and she was ashamed.

Mary left the church, and walked to the bank on 116th street and First Avenue. She asked the teller what her balance was. It was a little over five thousand dollars. Joe had obviously taken forty grand out earlier in the day. She closed the account and left with the balance. Mr. Donovan asked Mary if he could take her for a pizza, but she looked pale and sick. "Perhaps next time, Mr. Donovan," Mary said weakly.

"You do look pale," he said, "I hope you feel better." Mary thanked him and went home to bed.

Chapter XV

Drastic Changes for Mary

Mary's life was shrouded in a veil of secrecy from the prying eyes of the older women in the neighborhood. Philip was instructed to write to her in care of Tess's address until she made her move to Yonkers.

Mary had other emotional housekeeping chores ahead, and one of them was to meet Vito's mistress. Mary assigned Schlomo the task.

Schlomo called Mary with a date to meet Mrs. Martha Battaglia in Mulberry. Mary was pleased. She appreciated Schlomo's support in this important and nerve wracking quest.

Meanwhile, Mary's loss of weight, nausea and inability to keep food down was plaguing her. She made an appointment to see Dr. Stivale.

He examined her thoroughly, and though there were clear signs of malnutrition, something else was going on. He did an internal exam, and had her blood and urine specimens checked. He told her to get dressed and come into his office.

"Well, Mary, your symptoms clearly show that you're pregnant. Does this make sense to you?" Mary nodded and looked down at her hands, a gesture she made when she felt cornered. She had missed her period for two months, and had suspected it.

"Yes it makes sense," she whispered.

"Remember how rough a time you had had with Tess, and I came to see you in the hospital after your transfusion, and told you that you should not have another baby?" Mary's eyes filled with tears, "Yes, Doctor." He realized that a reprimand at this time was foolish, the deed was done.

"I wanted to tell Vito, and you told me you'd take care of it. Did you?" She nodded, "Yes, I told him never to touch me again." Dr. Stivale was perplexed. "Mary, did you tell him to see me? It's been eighteen years, and he never came to see me. What happened?" Mary shook her head, "Doctor, this isn't his baby. Vito died in August."

"I know that Mary. I didn't want to seem indelicate by asking you about the father. Did you marry?" he asked.

"No, I was intimate with someone, and it's over." Mary felt trapped, there was no way out.

"What are you going to do with this pregnancy?" he asked and Mary sensed the Doctor's meaning.

Mary cried, "No abortion, no abortion."

"I didn't suggest it," he said. "No abortion."

In the event she wanted one, he knew of a good doctor who did abortions on 103rd Street in the Puerto Rican neighborhood.

The doctor called his nurse and told her to bring in a blanket. Mary was shivering from having to face an illegitimate birth.

A Sicilian woman, with no husband, pregnant, in **this** neighborhood.

"Mary, listen to me. Don't go to any doctor around here. There's a specialist in New Rochelle who takes care of many high risk pregnancies. I strongly urge you to go to him. I'll call him, and if you want, I'll drive you there on my day off and hold your hand. Let's see what he says, okay?"

"Thank you, Doctor. I need for you to say nothing about my pregnancy to a soul. Soon I'll be visiting people out of state for a few months. I don't know what I'll do about the baby yet. I'll accept your offer to go to New Rochelle to the high risk doctor you recommend," she said softly.

"Mary, he's a staunch Catholic. You realize what his stand is on human life."

Mary nodded.

"In the event of complications, he'd save the baby and not you. Do you understand?"

Mary stared blankly.

Dr. Stivale wasn't sure if Mary had heard him. She sat there without a reaction. He reiterated it.

Mary started to shake. "I understood Doctor, but I'm going to make it. I have faith."

Mary stood up and stumbled, the doctor grabbed her arm.

"You okay?" he asked, very upset over the situation.

"Yes, I'll call you when I get home." She braced herself, and walked out. Her move had to happen within ten days. The house was ready, closing was imminent, and the movers had to be alerted to ship her belongings at midnight to her new home as soon as possible.

She went to bed, and prayed for her life, for a healthy baby, for the baby to look like her father, and in the event of her death, that the baby would remain in the family, brought up by Tess. However she wanted Sean to know that he had fathered a child, should Mary die. In the event that his life would be stable and he wanted his baby, Mary wanted him to have it. A dark corridor of difficult situations faced her, and she braced herself. She would not have to bear the brunt of being an adulteress when she moved to Yonkers. She'd be moving soon; a pregnant widow who had just moved into the neighborhood. She'd be treated with deference and compassion. It was the only way.

Without a husband she had to explain her baby to her own family. But first she must alienate herself as quickly as possible from Sean Quinn. He was not to know that Mary had conceived his child. Mary made a mental list: he slept with Maggie; he hates marriage, is afraid of attachments; couldn't say I Love You; his first letter took two months; was still corresponding with Maggie; had probably used her and made a fool of her, he with the grace of a snake charmer had mesmerized her with reference to the Blessed Mother full of grace, reminding him of her and how she winced at the reference soon after he said it. Sean Quinn would never know, and it was time to discourage him and terminate the letter writing. Had she been so blinded by love of this man that she had cast all her caution away and knowingly stepped into his love nest? Yes, but now it was time to change. Her family's reactions would be disastrous. Tess would not judge her, but accept it, and keep her antagonism to herself;

233

Maggie would disown her and label her a *puttana*. Marco would be shocked, keep his opinions to himself, but never look into her eyes again, and Philip's directive had been clear: "Don't destroy this family."

Mary made her decision. She had tried to build a case against Sean, and almost succeeded. Guilty as charged, a scoundrel, to be discarded like a common criminal. She went to bed and couldn't sleep. She got up and walked into her husband's den, now empty of his desk and his couch. She sat on the floor and folded her hands and prayed. She had prosecuted Sean so meticulously leaving nothing unsaid in her mind, that it gnawed at her sense of fairness. What court had she condemned this man at? Was there no spokesman to give his defense? She continued to pray, and as she took deep breaths and exhaled slowly, the defense presented its case in her inner room where her conscience dwelled.

What crime had this man committed if he, by loving her, had given her back her self esteem? Hadn't he given her life definition? Hadn't she been filled with the joy of love from a man who had loved her so deeply? Hadn't he, by Maggie's own admission, stopped sleeping with Maggie after he met her? Hadn't he fought his desire to be with her knowing how culturally forbidden his intentions would be for her? Hadn't he been painfully honest with her when he didn't tell her that he loved her until he got to Korea? Hadn't she looked into the mirror of his eyes and seen a reflection of a beloved and beautiful woman? In the final cadence of his defense, hadn't she become the woman she was because Sean Quinn had loved her?

Mary opened her eyes. The inner voices in her head were stilled. She waited, but she heard nothing else, and so she thanked God, and said an Our Father and went to bed at peace with her soul. She would not condemn a man who had made such an impact in her life, whether or not she would ever see him again. She must not taint his memory by anguish over her trials.

The following day, Mary got up early, carried the trash outside and stuffed the metal garbage cans, and saw Donna Binna coming out of the building.

"Buon giorno, Maria, I never see you any more. I wanted to thank you for the cookies you gave me, but you're always running." She unfolded her metal chair on the stoop, and Mary was already inside the vestibule. "I'm glad, Donna Binna, I gotta go." Donna Binna walked in the hallway behind her. "Maria, why are you so busy these days, you have no time to make coffee for me, we don't visit, *em beh* what's going on?" Donna Binna wailed.

"Donna Binna, with my children grown up, you would think that I'd have nothing to do, right? Well, that's not true. I have to clean out their closets, books and journals they don't need, so my house is not in perfect shape. There aren't enough hours in the day."

Donna Binna had a solution, "They could do it when they come home, meanwhile you keep yourself so busy, coming and going, but where do you go, Mary?" Mary stepped around her, and brightly answered, "All over." She ran upstairs, and Donna Binna waited until Mary shut the door.

"Something is suspicious," Donna Binna said to herself, "she's gotta have someone on the side. Vito dies, she gets her hair cut, new clothes, disappears for five days in March. *Managia la miseria,* that's what happens when a good man dies. The wife become the Merry Widow."

It was 8:00 o'clock in the morning, and her friend Donna Rosa didn't get up until 9:00. Donna Binna couldn't wait, she'd discuss her suspicions with Donna Rosa, and if she agreed, then Mary was having an affair.

* * *

Mary had an appointment with Schlomo at Luigi's. She got dressed and took the train to 42nd Street. As she was lulled by the *ca bum, ca bum ca bum* of the third avenue el, she recalled Sean's goodbye kiss on the train, and she put her hand to her mouth to hold back her involuntary cry. She missed him so much.

Mary walked to Luigi's and Schlomo was already there. They sat in the back where they ordered a light lunch and Mary talked.

"Mary, you sounded urgent, what's wrong?"

She told him that she was pregnant, that she loved the man whose baby she carried, and that she met him in her house when Maggie took him home as a guest of hers, for Christmas.

Schlomo was speechless. He asked the waiter for a bottle of Rheingold beer. Mary said, "Make it two."

Schlomo grew anxious. Did she need a husband, and maybe she was going to ask him? He was uncomfortable, he'd never been married, how could he take on a wife who was carrying another man's baby? Schlomo was upset, but Mary didn't know why.

"What is it, Schlomo? Do you think I'm a slut?"

"No, but what is it you want of me? Do you need..I mean.."

"I need you to be a friend I can talk to. I'm about to hurt my family, and I can't avoid it. Maggie will disown me, so you see, Schlomo, you're my only friend." He ordered another beer, while Mary buttered his bread, "Eat something Schlomo or you'll get drunk." He gave a caustic little laugh, "I'm drunk already, even without the beer. Your problems are intoxicating, enough."

"I know," she said. She felt sorry for Schlomo. His expressions gave away his reaction, even though he hadn't censured her verbally.

"Mary, did you agree to this affair?" she nodded.

"Schlomo, I love him. I forgot about consequences. So, it's my responsibility, not his. I won't tell him about the baby. In fact last night I decided to end the relationship. One more letter and it'll be over."

Schlomo asked Mary if she was going to terminate the pregnancy and Mary said, "Never!" This, he couldn't understand. He discussed adoption then, and Mary told him to look into it. She had not focused on the baby yet, but how to deal emotionally with her family. It looked bleak. There was no turning back, she'd have the baby and take it one step at a time.

"I'd like to suggest that you should let him know in your next letter," Schlomo said.

Mary's expression changed.

"No, he's not a marrying type, and I won't blackmail him into this. I can't."

"Mary, that's nuts. I'm not the marrying type either. I'm forty nine years old, but if I felt towards a woman the way you two seem to feel about each other, I'd marry in a moment."

Mary smiled. Schlomo married? He was an orthodox Jew, how was he ever to find someone if all his time was spent at the office or at the opera?

"You would?" Mary smiled for the first time. What a romantic notion.

"You still wanna meet Martha Battaglia?"

Mary nodded yes.

"Mary, why do you create turmoil?"

"I have to know what Vito's life was like with another woman. I know you told me it wasn't good, but I have to meet her. I'm searching for answers, Schlomo. I have to do this."

Schlomo paid the bill, and they left. Mary took the Third Avenue El home and got off at 106th street. She'd wait to hear from Schlomo after he contacted Martha Battaglia for a meeting at Mario's on Mulberry Street.

* * *

Mary got a call on Friday night. "Lunch on Saturday at noon on Mulberry Street, okay Mary? I'll meet you at Luigi's and then we'll take a cab from there." Mary was pleased. She looked forward to meeting the attractive blonde woman face to face. Mary was apprehensive, but she realized that if Martha agreed to meet with her, she couldn't be antagonistic, but it was something Mary was prepared for anyway.

Martha Battaglia had a call from her estranged daughter, Vivian. They had been polarized for years, but after Vito's death, Vivian sought to mend her relationship with her mother.

Vivian called Martha for a luncheon date. Martha told her she already had one, and Vivian was miffed. However, she wanted to see her mother, so she told her she was coming anyway because she needed some of her publicity shots which Martha had saved for her.

"Okay, come between 11:00 and 11:30. I don't have time. If you wanna see me, make it some other Saturday." Vivian smarted from the rejection she heard in her mother's voice. An angry woman, a volatile woman, a woman who had given her father no peace.

Vivian came, collected her old publicity shots which were a ruse to gain entry into her mother's life again, and though it was cordial between them, no physical contact was made.

Martha walked out of the apartment at Hester Street at 11:45, to Mulberry street. Martha seemed even more secretive than usual, so Vivian's curiosity was whetted.

She followed her mother and saw that she was exchanging greetings with a man and a woman. Vivian got closer. Who could it possibly be? The woman was dark haired and beautiful. A familiar face, but one that she couldn't place. She needed a better look, and then she'd leave.

Her curiosity got the best of her, and she walked in the restaurant and asked to see their menu. Martha's back was facing Vivian. Vivian saw the woman whose face was familiar, but she couldn't place it. Just as Martha was turning to find the waiter, Vivian ran out.

Schlomo made the introduction, and Martha thought, What a beautiful woman. They ordered a light lunch of *mozzarella in carrozza*, an Italian specialty, beer for Schlomo, water for Mary, and wine for Martha. The women liked each other right away. Conversation was hesitant at first, and they talked about safe subjects. Then Mary skillfully eased into the subject of Vito.

Martha's expression changed, and suddenly she became short with Mary.

"What do you want to know?" she asked as she sat up straighter in her chair. Mary was treading on quicksand. The woman seemed to have so much anger against him.

"Martha, please try to understand. Vito died of mysterious causes. He was in great shape, yet the coroner said death by natural causes. What does that mean? I have to know. Did he have enemies in his life with you?" Martha threw back her head and laughed sarcastically. Schlomo stared from one woman to the other. He ordered another beer. This was like watching a boxing match at the Garden.

"Yeah, me," Martha said. "I wanted marriage. He said no, we compromise, so I had a gold ring and part of his name Petra. It was a common law marriage. We fought, we split, and for spite I married a guy who hated him, a Sicilian from the Italian club. The bastard beat me. I found him repulsive and wouldn't sleep with him. I ran to Vito and asked him if I could come back. But you know what the Sicilian stallion answered? 'No woman sends me out of her bedroom and then asks to come back? Never! Go to your husband. I shall be here only for my daughter.'"

Mary was shocked. She had expected to get information from Martha about Vito's demise. Instead, she realized that they had shared a similar scenario with Vito. The man's pride had been formidable. Martha took money out of her purse for her lunch and put it on the table.

"You know?" she said as she got up to leave, "you had some hold on him. He wouldn't divorce you, and now meeting you I can see why. Mary he never stopped loving you."

Mary was touched, and put her arms around Martha. "Thank you for meeting me," she said. "I'm grateful to you."

Mary followed Martha to the sidewalk.

"Listen," Martha said. "nobody from down here killed your Vito. It had to be an inside job. He was set up, and God knows why, but I'm not Sicilian, I'm Polish. But having been attracted to their dark appearance and their mysterious look, I've hurt only myself. These men own a woman. They deal with a woman like a poker game, there's the hook, the bluff, and the killing at the end. Mary, look on 107th street. Vito was rubbed out by somebody in your neighborhood. I had to come to the funeral parlor to see if there were marks on his face or neck, but I couldn't see any. Well, that's my opinion. Take care, Mary, and if you wanna take the advice of someone who's been around more than you, get yourself a man from some other nationality. Irish. You have the Catholic religion in common and you're so different that life together would be an adventure. Yeah, I think I'm going Irish too. Make a life for yourself, you're young and beautiful."

Mary and Martha embraced.

"Thank you, Martha," she said.

Schlomo paid the bill, walked out and put the money Martha had thrown on the table in Martha's hand. "This one's on me." Martha thanked him, and walked home.

Chapter XVI

6/1/51 Mary Confesses

The phone rang in Tess's apartment just as she was about to leave for Yonkers. Tess thought she'd ignore it, but on second thought it might be her mother.

"Tess? What ya doing?" Maggie asked.

"I was just heading up to Yonkers," Tess said. "Mom needs help unpacking the boxes. She called you but there was no answer."

Maggie sighed. "Tell her I'll go next weekend," she said.

"Come this weekend. It'll get done faster."

Maggie obviously wasn't willing. "Didn't Momma hire a Neopolitan maid? Let her do it. I have papers to submit. Did you get your grades?"

"Maggie," Tess said, annoyed. "I gotta go."

"Wait!" Maggie screeched, "don't hang up damn it! What were your grades?" Tess usually didn't lose her temper, but Maggie seemed so insensitive about their mother. "You want to find out? Come to Yonkers. Your mom's not feeling well. *Ciao.*"

Tess hung up and grabbed her bag, but the phone rang again. "The hell with her," Tess muttered as she walked out the door.

Tess took the train to the terminal in the Bronx, came down the iron stairs and called a cab to take her to her mother's new home. When she got there, she was awe struck. The house was magnificent. The windows went from the ceiling to the floor. Each window had a small rail around a foot of balcony. Tess had never seen such beautiful construction. It looked like an Italian villa, the kind that Vito had always shown them in his books of Italy. She recalled her father's pride in being an Italian when he spoke about the Italians' contributions to art and architecture. Vito had spoken of the great engineers of Italy who had been solicited to Argentina to teach them how to build homes on a mountain side. Vito had been proud of his heritage and spouted out the accomplishments of men in all fields at the table, in the saloon and at the gym.

When Tess walked into the sun filled house, Mary held her in her arms and rocked her. "Tess, you came, thank God."

Mary introduced Tess to her Neopolitan maid, and Tess and Giovanna liked each other right away. Tess offered her hand in a handshake, but Giovanna embraced Tess in her arms. "You are as gracious as your mother said you were," Giovanna said.

Mary showed Tess the house. Every box was numbered and had a table of contents on one side. Mary had made a map with room numbers on it, and gave it to the movers who looked at it in awe. "This woman is a good draftsman," the driver and foreman of the men said. "I'll bet she gets these boxes unpacked in two weeks." He laughed, "Boy, I'd sure like to hire her to organize my life."

Mary seemed piqued and she had dark circles under her eyes. The transformation was startling to Tess. "Mom, are you sick?" she asked.

"Well, I'm not feeling well." Tess asked her what was wrong, and Mary said, "No, let's just unpack. We'll talk tonight. Tess, stop worrying, okay? I'm fine." But she wasn't, Tess thought.

Mary showed Tess the level on the first floor towards the side of the house. It had two rooms for the maid's quarters, and a large all purpose room, which could be another bedroom or a den. Towards the back of the house overlooking the huge drop of the property to the next street, was a large 20 X 30 foot kitchen with glass-fronted cabinets and hand-painted ceramic handles imported from Italy. The tiles were Italian tiles from Bologna.

The ceiling went from fifteen feet and sloped to twenty feet. An elongated skylight filled the kitchen with light.

Mary proudly showed Tess the two sinks at either end of the kitchen, one for washing vegetables and the other for washing dishes. The pantry was at the far end of the kitchen with cabinetry which blended in with the walls. "Stunning," Tess uttered, "Momma, this must have cost a fortune." Mary smiled, "No, the man wanted to return to Italy, and Tess, because it was so big, people walked away from it. I could just hear your father's voice in my head: A work of art! So I bought it. Your bedrooms are upstairs."

By 8:00 o'clock they were finished unpacking the boxes for the five bedrooms upstairs. Giovanna helped, but quit at 6:30, to shower, and to prepare supper for them. They had a good dinner of chicken soup with tortellini and small turkey meatballs, a salad and fruit. Mary couldn't keep meat down, but Giovanna did make a small roast for Tess and herself.

Giovanna cleaned up, then retired to her quarters. They had worked for eight hours straight, and Mary took a shower, then collapsed in her bed. Tess took a five minute shower, anxious to learn what was wrong with her mother, but when she came to her mother's large bed, Mary was already sleeping.

Tess stroked her mother's back, kissed her on the back of the neck, and with her hand placed on her mother's body, said the rosary. She was afraid that Mary had a terminal disease and did not have long to live. At midnight, Tess stopped struggling with her anxieties, and went to sleep.

Mary dreamt of Vito. He spoke to her through the thought process of dreams. He told her that she had done the right thing to move away from 107th street. She asked why he had said that, and he walked away nodding his head in a repetitive movement, then he disappeared. Once more even in the dimension of nocturnal thought travel, Vito and Mary had parted. As Mary ran after Vito, she flailed her legs, and fell out of bed waking herself by the thud. Tess jumped up and ran to her mother's room where she found Mary on the floor moaning. She knelt down and focused her eyes in the darkened room.

"Mom, what happened?" Tess asked.

"I had one of my dreams," Mary said. "Look at me, I'm like a baby, I need bars on my bed. I used to scare your father when I fell off the bed."

"Mom, who were you running away from?"

"I was trying to catch your father," Mary said.

"Is Poppa calling you to the next life?" Tess pleaded.

"Tess," Mary said quietly. "I'm three months pregnant."

Tess cried out, and covered her face. What shame must her daughter be feeling about her. The fallout of her situation, was only beginning. She was afraid that her children would turn away from her one by one. She mustn't lose Tess.

"Tess, come here. I'm alone in this, and I need to talk to you. Come, sit by me." Tess was reluctant, and Mary opened her arms to her daughter and Tess came to her. She looked at her mother as though she was asking her why, but the words would not come out of her mouth. Mary sensed it.

"I fell in love with Sean Quinn," Mary whispered.

"I don't give a damn about him, mom. This is about you. How could you have allowed this to happen after my birth? Oh yes, I found out about it. You were torn inside and you almost bled to death. I believe you were told no more babies. What in God's name were you thinking?" Tess cried out.

"I wasn't thinking Tess. You're right in every way, but now I have to deal with so much more," Mary said, "Look let's go back to bed, we'll talk some more tomorrow." Tess was relieved. She just wanted to shut her eyes to the nightmare her mother was about to go through.

The next morning Mary and Tess went to mass, and then out to breakfast. At the coffee shop, Tess admonished her mother to make sure she had the best of pre-natal care.

"Tess, the doctor is very good. He's a high risk doctor."

"Why high risk? Are you?" Tess was worried.

"He's Catholic. If complications arise, I want the baby to survive. I'm prepared for that," Mary said quietly.

"Jesus, mom! What am I to do?" Mary held her daughter's hand, "If that happens I want the baby in your custody. Sean has to be told and if he wants his child, he should have it. I'm putting this in writing."

The baby would be given the name of Petracca, which would make it legitimate.

Tess went back home on Sunday night and called Maggie who wasn't home. Maybe she had gone to stay with Marty in Virginia. Tess didn't approve of pre marital sex, and she always asked Maggie to spare her from listening to Maggie's romantic interludes with men.

At 11:00 o'clock Maggie called Tess. Maggie bubbled over with the great fun weekend she had had with a friend of Sean's, and when Tess asked about Marty, Maggie said "Soon

I'll speak of him only in the past tense." Tess asked no more questions.

"And how was **your** weekend?" Maggie asked caustically. "How many grocery boxes of mom's things did you unpack?"

"All of them," Tess responded, and Maggie apologized. Tess told her that their mother was in a delicate situation. Maggie got upset. "What is going on? Is she sick?"

"Sort of," Tess said. She wanted to cry. She promised her mother she wouldn't say a word about her predicament.

"Look, hang up. Call your mother. Good night, Maggie." Tess hung up and burst out crying again. She was terrified.

"Don't hang up, damn it," Maggie shouted.

Tess couldn't sleep. She thought about her parents. What had happened to them? Even at the most difficult times between Vito and Mary, the children were aware that the electricity between their parents had still existed.

Growing up in the household, Maggie was the most observant. A story teller, a writer, she studied her parents' dynamic and commented on all she saw.

Tess loved her father. As a father he was the best. He nurtured his children, gave them confidence to follow their dreams and moved mountains to help them out.

She recalled when Marco showed some interest in studying the violin how Vito went directly to the conservatory on 105th street, Manhattan School of Music. He hired a violin teacher, whom he asked to help him find the best violin for his son. Marco was given lessons twice a week instead of the usual once. Marco was precocious, and musically gifted. He started at seven years old and by the time he was ten years old, he was performing concerts by himself on Saturdays. By the time Marco was in his teens, he was asked to teach other children from the neighborhood. In the apartment, Marco's quarters were like a mini studio.

Vito had adorned the walls with art subjects which dealt with music, musicians and composers. Vito had bought a solid brass music stand for Marco. With Vito's encouragement and pride, the environment Marco lived in eventually created a brilliant violinist, composer and conductor.

For Philip, a brilliant human rocket, who danced and did acrobatic stunts all over the house, Vito had concerns. Initially, Tess remembered how very upset Vito was when Philip expressed a desire to be a dancer in the ballet. As much as Vito had supported Marco's ambitions and talent, he turned away from Philip's. A stigma of male dancers being 'sissies' soured Vito on Philip's choice.

At ten years old, after years of being asked nightly "what do you want to be Philip?" Philip had answered "an acrobat with the circus. A high wire walker." Once more Vito put his hands up in despair and gave his disapproval. Philip, was upset. His mother called him Mercury, and all his life Philip had imagined that he would be flying with his body because he was fast and quick and graceful. However, Vito had not been amenable to any of his young dreams.

Nightly after supper, Vito would ask the inevitable question, "So, Philip, what do you want to be?" Only when Philip answered: "Rich!" did Vito stop asking him, but as soon as Philip had concurred with Vito's expectations, Vito had put aside thousands of dollars to purchase a dress factory. From that night on, Vito made efforts to investigate the garment manufacturing business.

In post-war America, Italian dress makers were invited to come to America to study the production line system of dress manufacturing. After weeks of being shown the techniques, the Italian manufacturers were duly impressed with American's innovative piece work manufacturing process. A person didn't even have to know how to put a dress together. They just learned the one process on the production line, and were paid accordingly. Clothes manufactured in the production line were stylish, well made, and affordable.

Vito had followed this story in the newspaper, and being the head of a union, had made it his business to observe as a guest, the tour which the manufacturers in Milano had been shown. Mass production then began in Italy, so that good looking affordable clothing would be available for the Italian woman without being custom made.

Piece work was an innovative technique in the manufacturing of clothing. Each operator did one task. The first operator sewed the sleeves on to the bodice, then placed it in a bin on the right of the sleeve operator; picked up on the left by the next operator from the bin, who would then attach the bodice to the skirt, and place it in the bin to the right so that the process continued down the line until the entire dress was made. Button holes were put in by a special machine and a single operator. No one operator made an entire garment except the sample maker who put one garment together for the rest of the operators to see a finished product.

Tess remembered that the easiest turf her parents had when they conversed was their interest in the children. There they met on common and affable ground.

Vito's biggest concern was the free spirit of Maggie. Once more the Sicilian code of honor came into play regarding their first daughter. When Maggie was only 13, Vito told Mary, "I think she'll defy traditions and will probably have affairs." Mary was astounded.

"How can you say this?" Mary said.

"Just a gut feeling," he had said.

"Watch how she flings her arms around boys as well as girls. There's no modesty, no concern for proper decorum, and frankly she doesn't give a hoot about anything I say. So, yes, Maggie will fly the coop early, and perhaps even earlier than her brothers, and she'll experiment with her sexuality. She'll bring home a rebel like herself. Free spirit, unreliable and difficult to understand. We might be stuck with bringing up an illegitimate child, Mary," he had said prophetically. Tess was eavesdropping in the bathroom when her parents talked about Maggie.

"I don't worry about Tess, she's an old soul, Mary, so I don't concern myself about her future. She'll probably teach, a good profession for a girl. When I'm gone, Mary, she'll be the one you'll turn to," he had said prophetically.

Tess had a rough night, going over the scenes of her parents and her siblings. As she looked back she saw something that she had never seen before. She realized that Vito's support of them in their passions and dreams only happened if it agreed with his idea of what they should be when they grew up.

She was sure that if her father ever knew that Tess wanted to be a lawyer, he would not have supported it. He had bought her chalk as a child so that she could play "teacher," a profession which women gravitated to. Careers which were dominated by men were distasteful to Vito.

Journalism for Maggie? Never! he would have shouted. "No! It's a man's world." And so the stigma of Philip's choices were turned down with disdain by Vito.

Tess thought about the new baby. She prayed that it would be normal and healthy, and that her mother would be alright.

Mary drove Tess to the station. Mary asked Tess to arrange a meeting with Maggie at Tess's place. "I can't tell her about this unless you're near by," Mary pleaded. Tess agreed to be the buffer between them.

The following week on Saturday night, Maggie was invited to Tess's apartment. Mary was already there. Maggie saw how terrible her mother looked and she got frightened, thinking that Tess couldn't tell her just how sick her mother was.

After dinner, Tess told them to sit in the living room while she did the dishes so that they could talk.

After a half hour of Maggie's interrogation over Mary's health, Mary put a stop to it. Her courage was failing her as each moment passed.

"Maggie, I'm not terminally sick as you suspect, I'm pregnant. This is so difficult to do, but the father of the baby is well known to you. Don't ask me how or why it happened, only that it did. It's Sean." Maggie paled and looked as though she was going to faint. "Oh my God!" she cried out as she ran into the kitchen. Tess stopped cleaning and tended to her sister's shock. She wet a small towel and put it on Maggie's head. Maggie almost swooned, and Mary ran in and saturated another towel with vinegar putting it under Maggie's nose.

"Maggie," Mary implored as she sobbed, "forgive me, Maggie." Maggie pushed her mother away. "Get away from me. Stay out of my sight. I don't want to talk to you." Mary ran out of the parlor to Tess's room and collapsed on Tess's bed.

Maggie screamed at Tess calling her a traitor, and ran out shouting, "Damn all of you. I have no family."

Tess chased down the stairs after her sister, and caught her by the back of her neck. Though Tess was six inches shorter than Maggie, she had the strength to pull her to the floor of the vestibule of her building. "You brat!" she screamed, "that woman upstairs is your mother, how dare you talk to her like that?" Maggie got up and swung at Tess knocking her to the ground. "I have no family, do you hear? I don't want to see you and that *puttana* of a mother ever again."

Tess pleaded, "Maggie, maybe you're justified, but she's your mother." Maggie spat on the floor and hissed, "That's what I think of your mother."

Tess said with resignation, "I'm calling you in a few days when you calm down."

Mary left the next morning. Philip's admonition was becoming a reality. Loving Sean Quinn, was destroying the family.

When she got home, she felt dirty. She took a shower, then went to the local church to confess her sins. It was Sunday, masses had all been said, but Mary went to the rectory of the church and asked for a priest. The parish priest asked Father Peter Sullivan, a visiting priest to oblige the distraught woman.

Mary walked in the darkened confessional, knelt and did the sign of the cross. The priest slid the panel open to the screened window, so that he could hear her. "Bless me Father for I have sinned, it's been a year since my last worthy confession." The priest looked down at his breviary, put his hand to his face and leaned towards the screen.

Mary told the priest about her affair sparing no details of her duplicity against her daughter.

"You realize the seriousness of this sin puts your soul in jeopardy."

"Yes Father," Mary whispered.

"You must avoid further occasion of sin with this man," the priest said.

"Father I already have. He's in Korea covering the war. Father, there's something else. I'm frightened. I'm pregnant, and it's a high risk pregnancy. If there's a choice of life between me and the baby, I shall die." Mary clutched her hands tightly to control her tremors.

Father Peter gave an almost inaudible gasp, as he realized that he was listening to the confession of Mary Petracca.

"I shall keep you in my prayers. Like you, the Blessed Mother was frightened when she was told that she was going to have a baby. Only she had not known man, and she was confused. The Holy Spirit would come upon her and she would become the vessel for Christ's birth. Young, unmarried, and betrothed to Joseph, she accepted her fate. You have chosen to bring new life into this world. Focus on your child. Have faith, you will not be alone. Do you understand this?"

"Yes, I do Father," Mary whispered.

"For penance say a rosary meditating on the joyful mysteries. Now please say a good act of contrition."

As Mary began her prayer "Oh my God I am heartily sorry for having offended Thee--" Father Peter raised his right hand and said the prayer for absolution of her sins, in Latin. *"Deinde ego te absolvo a peccatis tuis, in nominee Patris et filii, et spiritus sancti, Amen."* He did the sign of the cross, and as Mary got through with the Act of Contrition, he blessed her.

"God bless you," Father Peter said,

"Thank you Father." Mary got out, and walked to the altar.

Father Peter Sullivan remained in the confession box and wept.

Chapter XVII

Hidden Agenda

In October, as Mary was swollen with child, she stayed close to home. Schlomo became a constant visitor, and a dear friend to Mary. He handled everything for her, but always with paper work and proof that he had done what he had said he had. He understood the Sicilian mentality of mistrust of anyone, especially (Vito used to say,) those who are closest to you.

Schlomo came to tell Mary that an offer had been made on her tenement building. Mary inquired about the offer, and from whom it had been made. Schlomo hesitated, and spent some time opening his briefcase as Mary sat on the chair quite uncomfortably, holding the heavy burden of her stomach.

"I got the offer here. Twenty grand, not bad."

She grimaced at the low offer. "Nope," she said. "Not enough."

"Mary, come on, this isn't an offer from the man on the street, you know what I mean?" Schlomo wiped the nervous perspiration from his neck. "The boys came to my office. I almost croaked. They wanted to know where you were. I implied you're not well, and can't see anyone. Joe Marra lifted me up and I swear I thought he was gonna throw me out the window. I almost choked. I swear to God, I thought they were gonna kill me, but then, Louie mentioned the building again. Sell, it Mary. Get the mob off your back. " Mary was single minded, she wasn't intimidated.

"What about the rumor that the city will buy it from us?" she asked.

"Mary, wise up. The city will buy for dirt cheap. If you don't take their offer, they'll condemn the property and it'll be worth nothing. Take this offer, you cannot afford to refuse this. Twenty grand? Better than what the city will offer."

"Who made the offer?" she asked undaunted by Schlomo's nervous reaction.

"Louie the Lip did." Suddenly Mary got up from the chair with difficulty, shuffled to the kitchen for a pen and paper, and came back to the living room. "Give me his number. I'll call him." Schlomo started to sweat. He told Mary that she had to be nuts to even deal with such low life. Schlomo was surprised when Mary sat down and dialed Louie in front of Schlomo. "Louie? Finally! How are you?" she was upbeat and charming. Louie muttered, "For Pete's sake, we thought you had died, cuz nobody could find you," and she responded weakly, "Better, Louie. I couldn't see anybody." He believed her, "I'm sorry, Mary, look I won't keep you. Let's get to business. I want to buy the building." Mary wanted to know why so little was offered for the building with a custom built eight room apartment.

"What do you want for it?" Louie asked impatiently. He sounded annoyed.

"Twenty five grand would be a better number," Mary said clearly. Schlomo was taking deep breaths. Mary was as cool as a politician. Where the hell did she get this enamel façade?

Louie shouted an expletive in Sicilian, *"Azzo!"*

Then he continued. "Hey Mary, you want a job as loan shark? Agh, what the hell, I'll do it for Vito."

Mary gave Schlomo a thumbs up gesture, and he shook his head incredulously. Who would have believed the nerve of this woman.

"Cash deal, Mary," Louie added, not wishing to tax Mary's energy.

"Good. I wanna be paid in hundred dollar bills, no bigger. I'm going to count it." Louie wanted to strangle her, but she might change her mind. He had to be patient.

"Anything you want, Mary," he said as he bit his finger as a sign of a vendetta, "by the way what happened to you? Are you dying, or what? For God's sake, tell me what's wrong?"

"It's a woman's problem, Louie, I can't talk about these things to a man." Louie gave a big sigh of relief, "Ah," he said, "I knew it. I even told Joe Marra, that I thought you had surgery. I'm glad you told us, because rumors were flying all over the place. There's talk, there's always talk, you know how the block is. Alright, you're okay, and we have a deal. Mary, call me."

"As soon as I recuperate, I'll call you and we'll have lunch." That seemed to satisfy him.

"What about your phone number?" he asked.

"No, I can't take calls. Just call Schlomo, then I'll call you."

"Okay, good enough. Mary, before we hang up, I just gotta tell ya this, Joe Marra's goin' nuts cuz he can't find ya."

"Louie, I'm feeling faint, I dropped the phone, I didn't hear what you said, but I gotta hang up." She dropped the phone on the floor on purpose, so that crash of the phone startled him, and she retrieved it by pulling the wire up and placing it on its cradle.

"Go to bed, Mary, I'm sorry," Louie said, but Mary didn't hear him, she had already hung up. She looked up and Schlomo was laughing to himself. He kept shaking his head and muttering, "Incredible! Worst than any Mafioso."

Mary stood up, and Schlomo followed her into the kitchen as she poured him a glass of cold beer which was all Schlomo ever wanted. Mary had stocked the refrigerator since he'd been coming up to visit her.

"Those guys are not to be trusted, Mary. You're making me nervous hearing you tell 'em you're gonna go out for lunch. Nuts, that's what you are," he muttered as he guzzled his Rheingold beer right from the bottle.

"This is the best beer," he said as Mary took out another bottle.

"Stay over, tonight, Schlomo. I don't feel well. You'll sleep in the guest room, and if I need to get to the hospital, you'll drive me, okay?" She was sweating, and it was October 30, the day before halloween.

"You think it'll be born tonight?" he asked.

"I feel like a helium zepolin about to burst. Schlomo, my housekeeper made chicken for you. Please eat, and don't get too drunk. I need you to be sober."

Mary went up the stairs, then after two steps she couldn't continue. Giovanna came out and helped Mary to the second bedroom on the first level, the one which Giovanna's son, Rafaelo, was going to occupy. Giovanna went into the kitchen and despite her broken English and Schlomo's thick Jewish accent, they were able to communicate. Giovanna was forty years old, Schlomo forty eight, and they sized each other up as prospective partners. She thought, Eh? do-able. He thought, I've been alone long enough. Mary is too complicated, but with Giovanna, at least I'll learn how to eat, and she has a son of twelve coming soon. Yeah, there would be my family.

After he ate the chicken, she said that he was eating the wrong foods, and he asked her what he should eat. "First of all get rid of the beer drinking habit, it makes you look like a pregnant woman, like Mary." Schlomo guzzled the last drop of beer he would ever take again. He was ready for a drastic change, and a mother figure who would take care of him. He lost no time. "Giovanna, would you marry me?" She blushed, but not for long. "Yes, when?" she asked. He answered, "As soon as your son comes and approves." Giovanna said, "Don't worry, he'll approve." They kissed and Schlomo and Giovanna became engaged.

That night after three pots of coffee, Schlomo sobered up and was ecstatic. He now had a family, almost, that is, until her son Rafaele came to America. When her water broke at eleven o'clock, Mary had no idea that the housekeeper was engaged to Schlomo and would soon be gone leaving Mary alone in the Petracca Palace.

With this additional drama, the beautiful nine pound four ounce baby girl named Grace came into this world in Lawrence Hospital in Bronxville. Mary's pregnancy was problematic, but the birth of her baby came quickly and without any adverse event. Mary did her screaming and yelling as the labor pains came frequently, and finally the obstetrician Dr. Dell'Aquila, gave her a shot to calm her down, and Grace made her debut in the Petracca family.

In the recovery room, Mary cried "Doctor, I'm going to live?" Dr. Dell Aquila assured her. "You made it Mary, Yes."

As she came out of the recovery room, she talked to Sean in her semi conscious state, as Schlomo and Giovanna sat by and listened. "No fences, Sean, no shot gun wedding, you're free-when I'm strong enough, I'll let you meet your baby girl, no fences, Sean." Mary moaned and fell asleep again. Giovanna was stunned. Who was Sean? Schlomo confided that he was the father of the baby because Vito was dead. "I'm not surprised," Giovanna commented. "Mary and her daughter Tess, seemed upset over the pregnancy. Now I know why. Sicilians don't talk. How come she talked to you?" Schlomo explained that Mary had to tell someone and he was flattered that she had put her trust in him.

Schlomo called Tess in the morning, and she came up in the afternoon. Maggie got called too, and she thanked Schlomo asking only if her mother was alright. Schlomo sensed a rift between Maggie and Mary.

* * *

In Korea, the winter battles were fierce, and many died. However, one Sunday, in a sunny quiet field near army quarters, a Catholic service was being said. A long piece of wood with a cloth became a makeshift altar. There were many denominations there, including Jews, who were identifiable because they did not do the sign of the cross. A sense of peace and deep worship permeated the quiet multitudes of soldiers.

Philip had been caught in a skirmish, and two of his men were badly wounded. In the dark, swiftly and deftly, Philip had carried them on his back one at a time to safety.

The small group of seven men were amazed that they were still alive, so when on Sunday the mass was put together impromptu, Philip and his men stood in the front. Philip looked impeccable in his uniform, and as the men gathered humbly, and silently for worship, sitting on rocks, standing or kneeling, the news reporters joined them too.

Philip looked to the left, and there was Sean Quinn. Ironically they were happy to see each other. Sean gave Philip a little salute, and Philip smiled. As the priest spoke of the life of Christ, the men wept, looked pensive and knew that they were not alone in this *inferno.*

As each soldier and officer went up for communion, Sean waited until Philip passed in front of him, then he offered him his hand in greeting. Philip took his hand, then put his arms around Sean, and they hugged each other, and went to communion together. It was a touching moment, leaving many who had witnessed it a poignant feeling of camaraderie between two friends.

After mass, they united for a cup of coffee at the tent canteen, and talked. Sean asked questions about the family, and Philip opened up. What in heaven's name did he have to lose now? *Omerta?* He laughed at the old values which did not apply here. One bullet, and it would be over.

They found a rock near a tree, and sat facing each other sipping their coffee and eating dried up crackers.

"How's your mom?" Sean asked.

"Fine. Don't you two write?"

"No, she dumped me, Philip. That should make you feel good." Sean's anger oozed out. At that point a photo journalist saw the two men who apparently knew each other, and he stood in front of them with the camera poised.

"Quinn, how about one for the states? You two know each other?" Sean was pleased. Mary might get to see them together. "Sure, we're old buddies," Sean quipped. Philip grimaced. Had the photo journalist not stepped in, he would have given Sean a nasty retort, but he had time to think and reflect. The guy was obviously hurt. Thank God his mother had listened to his pleas.

Sean put his arm around Philip's shoulders and they held their coffee canteens up in a toast to the folks back home, to boost morale which was quickly waning.

The photographer took two shots, and then walked away. Sean dropped his arm, and he too had time to reflect.

"Philip, I have a big mouth. I didn't mean to hurt you. You know when I heard what battalion you were in, I swear to God I thought you had been killed. They were all wiped out at the 38th parallel. Somebody up there's praying for you big time." Sean smiled in anticipation of Philip's answer.

"My father is, Sean. Let's go back to the women in my family. What the hell were you thinking of when you seduced my mother?"

"We don't have time," Sean explained. "Let me just tell you, that I fell in love with your mother from the first time I saw her. Maggie and I had had a brief romantic interlude--"

"In other words, you fucked her," Philip interrupted.

"I didn't call it that. She was young, beautiful and smart. She did the pursuing and I'm not made of rock, so I went for it. I swear as I'm standing next to you, I stopped sleeping with her after I met your mother. Maggie knew that it was over, but she hung on. I feel like the biggest shit in the world. I didn't plan this, Philip. Damn, I love your mother, and I like Maggie. She writes to me and I write back cuz I ain't got a soul in the world outside of my old friend Father Peter who writes me."

"You want me to feel sorry for you?" Philip snarled, "Screw you. I can't swallow the whole scene. You're a Catholic and you go after two women in one family? Sean, my stomach turns into knots when I think of you."

"Look Philip, once more, your sister hit on me, okay?"

"She was a kid, you son of a bitch," Philip was ready to swing at him, but he walked away, and then walked back "you ruined her honor."

"Man, that Sicilian bullshit doesn't work in America." Sean was stunned by Philip's thinking at the edge of hell in Korea, he spoke about honor? It was laughable, given Maggie's promiscuity.

"Get the hell out of my sight. Stay away from my family. You're poison," Philip spouted out. Sean smarted. However, from his point of view, he had acted honorably, because after meeting Mary he had stopped sleeping with Maggie. Were his actions so horrific, that Philip couldn't go beyond what he believed.

Philip walked away, but Sean went after him, "Damn it Philip, tomorrow we might both be dead. Let's for heaven's sake not end on this note, okay? I'll never pursue your family again. It's a promise I intend to keep. I won't go looking for your mother or Maggie, I swear to God, Philip." Philip's eyes were teary, "Yeah, right Sean. Right on all counts. Okay just get your ass out of my presence, and save yourself. I'll try to do the same."

Sean shook his hand, "Philip, you're lucky. Your mother was deeply concerned about you. That woman loves you."

"I know that. I don't need you to tell me anything about my mother. I had her on a pedestal. You brought her down to your level Sean Quinn. You contaminated my mother, you son of a bitch. Screw it. I gotta save my anger for the enemy. Try to survive, you got big lessons to learn."

"Right Philip. I'm sorry all this happened, and for whatever it's worth, I love your mother. Stay alive, buddy."

Sean's eyes were teary.

Philip wrote a letter that night. The battalion was moving out in the morning.

"Momma, today I went to mass in a church with no walls, and a sky for a ceiling. I looked over across the seven survivors in my battalion, and there was Sean Quinn. We spotted each other, and as I went out of the row to receive communion, Sean embraced me. It was nice to see him. He's skinnier than ever, but otherwise is making a splash in his articles, many of which we get to read first hand. Half of Korean history none of us knew, but Sean knows. He educates us, and maybe even the

American public. He asked for the family and I told him you were all well.

Tess wrote. She loves the new house. By the way, Sean told me you dumped him. I'm so proud of you. Oh yes Mom, did you know that my sister Maggie writes him? That's still going on mom, and I don't think it'll ever end. So have no regrets in that department and for heaven's sake don't look back, okay? I dreamt of Poppa. He told me I'm gonna be alright, and I swear to God, I'm not afraid. I saved two of my men in a battle. They were wounded, and I took one at a time out of the fires of the forest. So, my C.O. told me he's recommending me for a medal of bravery. Why should I get a medal of bravery? Isn't this my job as an officer? How the hell do you let people burn alive because their leg's been shot up? I can't do that. Whatever you're doing keep praying. Funny, I didn't want to mention him again, but Sean said I was lucky. I almost felt sorry for him, mom, he's got nobody, except his best friend a priest back in New York, and Maggie. What's her problem? Why can't she write? I'd like to give her a good smack in the face, as I did when she'd mess up my room just to get my goat. She's mean, mom, I swear to God, she is, but she's my sister. You call her and tell her to write. Take care of yourself, I love you. Pray and don't stop. I'm coming home. I think that's why poppa came in my dream and told me not to be afraid. One more thing, I almost forgot remember the troop I was with at Ft. Dix? I was supposed to be with them. Sean told me that they were all wiped out at the 38th parallel. so..yeah, Poppa's with me. If I hadn't been fast on my feet, they might not have noticed me for officer's training school. Funny how things work. Poppa thought being fast didn't matter much, I just had to know what the hell I was going to do when I grew up, now I can tell him. Being Mercury saved my life...think about it.

Momma, gotta go. I love you and when I come home, I want my linguini with anything.love you. Philip."

Chapter XVIII

Marco comes home

On November 6th, 1951, Marco came home after an extended tour. Marco's timing was in tune with Grace's birth. Marco was exhausted but exhilarated to finally be able to spend time with his mother.

When he arrived, the surprise of finding a baby sister in his mother's arms was a jolt and took getting used to. Marco was in shock. However, Mary's position was that each of her children would have to accept their newest sibling.

Grace Petracca was a large baby, and looked more like a month old baby, than a newborn. She was fair of complexion, had blue eyes, and had long wispy straight hair. "Just like her father," Mary commented as she stroked the child's silken hair.

Mary held Grace, and radiated joy. Marco was anxious to know the particulars. "Who's her father?" he asked.

"Sean Quinn, Marco. I couldn't tell you this on the phone." She was defensive, then she smiled, "the baby looks like him." Marco grimaced.

Marco was speechless. He was enraged at the very idea that the lascivious Sean Quinn had been intimate with his mother. Yet Mary was happy with this new baby. She whispered to her, "*Bedda fighia mia,* my Irish bambina."

After the first night home, Marco had chosen the two bedrooms at the top of the stairs, one as his bedroom, and the second one adjacent to that, as his music studio. Maggie's room remained vacant except for the furnishings.

Marco asked about Maggie. Mary didn't want to comment on her daughter. "Right now she's not feeling generous towards not only me, but all of you. In time, she'll have a change of heart. At least, that's what I'm hoping for. I wish you'd call her, go see her, Marco, she must be hurting so much." Marco's cold demeanor hurt Mary, but she expected it. In fact she anticipated worse.

"Do you like this house, Marco?" Mary asked.

"Like a villa, Mom, but, the house is too big, and I can't imagine what you were thinking when you bought it." He waved his hand around in a semi circle to emphasize the grandness of the house.

Mary felt his censure, in a diversionary way. Marco had no strong opinion about the size of the house, but he did have a strong opinion about her affair and illegitimate baby. There was something else that bothered Marco, and that was that Mary had become stronger, decisive and sure of herself. He didn't know how to deal with this at all.

"Marco, the size of the house is not bothering you. What is?" He followed her to her bedroom upstairs, and sat at the edge of the bed, "I can't get over it." Mary realized that he still wouldn't articulate what he was really feeling.

She looked at her son, who couldn't look into her eyes, "The telephone is a wonderful invention Marco, it's good for brief messages or conversations. No mother should have to use it to tell her son that she had given birth to a baby. I had to see you in person." He skulked away from Mary and wanted to go to his room, "I have a major headache," he said, "But why couldn't you have turned to my father instead of your daughter's boyfriend for the affection you craved?"

"Intimacy, Marco begins with the brain, not the body. Your father and I had become strangers. I love you Marco, you're my son, but I'm not going to crawl like an insect because I've sinned. Grace was conceived in love, not lust. My son, please think about what I've said." Mary drew his face towards her and she kissed Marco on the cheek. He shut his eyes and wanted so much not to hurt his mother, "Momma, give me time, I was not prepared for what I found." He returned Mary's embrace and went down the hallway to his room.

* * *

Marco liked Giovanna. She didn't seem like hired help but like a relative. She took excellent care of Mary, adored the baby and was a fabulous Neapolitan cook and housekeeper.

He was happy that she and Schlomo Schwarz were already a couple, though Marco felt, an unlikely couple. Between her broken English and his thick accent, they were hilarious to listen to. How they understood each other was a mystery.

Schlomo spent many nights with Giovanna in her quarters. His whole demeanor changed. He learned how to drink wine, and water, and had given up beer. Already his color improved as Giovanna introduced him to broccoli, broccoli rape, swiss chard and spinach omelets.

Tess came home for the weekend, and she and Marco were happy to see each other. Privately they voiced their opinions about Mary, and it was Tess who said to her brother, "Marco, you either don't accept it and make yourself and mom miserable, or you begin to see that mom has changed for the better. Look at her, she's moved mountains, Marco. With Poppa, she was a shadow, a silhouette. I like the change, and I'm supporting her."

"Okay," Marco said as he sighed, "you're right Tess."

* * *

Philip's letter came, and they read it voraciously. Mary read the letter over and over, picturing the reunion between Philip and Sean, hoping that their warm impromptu meeting at the outside church had healed some antagonism between them. Mary continued to hope for that. Philip had not been told about Grace. In her next letter, now that he had seen Sean, she'd tell Philip.

After the family dinner, Mary sat at her desk in the den off the main floor and wrote to her son Philip.

"Dearest Philip: I was so happy to receive your letter. It was a wonderful surprise to see that you and Sean had connected. Now that a certain event has taken place on October 30th at 11:50 p.m., I can tell you. I've given birth to a beautiful baby girl whom I named Grace. She is 9 pounds and 4 ounces, blonde and blue eyed. I couldn't tell you anything before this, because the pregnancy was so terrible, that I never thought I'd survive it. I was filled with terror about the normalcy of the baby that

I couldn't even "talk" about it to you in my letters. You didn't have to worry more than you already are doing in the middle of this horrible war.

I was glad to learn that you and Sean saw each other and went to communion together. We need a healing in this family. We need to forgive one another. I fell in love with him, Philip, and I followed my heart. I don't regret the time I spent with him. I have to make that clear to you especially. Maggie still won't call me or come here.

I recall your words "don't destroy this family, Momma." Rest assured Philip, I did as you requested. I've severed our relationship. If you see him, say nothing about the baby. Her name is Grace Petracca. She has blue eyes like her father and the golden wisps of hair sticking up just like his. She's beautiful. I nurse her as I did each of you, and it's like being a kid again. Yes, as a kid, I had kids too.

My joy is not complete until you come home. Marco is here, as is Tess. They'll add a few lines to this, my letter to you.

A candle is lit in front of the Sacred Heart of Jesus in my bedroom for your safe return. Our family will not be complete until you and Maggie are home again. I love you dearly. My love always, Momma."

Tess added a few lines:

"Hi Philip:

So happy to read your letter. Things are different here. We now have another Petracca baby. Momma's household is full. Giovanna and Schlomo are engaged. An orthodox Jew with a Catholic widow? Unlikely you say? Incredible, I say. I don't understand his thick Jewish accent, and even Giovanna's fractured English is spoken with a mix of Neapolitan words which I don't get because it's not Sicilian. Both of them speak bastardized English, his dotted "*mit cherman vords*" and hers "*parlammo ma no understand-a*" They'll have a perfect marriage. A marriage with no arguments because they won't know what the other one is saying.

Our sister Grace is a miracle. She is blonde, blue eyes, beautiful, her mouth is always open like a little sparrow waiting to be fed, and she sleeps a lot. Momma's had a rough time with this whole business of a baby, but thank God she's okay and the baby is normal.

This baby needs to know that her family adores her. How she got here, and why, is not our concern. I told this to Marco who's so hard on mom, but it's done. The fact is the baby is here. She needs us to love her, okay? Take care, do write if you have time, or include a few lines in momma's letters. So my darling brother Mercury, I miss you so much. When you come home, you'll visit me in the village, and we'll have a linguine tour of all the restaurants in the village. I love you. Love Tess."

* * *

Marco sat down to add his few lines.

"Dear Philip: I read your letter. Thank God you're alright. I also read Sean Quinn's articles. The guy is good at what he does. (even beyond writing.) The baby looks exactly like him, even her hair sticks up like quills. She is knock out gorgeous. Does she look Sicilian? Not at all. Momma's given birth to an Irish baby, and I held her and it felt so weird seeing new life in this house, and hopefully the process of all of us accepting it.

Momma calls this the Petracca Palace, nice touch I'd say, kind of brings Poppa's good name from East Harlem to Yonkers. She's also given Poppa's good name to Grace. The baby is Grace Petracca. Nobody up here knew Poppa, so the neighbors think that Poppa was the father of the baby.

Next week the Petracca Palace greets Rafaele, Giovanna's twelve year old son from Naples. They'll marry as soon as her kid approves. (How nice to see a mother consider the feelings of her son before acting.) Anyway, it seems that they lost my draft card, but they caught up with me. I'm reporting in two weeks. I'll keep in touch. Talk to you later. Love Marco."

Mary read her children's letters, and felt guilty at Marco's line about Giovanna waiting for her son to approve of Schlomo before she married.

* * *

Tess took over the kitchen as Giovanna helped her mother with the baby diapers, and the additional laundry which belonged to both she and Marco.

Schlomo was a very welcome addition to the household. He truly tried to become Italian overnight, but it would be a life long process for him. However, the man was ecstatic, and he no longer shuffled when he walked, but he lifted his feet. Tess noticed that, for her powers of observation were keen as the future lawyer and judge she'd become.

Marco softened his attitude towards his mother, particularly after he saw her deep concern for Philip. Anything could happen out there, thousands of American troops dying for the cause of freedom, the banner behind which precipitated many American wars.

Marco got up at 6:00 a.m. and practiced the violin for four hours. At ten, he showered, came to the kitchen, and Giovanna made him a huge omelet with broccoli rape. Marco loved the unusual breakfast, and kissed Giovanna on the cheek. *"Delizioso! Giovanna, grazie,"* he said. She blushed and said, "I'm so glad you enjoyed the breakfast." Giovanna was in awe of this exquisite young man. Marco left for the city, and met with Maggie after school. They had a wonderful reunion, and Maggie was so proud to show her brother off at the bar to her friends. Marco was the younger version of Vito Petracca, handsome, a full head of black wavy hair, a strong Roman nose, big eyes with dark long lashes, and a full mouth with a cleft chin and a dimple on the right cheek. He was tall and slender of figure, not as muscular as Vito had been.

Because he was a musician, Marco's ego was not filled with himself but with the muse which owned his intellect and his spirit. His great heroes were Isaac Stern, the violinist, and Arturo Toscanini, the conductor who inspired him with his innovative style.

Maggie and Marco talked at once and laughed because they were excited to see each other. "Me first, Marco, tell me about yourself." Marco spared no details of the tour of the symphonette orchestra he had been on the road with for close to nine months. He asked about her life and she told him about school, and then talked about Sean Quinn. She was bitter towards her mother, and told Marco that her opinion of Sean had fallen into a pit. "He's got no heart, Marco, your mother has lost her soul over this whore master, and I'm deeply wounded. I don't know if I can ever forgive her."

Marco empathized. "Maggie, you can hold a grudge all your life. You'll be cynical, bitter, and empty. Mom's ended her relationship with Sean. Why? Because of you. She loves the guy, make no mistake about it, he loved her too. You're right he's a shit, but them's the facts Sis, hang it up, don't keep this damned vendetta any longer. You'll be the one who suffers." Marco stroked Maggie's hand.

She listened and didn't argue any of the points he made. Marco invited Maggie to dine with him and his girlfriend Vivian. Maggie was thrilled to see the soprano again and happy that her brother had taken his heart out of a musical score to fall in love with a woman and join the rest of the human race.

The whole evening was so perfect for Maggie. She realized that her anger had put a huge weight upon her spirit, and she hadn't laughed with such total abandon in months. Vivian was wonderful to Maggie, and the girls hit it off as they discovered their mutual sense of humor.

Ultimately, Marco had penetrated the ice wall Maggie had surrounded herself with, and the Petracca family would be unified, but it would take time.

Chapter XIX

Mary's Investigation

Mary was concerned with the events and mysteries surrounding her husband's death. One of these burning questions was how deeply had Vito been involved with the mob? Mary did not wish to arouse suspicion so she had to take charge herself until she found the answers. Just why was the mob anxious to buy her building?

She had recuperated from the birth of Grace, and devised a plan. The plan was to get into her tenement building's cellar. No one had access to it. Vito was the last to have the key to the padlock. Mary suspected that the cellar was rented, but to whom, exactly, she didn't know. Vito collected fifty dollars a month for the rental of his cellar, that much she knew. Yet she never saw anyone come there during the day. Her intent was to investigate it at night when no one was around.

The tenement buildings were attached to each other like matchboxes. Cellars had small cubicles for storage for each of the tenants in the building, yet in Vito's building, no cellar or storage privileges were given to any tenant. The cellars opened up into the small backyards, facing the backyards of the southern row of tenements on 108th street.

Backyards featured short fences in some of the yards, and sticks in the ground in others. Huge utility poles were planted in the backyard of each building to hang the clothing lines on. Backyards had to be open fields to accommodate the free movement of the line-o man who came once a month howling his trade, "Line-0, here, line-0" he'd shout. When a housewife needed service on her clothing line, he climbed up the iron rungs stuck into the utility pole to repair the pulleys or ropes.

Landlords planted fig trees and peach trees in the back yard. Small tracts of land were utilized for the tomato, lettuce and basil gardens. On the rooftops between the two blocks were pigeon coops. Their "cooing" created the sounds of the common backyards. On occasion, as a housewife reeled in her sheets, she'd find the excrement of pigeons on her sheets, and cursed the pigeons shouting: *"Disgraziati!"*

Often cellar doors were not locked so that the line-0 man could get into the backyard to service the neighborhood's clothesline needs.

Mary's plan was to get in to her former home through the backyard cellar of 108th street, opposite her own building after midnight. Disguise, speed and proper tools to break in were important.

She shopped at the local hardware store in Yonkers and bought a crowbar, tools to bend steel, flashlights, and clothes at the second hand store. She tried on various old clothes in front of the mirror, and when she no longer recognized herself, she chose the means of her own disguise.

Although she could have borrowed these tools from Battista, who had his own construction company, she did not for reasons of secrecy. Mary was exhilarated by the adventure, and felt as empowered as a high level spy.

She shopped for Schlomo's and Marco's disguises at the second hand store in town. Grungy, ugly clothes, and caps together with glasses with no lenses attached to fake noses with a mustache were perfect. She tried one on and laughed.

She met with Schlomo and Marco, and as she unfolded her plan of entry and explained their role in the break-in, their eyes opened wide with dismay. Marco got pale, he perspired profusely, and was astounded to hear his mother's calm explanation of how and why they were going there, precluding any further queries from them.

Schlomo took out his handkerchief and wiped his nervous perspiration.

"Mary, what do you plan to accomplish?" he asked. She shot him a look of surprise. "Are you kidding? Vito comes in my dreams almost every night. He told me that bad things were going on in the cellar. I owe him and I owe myself. I want to know if he was involved with the mob, and he? I think he wants me to know that too. He made some bad decisions. This is one of them, the other one was walking out on our marriage. I loved him. Look, if you don't want to help, I can do it alone."

Marco sighed. "Alone? No! I'm with you," he said with a resolve he did not feel at all.

"Well, Mary, count me in," Schlomo answered.

It had to be on a weekend. Tess could help Giovanna with the baby. East Harlem on a Sunday night was a quiet night. After the three hour Sunday *pranzo,* there was a lull of activity as people stayed home with company and played cards.

"Okay!" Mary said brightly, "come into my bedroom, I have great disguises for you. Schlomo, try on these glasses." He did and burst out laughing. Marco found this hilarity bizarre. He tried his on, and Mary and Schlomo laughed. Marco didn't.

"Marco, laugh!" she said, "this is funny." He looked at his mother in disbelief. "You know, Momma, you're actually enjoying this. I can't get over it. You're not scared, are you?"

"Why should I be scared? This is what Poppa wants. Don't worry, he'll protect us." She patted her son on the back condescendingly and asked them to come into the kitchen for a shot of sambucca to calm their nerves.

On Saturday evening, Tess came home. She was briefed on Mary's investigation. Tess's reaction was exactly like Marco's. Like a good prosecutor, she cross examined her mother's motives. Mary refused to fall into Tess's mindset, and simply said, "your father wants this." There was no further discourse after that statement. Marco looked at Tess and pulled her aside and said, "I think momma's going nuts." Tess smiled, and said, "Do you know how much guilt she's feeling over the life she and poppa led? She's gotta do this. Notice she stages this based on his nightly appearances in her dreams? I don't know if this is true, but Marco, she's got to play this out, to get it out of her system. Just do it. You, my dear brother look like Groucho Marx in those eyeglasses and nose...impressive." Marco asked

"Don't tell me you're enjoying this too, Tess."

She smiled, "Yes, I am. Tell me Marco, do you get as nervous when you're conducting an orchestra?" He gave her a dirty look. "Spare me Tess, there's no comparison."

Mary pumped her breasts to gather milk for the baby and she also prepared some bottles of formula.

At midnight Sunday, in a rented black Plymouth, Mary drove Marco and Schlomo to 108th street. They drove in silence. Marco tried to relax. After all, according to his mother, his father was behind this caper. He was incredulous over her determination. It was a dangerous project, but that never entered his mother's mind. This was a side of Mary her children had never seen before.

Mary, Schlomo and Marco walked into the building on 108th street opposite their building. Mary carried a burlap bag with each tool wrapped in small cloth towels so that they wouldn't rattle.

Damn! My mother could rob a bank. Marco thought. Look at her. No nerves, just forges ahead as though she was shopping in a department store. I can't believe this woman is my mother.

She climbed over the short barriers in the back yard to her own building. She tried to open the door but it was locked. Mary prodded the crow bar between the door and the frame. The door creaked open, and she took out the flashlight. She shone it on the walls and floor. Suddenly she and Schlomo gasped. They almost fell into a square hole where a group of large stones had been moved out of the floor to the side revealing a gravesite of bodies. The stone had been moved probably to put more victims into the hole. Mary couldn't speak.

The stench of death was all around them. Marco coughed. "Hush!" Mary whispered, "Go in the backyard, Marco."

Mary held a handkerchief to her mouth as did Schlomo and they stared in disbelief at the hole. Suddenly, they heard footsteps.

"Jesus, Mary and Joseph. Let's go." They fled from the back door, Mary tried to push the jimmied door back as it was, but it wouldn't close entirely. They fled across the back yard to the building of entry on 108th street.

Mary turned and saw a light turned on from the cellar window. "Oh my God! I want to see if they're burying another body. I'll meet you on 108th street, Go! I can look through the.."

Marco grabbed her arm and pulled her towards the building. "Momma you'll be the next victim, let's go." He pushed her back into the building on 108th street to their waiting car under the Third Avenue El. Marco was shaking.

"Son, sit in the back, I'll get us home."

"Yeah, if you don't get us killed first."

Schlomo whimpered, "Mary, that's why Vito got killed. He found out how they were using the cellar. Mary, this proves that he wasn't in on it, or he'd be alive today."

Mary sighed, "Okay, Schlomo, now you can see why we had to do this?"

Schlomo commented, "In Europe, they'd throw lime in open graves so as to speed up the deterioration of the body. Mozart was buried like that."

Mary was enthralled. Schlomo knew so much. The man was a walking encyclopedia.

"Schlomo, why don't we open a funeral parlor?" Mary suggested and Schlomo laughed, while Marco screamed, "For heaven's sake Momma, what the hell has gotten into you? I'm sick to my stomach and you? You're enjoying this."

Mary ignored her son. She told Schlomo that she was going to inquire about embalming school. "I bet they make out like bandits."

"For God's sake, Mary, you don't need money. Do you know how wealthy you are?" Schlomo asked.

"No, but you just can't have too much these days. Schlomo sell the tenement for twenty five thousand dollars. No! no wait. They killed Vito. Let them pay through the nose for this house." Schlomo groaned as if he was in pain, "Mary, sell it, I implore you. Sure there's talk about putting up the projects, but when the government steps in, I'm telling you again, they'll give you peanuts. You have no idea what you're up against." Mary patted him on the arm, "Yes, I know. I'm not waiting till then, but don't worry. I have a plan."

* * *

They got home at 2:30 in the morning. Tess fed Grace the last bottle, but she was still hungry. "Good timing, Momma. Thank God you came home." Mary threw off her coat, washed herself well, and took her baby to her bedroom to feed her.

Marco told Tess how the break in occurred. "It was like a cops and robbers movie, only Mom was the star. I was shocked at this woman, breaking in, and finding the hole in our cellar with murdered victims in it. It was a horror. I had to run out so that I wouldn't throw up. I didn't want to leave evidence that anyone had been there. And then, you know what she did? We're almost out the cellar door on 108th street, and Momma sees a light go on and starts to go back. "I gotta see who it is." She said, I grabbed her and pulled her away. I swear to God had they seen her they would've killed her."

Tess gasped in disbelief. The scene Marco described was horrible, but her mother's actions were completely out of character. "Who is this woman, Marco?" she asked. Marco shut his eyes. "Who knows? Is it possible that Poppa haunts her every night in her dreams? We believe in an after life, and if he's been murdered, he wants her to find out who did it."

"Don't be silly," Tess said. "If this is true, then as a spirit he'd know this, wouldn't he?" Tess thought that Mary was involved in Vito's death in a way she hadn't been involved in his life, and all of these nocturnal visitations by Vito were staged by Mary's subconscious. Guilt!

Marco was exhausted. "I'm turning in," he said sleepily. "Who the hell has to go see an opera, when my own mother is staging her own?" Tess laughed aloud, "And she does it with style," Tess added.

Mary was groggy the next day, but fired up about her discovery in East Harlem. Schlomo came in this time dragging his feet with exhaustion from lack of sleep. Giovanna made coffee, and breakfast for whoever wanted it.

Now that Schlomo was not paralyzed by fear, he realized how bizarre the whole scene was with the funky outfits, reminding him of the Keystone Cops in the silent films, and suddenly he burst into uncontrollable laughter. Marco, Tess and Mary joined in Schlomo's infectious laugh as Giovanna was perplexed. Dear God, she wondered, where had they gone to last night?

That afternoon at 2:00 p.m. Mary called Louie the Lip.

"Louie, it's me, Mary. I have another offer. A clean cut guy-sort of like an F.B.I. type-offered me 30 grand for the house. Your offer is too low." Louie the Lip screamed, "Mary, you can't do this. This is blackmail." Mary smiled, "You ought to know, Louie-I could have sold it, but you're a fellow Sicilian, so I'm telling you."

"Okay, thirty grand. I believe you because the cellar door to the back yard was jimmied with. Must have been the feds." Louie was scared.

"When I lived there, I got strange calls about the cellar in the middle of the night." Mary thought she'd continue the drama, but Louie cursed, "Mary, damn it to hell, hang it up. I'll pay, let's do this fast. Get Schlomo to come down. We'll close with

Lawyer d'Onofrio's in the back of the saloon with cash." Mary felt smug. "In hundred dollar bills," Mary suggested. He had a moment of hesitation thinking maybe Mary had pulled a fast one, but she was a woman, she couldn't concoct such a plot against him, too innocent. Nah, not possible, he thought. "Okay Mary. I'll call Schlomo."

The transaction was completed the next day and right after the deed had been signed, Schlomo was perspiring from nerves, and Mary shocked him even further. The lawyer offered Mary and Schlomo a cup of demi tasse coffee. She put sugar in it, stirred it then put it to her lips. Suddenly she put the cup down.

"No, I won't drink this. Put it down Schlomo. This is how my husband died. There was nothing wrong with him. He was poisoned at his desk at the union. Forgive me Louie, but I have nightmares. Vito tells me every night that he was murdered. I can't make out who did him in, but the dreams persist. What should I do?" Mary asked, and Louie was red in the face, sipped his coffee, and he stood up as though he was ready to run out of there.

"You know what you should do, Mary? Shut your mouth, and go home, and don't come back to 107th street again. A woman as attractive as you should get married." Mary stood up, and thanked Louie, then took her brief case with the thirty thousand dollar cash, which she examined, put her arm in Schlomo's and left.

"Mary, how do I say this without being vulgar?"

"Don't, Schlomo. I overheard my son say the same thing."

"How you pulled the story of the F.B.I. killed me. I almost laughed."

"Schlomo, I made a mess out of the padlock. I had to make up the F.B.I. offer to buy the building," Mary explained, "so I figured why not use a fake offer to cover my tracks as well as to get more out of him?" Schlomo looked at her in disbelief.

"Iet's go, if I ever decide to become a mobster, Mary, I'm gonna make you my right hand woman. You're better than any thief I've ever known."

"I know." She snickered, as she drove away back to Yonkers via downtown in case someone was following her.

They got home, and Mary put the money in the safety deposit box then slipped it in her closet underneath the floor boards and put the rug on it.

Grace was hungry, and Mary brought the baby to her bedroom where she filled the role of mommy, and nursed her hungry baby girl.

Chapter XX

Korea: Philip & Sean

Philip and his group of men met other soldiers who had already fought in World War II. The World War II veterans didn't even know what they were fighting about. Truman urged MacArthur to keep pushing North beyond the 38th parallel to the Yalu river, a border shared by Red China and Korea. America had been warned that if they came too close to their borders, the Chinese would attack. However, America did not pay attention to the warning. General MacArthur was sure that the Chinese would not attack, unfortunately, they did.

Casualties added up to huge numbers. The fighting was intense in 1951. Philip Petracca led his men in a futile attempt to gain ground. However, during the winter of 1951, the United Stated retreated, back to the 38th parallel.

It was there that Philip Petracca fell. He was left for dead, his face down in the cold ground. At night, South Koreans scoured the fields trying to steal arms, or money or valuables from the soldiers who had died. Philip was in a semi conscious state, having been wounded on his legs and arms. His face had not been damaged.

During the night a group of South Koreans came through the forest and found a few live soldiers. Philip was one of them. He heard them talking and he moaned in pain. One of the women spoke in Korean, and Philip opened his eyes, realizing that they were not communist Koreans. He was lifted gently on to a makeshift stretcher, and carried away.

Philip was carried into a hut on the periphery of the woods. There he was placed with other survivors on cots, and ministered to by a young woman who spoke English. She was beautiful, like nothing he had ever seen before. His soul was lifted at her gentle touch.

"I help you," she held his hand. "Thank you," Philip said and smiled. She cleaned off the caked on mud and as she uncovered his face she thought to herself that she had never seen such a handsome young man. "I'm Philip," he said softly. "I'm Inchon," she said and deftly cut open his trousers and cleaned off the mud on his wounds. "You are beautiful," he whispered as he fixed his eyes on her face. She smiled. "You too are beautiful."

Philip had been rescued at the South Korean section of Panmunjam. The United States Army listed him as missing in action. All of his mail had been held up and his family had been informed.

Mary Petracca was struck with shock when she learned that her son Philip was missing. She shuffled to her bedroom, the sun was dancing through her lace curtains, and she pulled the window shades down half way to shield her eyes. Mary stared at the statue of The Sacred Heart of Jesus for a long time as the numbness of unfeeling permeated her body like a paralysis. Grace cried, and Mary went to her.

* * *

When Tess called and heard the monotone voice of her mother tell her about Philip, it sounded as though it had happened to someone else. Mary still hadn't been able to accept the news in the telegram. Tess called Marco at Vivian's but he was out of town, so she asked Vivian to have Marco call her as soon as possible.

Tess called Maggie. Her reaction was disbelief. Philip? Impossible, if anyone could capture the spirit of life, it was Philip. She crumbled into a heap after the phone call, and knew that she must see her mother. God would not forgive this *vendetta* she had decided would last forever. Distraught and alone, Maggie told her mother that she'd come on Sunday.

Mary made arrangements to have a baby sitter for Grace; a high school teen-ager who lived across the street. Mary went to mass alone, and left early. She could hardly concentrate on the mass. Her anxiety was increasing. She put her car in the garage, and ran in the house. Grace was just waking up. Mary told Analise the sitter that she'd have to take complete charge while Mary devoted her time to her daughter Maggie. Analise told her not to worry and to calm down. "Oh I wish." Mary said.

Mary waited outside the house and paced on the path around the circular garden. She was apprehensive to see her daughter again. Maggie had disowned her mother, yet the tragedy of Philip's situation had precipitated a call from Maggie. How strange God works His blessings. Mary felt light headed. She was shivering more from anxiety than from the cold.

Maggie got out of the cab, paid the driver, and carried her cloth bag on her shoulder. She was beautiful, thought Mary. Blonde, tall and beautiful.

"Maggie, welcome home." Mary opened her arms and hugged her, but cringed when she felt no response from Maggie. She let go and they both walked into the house.

"I'm here because of Philip," Maggie snarled as she took off her coat, and dropped it on the sofa chair. She looked at the elegant large home, without expression or reaction.

Mary bristled with shock. "You're here because of yourself. How long are you staying?"

Maggie did not expect this reaction from her mother.

"Why? You got plans? I made time to come here," Maggie snapped.

"Yes, I have plans," Mary said. "Do make time when your brother is here, as well as Tess. Then you can see your siblings."

Maggie paled and stood up.

"Do you want me to leave?" she asked, as her mouth quivered.

"It's up to you," Mary said.

Grace was fussing and Analise the baby sitter came into the huge living room to Mary who was sitting in the love seat opposite Maggie.

"Mrs. Petracca, Grace is antsy. Do you want me to give her a bottle?" Mary didn't want to parade Grace in front of Maggie. She didn't deserve to be privy to meeting her new sister, not with such antagonism in her demeanor.

"Analise, put her in the high chair and give her a piece of bread please. She's teething and needs something to chew on."

"Sure." Analise went back in the downstairs bedroom which was Grace's bedroom during the day, picked up the baby and brought her to the kitchen. Maggie's eyes were focused down the hallway as she tried to see Grace. Her mother had made it clear that the visit was over.

Maggie called a cab and waited outside for it. She had fumbled into her mother's house with antagonism instead of compassion. If her intent was to mend the relationship, she had failed. Maggie cried intermittently on the train to the city.

Maggie never looked back at the house. The Mary Petracca she knew and remembered would have taken so much more abuse than Maggie had given her. What had happened? Her mother was a stranger to her.

Maggie headed for Luigi's. There was always a cub reporter, or some of the seasoned journalists hanging out there. It was for many reporters, a home away from home.

It was a Sunday afternoon at 5:30 when the distraught Maggie walked into Luigi's bar and grill. A few of the old guard were there, recognized her, and sat talking to Maggie about the war, and the polarized mood of the country over this "police action."

Suddenly, the door opened and a few of the journalists ambled in, found a seat at the bar and said "the usual" to Luigi who had everybody's drink memorized. Sean Quinn was the last to limp in.

Shrapnel had exploded and lodged itself in his good leg, so now Sean sported two bum legs, one for each of the wars.

Maggie's heart leapt as she saw him. She approached him, touched him, and asked about his limp. Sean laughed caustically. "Yep, one leg got wounded in Italy and the other in Korea."

"Too bad about the leg. I didn't know you were back."

Sean asked Maggie if she would join him at a table for a bite to eat, and Maggie quickly acquiesced.

"Nobody wants to read articles about the Korean war. Our men are all but forgotten out there," he said.

They ordered an antipasto with Italian bread and wine. Sean's face was burnt by the sun. He looked gaunt, and his skin was prematurely wrinkled. He stared at Maggie and felt that there was an edge to her normally warm personality. She was, in a word, reserved.

"It's good to see you," she said.

She toyed with her napkin, feeling content to be with him, but she realized in looking into his bright blue eyes, that they never would go that route again. It was over, whatever "it" was.

"You're looking good Maggie. I saw your brother out there. We attended mass together. It was not a good scene," he mumbled as he picked at the antipasto, then enjoying the taste, ate with more determination.

"How is your mother?" he asked, and his look pierced Maggie's eyes.

"She's different, Sean. I haven't seen her in over a year, and then when we got the news about Philip, I felt obligated to make an appearance."

Sean put his fork down, his face grew red as though he had fire within him. "Is he dead?" he said, standing up.

"Missing," Maggie said.

Sean left the table and went to the men's room. He didn't come back right away, and Maggie was surprised at his reaction. For a man who's been through two wars, why would he become so despondent over Philip?

Sean came back to the table. The waiter asked if he wanted his food heated, but Sean pushed it away. "Lost my appetite, just bring coffee, black."

Maggie studied his face closely, and Sean couldn't look at her. He sighed deeply a couple of times, then strolled to the bar for a straight shot of vodka. He brought two of them to the table and downed them immediately.

"Where's your mother?" he said with a husky voice.

Maggie sat back. "Upstate somewhere."

"I want her number," he said.

"She doesn't want to see you again, Sean," Maggie said.

He was furious. "Damn it, give me the phone number."

Maggie scribbled something on a piece of paper, threw it at him, and walked out.

He brought the scrap of paper out to the street lamp to try to make out the number.

"Bitch! Damned bitch!" he uttered. Three of the numbers were illegible, the area code was missing, and Sean was sure that Maggie had made up the number sequence. When he realized that Maggie had deliberately misled him, he crumbled up the paper and threw it down the gutter.

Sean went back to the bar and ordered a beer. Dennis walked in having just arrived the day before from his own foreign assignment. The men talked, and Dennis wanted to know how Sean's love life was. Sean downed the beer quickly as though he needed something to numb him from the turmoil he was feeling. Dennis asked him what was going on with the Petracca women. Sean put his head back and shouted, "Hah! Drecht! That's what I am to them." Dennis nodded and looked at his friend with abject disapproval.

"Two women in one family? What the hell are you, a super stud?"

Sean felt like he was getting it from all ends.

"Fuck you, Dennis," he said. "I'm under fire tonight, and now you too, Brutus?"

"Look buddy, I'm not attacking you. I'd just like to see you join the rest of the human race, get a woman who's available, who loves you, and get married."

Dennis put his hand on Sean's arm as Sean tried to drink another beer.

"Let's go to your place," he said. "We'll get a couple of containers of coffee and chew the fat."

Sean staggered. He couldn't even flag down a cab because he was downright drunk, and no cab driver would stop for him. Dennis called a cab and got Sean home. Dennis picked up some coffee containers and called his wife and told her he'd be home late. Sean was having a crisis and couldn't be left in such an agitated and drunken state.

Dennis had stepped into Sean's life at a crucial moment. Sean felt victimized by Maggie's caustic tongue which had lashed at him like a cat'o'nine tail, and cut him to ribbons. He wondered how he ever could have found her enticing enough to make love to her. He had made many mistakes in his life, but the one which had distinguished itself as being the worst in the aftermath of its termination had definitely been Maggie. He talked about her as they sat in his living room downing the coffee.

"She whips me, Dennis, and I have no defense," Sean said. "And why? Because I fell in love with her mother."

Dennis looked up. Sean's track record in love affairs had never had any emotional residue in the past. Something was going on here, which for Sean Quinn was new, and Sean was reeling from it.

"Hey, buddy, you're still carrying the torch for Mary?" Dennis said.

"The woman's son is missing in action. I have a picture of us taken by Buddy Beckett. I want her to have it."

Sean took the photo out of his satchel and showed Dennis.

"Oh Jesus, he's only a kid," Dennis said. "If he's a prisoner, he might be tortured. Jesus, what a shame."

"So what do I do?" Sean said.

"Find her, Sean. You're a masochist to ask Maggie anything. She's furious that you chose her mother. This isn't love, this is a fucking Sicilian *vendetta,* and boy, they don't stop until they kill you. What the hell's wrong with you?"

"I feel jinxed," Sean said.

It was 1:00 a.m. Dennis had to go home. Sean walked downstairs with Dennis, and they talked about finding Mary.

"For God's sake, Sean, you're the *Trib's* best reporter. Use your skills, find her, and when you do, for God's sake don't let her go. You're so phobic about marriage that you're going to end up one hell of a lonely old man. I'm not your Brutus, buddy. All I want for you is to get a life."

Dennis got in the cab and Sean watched him drive off. Get a life. Sean was infused with energy. He had to approach his investigation as he would a newsworthy story. Three strategies.

One of them had to work. So, he'd improvise as he went along. He'd do that first, and then he'd think about the next two.

* * *

The next day, he took a day off, and went to East Harlem. He walked into the saloon, and told them that he was a newspaper reporter who had just come back from Korea. At first they glared at him, but Louie the Lip, still concerned over a possible tail from the F.B.I., gave the boys the high sign and waved them away. He invited Sean to sit down at the small table in front of the plate glass window of the saloon. Sean took out his wallet and showed him his credentials. He pulled up his trousers and showed him the scars from the shrapnel which had torn part of his leg off. Louie cringed. He asked Sean, "So how can I help you?"

Sean told Louie that he had to locate the mother of Philip Petracca. Philip was missing in action, probably dead. While they were in Panmunjam having coffee after an outdoor Sunday Catholic mass, a photo- journalist had taken a picture of them.

"I have to find Mrs. Petracca and give her this picture. I could mail it but I need an address."

Louie gave a sardonic laugh. "Yeah, you and a couple of other interested parties."

The earth had swallowed her up, Louie said. He told Sean that Mary didn't want to see anyone from the old neighborhood any more. She was so broken up over her husband's death, that she needed a new start.

"Get in touch with Vito's accountant, Schlomo Schwartz in the city,"

Louie the Lip suggested. "Call information for the number."

Sean thanked him and took out his wallet to pay for his beer. Louie told him to put his wallet away. "This is on the house. You're a hero, any time you wanna hang out, walk in. Let me know if you find her."

Louie the Lip hugged Sean. "Holy Shit!" he said. "You're like a fucking scarecrow. You know what you need? An Italian wife. She'll put some meat on your bones."

Louie slapped Sean's face lovingly and Sean smiled. "I'm working on it," he retorted.

Louie watched Sean until he got to the corner of 107th street and crossed second avenue to the drug store.

Sean was laughing to himself. Yeah Louie, I'm working on it. Just watch me. He walked in the phone booth and took out a pocket full of change. He called up information, and got

Schlomo's office. Schlomo was surprised to hear the voice of the man who had changed Mary's life so drastically. Sean explained the purpose of his call, and Schlomo explained that Mary did not want contact with any one. Sean said he understood. Again a stone wall, he thought.

Schlomo took his telephone number and said he'd pass it on to Mary.

"Thanks," he said, but before hanging up he added, "how is she?"

"She's fine," Schlomo said and he was pleased to hear the concern in Sean's voice. Schlomo thought of his wife. Maybe that saint room had worked out fine. Giovanna prayed for Mary and Grace, and talked to the saints and made deals with them, especially Saint Jude.

Sean said, "Will you tell her that I'll meet her wherever she wants? Give her my number and have her call me tonight. I'd appreciate it."

They hung up and Sean wasn't optimistic about the outcome of this call. Schlomo was cagey. What was the mystery with Mary? How could she simply have dropped out of the Sicilian community in East Harlem?

Sean walked to 106th street, and stopped at the corner candy store near Stroncone's pastry shop. He bought a pack of cigarettes even though he didn't smoke, and engaged the proprietor, Lena in conversation. He told her he was a newspaperman doing a story about a young soldier who was missing in action, Philip Petracca. Lena was thrilled. Sean showed her his credentials and then Lena talked.

"The mother moved out of the neighborhood months ago, and nobody saw her move, nor did anyone know where she had moved to. She was always running, but she had no close friends, so nobody knew nothin'."

This seemed like another dead end for Sean, and he probed further asking if Mary had been sick, or distraught over something. Lena nodded her head, "Yeah, very distracted. Sometimes I'd have to call her name from my candy store, and she'd answer, only if she heard me. She was not herself, I'd say. She looked sick, and people thought she had a terminal disease, so I can't help you more than that."

Sean was worried. Suppose Mary had a terminal disease, would she want the world to know it? And Maggie? Was her caustic bravado protecting Mary's privacy? And was it *omerta* that made Maggie act like that? Sean began to catastrophisize

Mary's life, and he felt the heat of panic well up in him. Yet, he took a deep breath and decided to investigate at one more place, Mary's building on 217 East 107th Street.

Sean thanked Lena and continued walking down the block past the funeral parlor towards the Third Avenue El. He approached Mary's building from Third Avenue.

On the stoop there were two old ladies sitting on folding chairs in their coats eating peeled apples and talking. Perfect, he thought, the neighborhood gossips. A font of information.

He introduced himself as a friend of the Petracca family, and a newspaperman who had been with Philip Petracca in Korea. Producing the picture of himself and Philip helped the old ladies to open up.

Donna Binna swore that Mary left town for five days, last year and nobody on the block knew where she had gone. After that, Mary had become secretive, and wouldn't let anyone in her house. She got herself a chain lock so she could see who was there, but she'd never let them in. That was weird. She was private, but always warm and caring. She used to make cookies once a week.

"She must have found somebody," Donna Binna said in a loud whisper as though the brick building was listening. Sean smiled. Yeah, me, he thought, I'm the somebody she was with.

"So was that after Vito had died?" Sean asked.

"Sure, we called her the Merry Widow, after that. Mary used to go out all day long when Vito was alive. You think he knew it? Nah, she was always home when he came home. But, Vito disappeared every weekend. Yeah, he had a *comare*. For a man that's okay, but for a woman, she becomes a *puttana*. Mary wasn't a *puttana* type, a church going woman who belonged to the Altar Society at St. Ann's. But let me tell you, their lives were not what they seemed to be. It was an act, one big drama, and they all suffered, and were all lonely. When the head of the house runs off, he destroys his family. I loved Mary. She never bad mouthed Vito. She always defended him, and I thought that was because she came from Corleone. Old habits, you know. Vito was the best looking man in Harlem, but I wouldn't give a plugged nickel to be married to him."

Sean had learned more from Donna Binna than from anyone. Maybe news reporters shouldn't have to look too far for stories. All they had to do was to approach two little old ladies sitting on a stoop, and get their scoops.

He took the train home and was lulled by the rhythm of the wooden planks under the tracks as the train passed over them. Sean was proud of himself. He had set out to investigate by three separate means: the saloon, the shopkeeper, and the neighborhood gossips on the stoop.

When he got home, Sean called Dennis to thank him, and they agreed to meet for dinner the next evening to discuss Sean's success.

Chapter XXI

The Schwarz House; The Phone Call

The phone rang as Giovanna got through starching Schlomo's white shirt. Giovanna let it ring three times, then ran to answer it. Mary had just called her with a crisis. Grace had a 103 degree fever, and she needed Giovanna to drive them to the pediatrician.

"Hello, *leibchen,*" Schlomo said, "I have news for you."

"Oh, *amore mio,*" Giovanna answered, "Mary just called and I'm putting away the ironing board. I have to take her and the baby to the pediatrician. Grace is screaming, and Mary is crying. What is it, amore?"

"Nothing. This I have to tell you when things are calmed down. What's wrong with the baby?" he asked, very much concerned.

"Mary becomes panicky so easily since Philip's news. She cries and worries if God is going to take her baby. Schlomo, I have the food ready, and.."

"*Leibchen,* go, don't worry about the food. Rafaele and I shall take care of supper. I'll see you when you come home.

I'm leaving now. Where is our son?" Rafaele and Schlomo had gotten really close.

"He'll be home from school in a little while, *ciao.* "

Schlomo hung up. What a nightmare Mary went through every time Grace was sick. It went beyond normal. Tess was the only child who visited her mother on a regular basis.

Maybe Sean's appearance at this time would be welcomed, but maybe not. Mary's state of mind had been of concern, and Giovanna spent a couple of hours of the day helping Mary with the baby and doing her laundry. They had grown as close as sisters, and the class distinction of former maid and employer simply didn't exist.

Schlomo put away his books, and locked up the musty office. Some day he'd get a carpenter to open the sealed windows and maybe he'd get some fresh polluted air from the city's streets.

He walked to the I.R.T. subway and took it to the last stop. He sat in the train reading the New York Times music section, and thought about Sean Quinn's phone call. Schlomo was certain that the timing of Sean's call must be prophetic. However, what if the guy just wanted to give her the photo of Philip and Sean in Korea? What if that was all he wanted to do? What if his romantic interlude was just that: an interlude?

Schlomo grew sad. He wanted to take matters into his own hands, but how could he? Mary being over sensitive these days, cried frequently, and was totally unpredictable.

* * *

Grace was teething. She was almost five months old, and already had two front teeth. Her fist was always in her mouth and she drooled constantly as she gnawed at her fingers. Mary was besides herself with worry. Grace had a temperature. It was 5:30. She called up Giovanna who lived down the block and asked her if she would drive them to the pediatrician.

Schlomo had met his soul-mate. Giovanna looked at him as though he was Clark Gable, she treated him like a king, and she took such prestigious care of him that he felt as he did when his mother doted on him when he was a child in Germany. Giovanna had given him a quality of life which gave him a sense of joy, one he never would have known without her. There was only one thorn in this domestic life of his, his house!

The Schwarz home was the neighborhood's Catholic monument to the birth and death of Jesus Christ, much to Schlomo's chagrin. However, it was a bargain. The owner Joseph Patrick Mele had died and his wife wanted to sell the home quickly so that she could follow her lover to Argentina. It was a difficult home to sell. Not everyone in Yonkers was as zealous a Catholic as Joseph Patrick Mele had been. People from the Bronx took the train and a bus to stop by and see the collection of statues in the Mele's stone garden. It had made the newspapers at least once a year as an icon of Catholicism.

In front of the house was the nativity scene stuck in cement. Statues of the stations of the cross went from the left side of the house to the back and up to the right side for the last station of the cross. For Joseph Patrick, the resurrection was the greatest miracle, so he hired Pasquale Cuppola, the greatest stone mason in Yonkers, to emulate the tomb of Jesus' burial. Pasquale built an igloo type of stone structure with a miller's wheel in front of the entrance. Joseph Patrick had a six foot tall crucifix with a white cloth draped around where Jesus had hung, planted in cement next to the cave with the miller's stone wheel, with a sign: HE HAS RISEN.

Schlomo had been deeply concerned about these structures. The neighbors wanted to know who had bought Joseph Patrick Mele's house, and when they found out it was an orthodox Jew, they screamed with laughter. He'd need a bull dozer to get the saints out of there, but Giovanna went crazy over the house, and he bought it for her. There was only one argument they would ever have. "The statues have to go," Schlomo said, and Giovanna responded, "if the statues go, I do too." So the statues remained.

The house had six bedrooms. It was so ostentatious that it looked almost like a *bordello* in Naples. The back of the house had a vegetable garden and grape plants climbing on a trellis called a *prevola*.

However, Schlomo had never known love before. Giovanna was his life and she looked up to her Jewish husband with great esteem. When he passed the garden of Catholic doctrine, he grimaced and often shut his eyes. Giovanna would poke him and tell him, "Open your eyes, my beloved, just remember Jesus is your *paesano*." She'd rub up against him and kiss his cheek and he managed to walk more tolerantly from the sidewalk to his front door.

Inside the house, Giovanna was convinced that a collection of saints had answered her prayers. What good fortune she had incurred. After the war, in Naples, her husband dead, half her family missing, and a mother who had snapped and been committed to the *manicomio* in Naples, left Giovanna in a desperate situation. She had been contacted by friends in

America to come there and do housekeeping. She'd have a roof over her head, and food on the table. She could always send for her son later. Without hesitation, she signed up, and left her son with her in-laws who took care of him but called her a *puttana* for emigrating to enemy territory: America.

Her novenas to St. Anthony, St. Jude, St. Ignatius, St. Peter, and last but not least, St. Joseph the patron saint of her husband, never ended. She had a list of requests before she left. "You know, I have no patience," she had said to the collective statues of saints as she surrounded herself with them and talked to them collectively. "I need a good family, I'm willing to work, but then I want a good husband. I need for him to have money, to provide for me and my son, and as long as I'm asking, please make sure that he's someone I could fall in love with. I'd rather he has no other family, like no kids from another marriage. Please not too old. I don't want him to be toothless. I want him to be young enough to fulfill my needs, because, frankly I'm dying for a man. Don't forget me. I'll pack each of you in my suitcase, and if you all get together and take care of my prayer needs, I'll give you a whole room for yourselves. Candles day and night, devotions every day, and I won't ever forget what you will have done for me. Thank you, and may God help each of you to hurry up with this request. Amen."

Recently Giovanna's entreaties to St. Jude were specific. The prayer began and ended in one sentence: "St. Jude, bring back the baby's father to Mary, and let them marry and live happily ever after, Amen."

At 7:30, Giovanna, Mary and the baby came home from the doctor's Schlomo was home. "Sit down and eat," Giovanna said to Mary. The baby was asleep after having screamed for a half hour. They put blankets on the living room floor and propped pillows all around Grace.

Mary guzzled a tall glass of wine and sighed with relief knowing that Grace wasn't deathly ill.

Schlomo was pleased to be able to sit with his wife at the table for supper, and Mary whom he loved like a sister had indeed been a source of inspiration for him.

Giovanna served pasta with broccoli, which Mary was shocked to see Schlomo eat. The second dish was veal a la saltimboca, with fresh sage leaves, butter and white wine. Side dishes were spinach balls, roasted pepper salad, and string bean salad. None of these foods Schlomo would ever have touched. Now, with an Italian wife, he had overcome his antipathy for vegetables. It was not easy, but she used garlic and oil heavily and it became palatable for Schlomo.

Rafaele loved his Jewish stepfather. He often asked him about the Jewish faith, and Schlomo talked to him about it every night. Giovanna thought it was cute, so she didn't interfere.

"Mary, I got a phone call today asking for you, and I almost forgot to tell you," Schlomo said. Mary filled another glass of wine, and was quickly getting sbronzata as they say in Naples.

"Oh? I bet it was Louie the Lip," she asked flippantly and threw her head back and laughed.

"No, someone who wants to show you a very special photograph."

"Not interested, Schlomo. I want no contact with anyone, please. That's your job to keep them away from me."

"Mary, stop drinking. You're inebriated and I need you to be sober, or this message I have for you will not pass my lips." Mary put the glass of wine down, and once more grew apprehensive. She shut her eyes and sighed with resignation, and Schlomo could see the level of anxiety grow in her. She was obviously bracing herself for bad news.

"What happened now?" she said and slumped in her chair expecting the worst. She covered her eyes, so quick to tear these days.

"Mary, have your coffee, it's good news, I think, I hope, and let's go into the saint room, okay?" Giovanna was shocked, Rafaele snickered, Schlomo was now acknowledging the saints in the saint room? Mary smiled, maybe it was good news, everyone seemed to be amused.

Giovanna poured Mary a half cup of demi tasse coffee, and Mary drank it quickly almost burning her lips. "Let's go," she said.

Schlomo took her arm and they walked into the saint room. It had four church pews in it with candles glowing, and casting eerie shadows on the walls behind them. Schlomo stood up and Mary knelt at the pew. There were no chairs in the saint room.

"Today I got a call," he began. "It was from a news reporter whom you know. Sean Quinn." Mary cried out, "Oh God! Is he alright?" Schlomo smiled, "Funny that's what he wanted to know about you too. He called to tell me that he had a newspaper photo of him and Philip in Panmunjon, taken after they met there at an outdoor church service. He wants to see you so that he could give you the picture." Mary stood up and did the sign of the cross.

"At least he's safe. How did he sound?" Mary asked.

Schlomo said, "I have no previous frame of reference, I never spoke to him before. He gave me his phone number. He told me that he'd meet you any where you want. Call him tonight any time. It's about 8:30 now. Here's his number."

"Oh my God, Schlomo," she said. Schlomo handed her the paper, but Mary looked at it and said, "No, I have that number memorized. Where can I call him? I need to be private."

"Our bedroom, Mary. If Grace wakes up, Giovanna and I will take care of her. Go, call him." Schlomo was well pleased with himself.

Mary was nervous, she walked into their bedroom, shut the door, sat at the edge of the bed, and dialed.

"Hello?" Sean said.

"Hi, Sean, it's me, Mary. I understand that you wanted me to call you."

"Yes, I had a hell of a time finding you."

They were like strangers, almost as though nothing had ever happened between them.

"But you did. How are you?" she asked.

"Fine. And you?"

"Also fine. Sean, what's this call about?" she asked.

"I have a picture which was taken of Philip and me one Sunday at an outdoor mass in Panmunjon. I thought you'd like to have it."

"Very much, especially now. He's missing Sean."

"I know." His voice faded to a whisper.

"How did you know?" she asked.

"Maggie told me." A long silence, he wasn't surprised.

"Look, Mary, it's not what you think. I hang out at Luigi's, Maggie walked in and she told me about Philip, and I asked her about--"

"Spare me the details, Sean. Tomorrow, Luigi's at 1:00." She spoke quickly as though she couldn't wait to hang up. The discourse was over.

She hung up and Sean did too. He felt as though the rug had been pulled out from under him, as the temperature of Mary's manner went from lukewarm to icy cold.

"You stupid bastard!" Sean said to himself in the mirror.

* * *

Rafaele and Giovanna did the dishes together, and he told his mother that he was interested in the Jewish faith.

"Why? You got the best Jew that's ever lived as your Messiah, what are you looking for? He's a tough act to follow," she said, and dismissed the rest of the conversation.

As Mary came into the kitchen, Schlomo and Giovanna sat at the table with her and asked her how the call went. Mary shrugged, "It went okay."

Schlomo started to laugh and couldn't stop. Both women looked at him and wondered what had amused him so much.

"The saint room. My wife goes in to St. Jude every night and tells him, tells him to make sure that Sean comes back to you and Grace. Can't you see it's happening?" Giovanna smiled and kissed her husband, "Ah, you begin to see how miracles happen."

Mary grimaced. "Nope, he called for one reason and that's to give me Philip's picture. He's already got another love interest." Giovanna raised her eyebrow, "for now," she murmured.

Mary asked Giovanna if she could watch Grace for a few hours tomorrow so that Mary could meet Sean, get the photograph, and come back. She'd have a late breakfast of eggs to tide her over because she was skipping lunch. Giovanna was most unhappy about Mary's sudden emotional chill towards Sean. But at least she was seeing him, at least it was a beginning. Mary insisted that there wasn't a beginning, that the end had already come and gone, and one didn't go back to a relationship whose embers had stopped burning the day they walked away from each other.

"Even then I knew that I would never see him again," Mary said with resignation.

Giovanna wouldn't accept that. Tomorrow was another day, Mary was exhausted and emotionally drained. Her face had lost its color, and she seemed so dejected. To say anything to her now would be futile.

It was agreed that Mary would sleep over. The baby was in a deep sleep and picking her up and bringing her home was foolish. Therefore Mary slept on the couch next to the baby, who was on a quilted blanket surrounded by pillows on the floor in the living room.

Chapter XXII

The Best Laid Plans

It was about 2:00 o'clock in the morning before Mary fell asleep. Schlomo wasn't feeling well, and she could hear Giovanna's worried voice comforting him. At 6:00 o'clock, he complained of chest pains. Mary woke up with a start as she heard Giovanna's hysterical call.

"Mary!" Giovanna called terrified. "I need you." Mary jumped off the couch, and Grace woke up. Mary called Emergency Medical Services, and they arrived within minutes. Rafaele brought them to the bedroom. Giovanna and Rafaele got in their car and drove to the hospital right behind the ambulance. The mood was somber, and Mary bundled up her daughter, locked the house and went home.

At 9:00 a.m., Marco called his mother with the news that he reported for the draft and they rejected him and gave him a 4F rating. He had a heart murmur. Mary felt drained. Oh God, not another son, she cried and held the tears back so as not to frighten Marco.

"Marco, see a specialist right away." Her voice quivered.

"I shall. Look, I've been in town for a few days and I was so damned busy that I didn't call you, I'm staying in the city with friends. I'll come home. You sound scared, and don't worry. I'm okay." Mary shut her eyes and said, "God spare him," and then as she thought those words, it occurred to her that God indeed had spared him. Maybe the murmur would go away. She had to hang onto something.

Mary had grown to believe that she was living under a curse, and that she couldn't get out of it. The verve she had had before Philip's news had been so strong that she hardly saw obstacles, but now every negative incident took on mammoth proportions.

Marco talked and Mary zoned out again, involved with her anxieties about his health and his life. As he spoke, she focused on him again, and she heard the end of his conversation, "and of course if you want me to pick up anything downtown, cheeses, breads, or fresh pasta, I'll get it this morning, okay? What do you want, Mom?" Marco said.

"Marco, I was supposed to meet Sean Quinn at Luigi's at 1:00, but I can't. Schlomo's in the hospital, and Giovanna was supposed to take care of Grace, so I'm stuck. Would you pick up Sean and bring him here? He's got a photo of Philip to give me."

Marco was surprised. Was that starting again? Had Sean called his mother? Yet, according to Tess's periodic bulletins about her mother, Mary was so overwrought lately that Sean was the least of anyone's concerns including Marco's.

"Sure Mom. Does he know about Grace?" Mary said, "No, and I don't want him to know. Let him come here. I haven't figured out how to deal with that situation. I never wanted to see him again, and now I'm not sure about anything."

"Mom, Sean meant a lot to you, and love's a good thing. You always told me that. I only wish my father was alive, and that you and he would have made your peace, and we'd be a happy family again." Mary heard her son's sadness, and it only magnified hers.

"Marco, is Maggie seeing him again?" She held her mouth with her handkerchief to catch the sob emanating from her lips, but Marco heard it.

"No, Mom. Do yourself a favor. You have his daughter. It's no time to be playing games, mom. Let him know." Mary said, "Oh of course, if he comes here, he'll know. Okay, tell him he's invited, if he can't make it, then take the photo of Philip, thank him, and come home by yourself. We're at a crossroad here, Marco." Marco nodded, and understood that Mary was in great conflict over this man. He promised he would do exactly as she asked. Marco and Vivian went shopping for food in Little Italy. He had a shopping bag full of *sopresata*, an Italian salami, *scamorzza*, an imported cheese with a center of creamy butter in it, and home made sausage with fennel. Vivian gave Marco a large cloth shopping bag to put his purchases in. The double paper bags would only tear as he carried the food.

He kissed Vivian and they parted. They had become lovers and they dreamed of a beautiful future together. It was 12:30, and Marco was still downtown on Mulberry Street. Vivian noticed the time and told him to get a cab, drop her off, and head for Luigi's on 43rd Street.

Traffic was thick with trucks carrying cargo and manufactured goods from the garment district. Double parked vehicles dotted the downtown side streets making speed impossible. At 1:30, Marco asked the cab driver to pull up in front of Luigi's. He saw Sean Quinn pacing and limping. The man had obviously been wounded. He walked with a cane, and he wore dark sunglasses, his blond hair was still in a crew cut, marine style, and his trench coat hung loose on his already slender body. Marco paid the cab driver, picked up his groceries, and walked towards Sean, who hadn't noticed Marco at all.

"Sean Quinn?" Marco stood in front of him, "you don't remember me, do you?" Sean didn't remember him.

"You look familiar, but I swear I can't place you." Sean looked at Marco carrying the bag with the pungent smells of Italian food permeating his senses.

"Jesus!" Sean said as he looked at the bag, "What in God's name do you have in that bag? I'm salivating." Marco laughed. "Yeah, Italian salamis. You don't even have a clue who I am, do you?"

Sean felt awful. Yes he knew him, but from where?

"Give me a clue. I hate guessing games."

"The Messiah, Washington D.C. 1950." Sean groaned, "Damn! Marco Petracca!" Sean shook his hand vigorously and was pleased to see him. "Damn! Who'd know you without the baton? You're looking great, by the way, I'm meeting your mom, and she's late, but traffic's been fierce.so Marco, what brings you to my neck of the woods?" he asked.

"Mom. She can't meet you, and I'm going home any way so she asked me to swing by, pick you up if you can make it and bring you home."

"Where's home?" Sean asked, as his shoulders straightened out with the anticipation of Mary's circuitous invitation.

"Yonkers," Marco answered. Sean asked Marco to wait while he called his editor. He went inside the bar, and used Luigi's bar phone.

"Sean," Luigi bellowed, "don't have any arguments on my fucking phone, you broke one once, so keep your Irish temper in your pocket, okay?" Sean laughed, "I'm only calling my editor." Sean's spirits seemed lifted and Luigi smiled knowingly. "Yep, you're gonna see Mary, right?"

"Yep," Sean said and called Patrick telling him that he was going to Yonkers for a story, related to Korea. Patrick laughed, "You seeing her?" he asked, "Yeah, Pat, it's in reference to a news event." Patrick burst out laughing, "Sure, Sean, it's called selective truth. Say hello to the little woman." Patrick gave Sean the Bronx cheer on the phone.

By 1:45, Sean came out of the bar, and Marco didn't want to take public transportation. Sausage needed to be refrigerated. So, they took a cab to the Bronx terminal, then a Yonkers cab to his mother's house. Sean kept taking deep breaths.

Marco was fascinated by Sean's brassy style as he described his chance meeting with Philip the war scene in Korea.

"A futile war. A no-win war, irreconcilable ideological differences, that's what's going on there, and I for one think we never should have gone there. Of course I never wrote that, but the American people smell a rat, and there's no interest here about why the hell we're sending boys there to be killed. There's a panic mode in our country, the hammer and sickle appear and what do we do? We send in the troops. Nuts, insanity, because it'll happen again."

Marco could see for the first time how Mary could have fallen for this man.

Meanwhile, Giovanna called Mary, and told her that Schlomo was okay. It was indigestion from having eaten too fast, and too much. Giovanna was relieved, and so was Mary.

"Marco's bringing Sean home. I'm a nervous wreck." Mary uttered.

"So, Sean Quinn gets to meet his daughter. Brava, Mary! Now you're thinking like a Sicilian woman." Mary smiled. Giovanna was puzzled. "Ah, but who gets to tell him about his baby?"

"Nobody. When he comes, he'll see her."

"*Madonna mia,* I got goose bumps," Giovanna said emotionally.

At 3:45 p.m. the Yonkers cab came to the back entrance. Mary ran to the window and peered out behind the ninon drapes.

She gasped as she saw Sean Quinn walking with a cane. "Oh my God!" she exclaimed. "He's so painfully thin."

She opened the door, and walked towards him and he opened his arms "Fill my arms Mary," he said as he kissed her face. He held her in his arms smelling her hair and he murmured, "I dreamt of this."

Mary edged away, and whispered to Marco, *"Fighiu mio,* thank you for bringing him home." Marco brought the food in the kitchen to put it away in the refrigerator, while Mary showed Sean the details of the living room walls and small terraces.

"My God, Mary, you have a palace here," he said in awe. Mary showed him the front view of the house which sloped over a hundred feet to the next street. He had been enthralled with Mary before, thinking she was a helpless exquisite victimized woman. His opinion was rapidly changing. She had burst out of her cocoon like a butterfly.

Marco walked out into the foyer, and told his mother that he was going down to Giovanna's to see how Schlomo was. Mary smiled at the delicacy and consideration of her son.

"Stay Marco," Sean said. But Marco insisted. "No, you two need to be together."

Marco bought Giovanna a *sopresata* and a round loaf of bread from Mulberry Street.

Meanwhile, Mary's heart was beating out of her chest. Grace was asleep in the downstairs bedroom off the kitchen, and Mary wished that she'd sleep at least fifteen more minutes. She wanted Sean to see her rather than be jolted into discovery by her cries.

"Come, I'll show you the downstairs first." She took him into the spacious kitchen, and he commented on its cabinetry and windows and the huge squares of white marble tiles. She took his hand again and strolled down the hall to Grace's downstairs bedroom.

It was pink and white, and the curtains filled the windows with plush folds of lace. Sean looked puzzled. The shades had been drawn and this was the only room in the house which was dark. There was a crib in the opposite side of this huge bedroom. "Mary?" he said as he became aware that this was a baby's room.

"Come Sean." Mary held his hand and brought him to the crib. Grace opened her large blue eyes and looked into the blue eyes of her father for the first time.

"Jesus, God!" Sean's voice cracked. "Mary, she's mine, isn't she?"

Mary was enjoying the changing expressions on Sean Quinn's face.

"Pick up your daughter, Sean. She's been waiting for you," Mary said, and Sean picked up Grace carefully and the child smiled at him and her arms flailed happily as a puppy dog wagging its tail.

"God, I know now why I wasn't killed. I had family waiting for me." Mary looked at father and daughter together.

"What do you think?" she asked.

He frowned. "There's no point in asking you why you didn't tell me, is there?"

"Sure there is." Mary led Sean to the settee and he sat with Grace in his arms. Mary knelt at his feet. "Sean, remember, you wanted no fences, no roots and the single life. I love you, but I'm not a hunter. No traps."

"I knew I had shot my mouth off once too often. I swear I knew it. I saw your expression. I knew it. Damn!" he said and the baby stuck her fingers in his mouth and he laughed. Mary explained, "She won't tolerate vulgarity, Sean, she almost choked me one day when I said the same word." He kissed the baby on the cheek tenderly not wishing to overwhelm her. Grace kissed him back by opening her mouth on his cheek. "Oh God, is that cute," he exclaimed. Mary invited him to see the rest of the house. The hallway upstairs was very large, with chandeliers every fifteen feet, and mirrors hung high on the walls facing the chandelier to reflect even more light. Cleverly designed after the mansions of the wealthy.

"Mary, this is beautiful. Are we going to live, here?" She looked at him, feigning ignorance. "What do you mean?" He laughed. "Marry me Mary." She kissed his mouth, "Sean, I can't think about that now. I wasn't going to tell you a thing about the baby. Giovanna was going to baby sit for Grace, and I was going to meet you for a few minutes to take the picture from you, and that would be it." Sean held his daughter as though she was breakable. Grace was a big baby, and at five months old, she was already making talking sounds, a jibberish which only she understood, and Sean was amazed at the miracle of her birth.

Sean had fathered a child who was exactly like him, with a woman who had woken his dormant soul to the wonders of the depths of a strong love. He asked Mary why she hadn't written him any more, and how she had managed the pregnancy and the censure from people that he was sure she had endured.

349

Mary described the events that occurred right after she discovered that she was pregnant. Sean was fascinated by her tales of secrecy in a home purchase, and keeping everyone out of her apartment while she was packing and getting ready to move, and how the move cost her so much more because it was done at midnight.

"And I'm here. I am so sorry that you went through all of this by yourself, and boy do you do things with style Mary. You had no help I imagine, did you?" Mary told him that Tess was in her corner. Maggie was not mentioned. It was still a sensitive issue for Mary, who had reacted coldly after the mention of her daughter's name in their phone conversation.

Mary called Marco at Giovanna's, and told him to come home for supper. She wanted her family together. Outside of the kitchen there was a huge patio with a barbecue stove. Marco made the fire with Sean, and the men got along wonderfully. Mary set the table, and they dined in the large kitchen. Sean frequently caressed Mary's hand, or touched her arm or touched her face. He looked at her, and Marco turned away, feeling as though he had seen something intimate which he shouldn't have.

After supper, Marco insisted that he clean up the kitchen, and Mary called Giovanna to tell her that she and Sean were coming over. Grace was tired, and sat in the play pen in the kitchen, while Marco cleaned up and sang to her.

Schlomo and Giovanna were ecstatic to meet Sean Quinn. He felt as though he had known them for years. The medical emergency they had had this morning had actually precipitated the meeting of Sean with his daughter Grace. Giovanna was convinced that "her guys" in the saint room had worked overtime, even if Schlomo was the unknowing catalyst to this miraculous event.

As Schlomo showed Sean the house with the Catholic history of Christ in the yard, Sean laughed.

"You can't even remove these statues, can you?" he said. Schlomo shrugged. "What can I tell you? Sicilians use cement freely, with their saints, and with the people they don't like. It's the way they are. I figured we'd dynamite them out, but my wife said we'll go straight to hell, so the statues stay. Who knows? They took care of me this morning in the hospital, because I sure take care of them. In the hot weather, I wash them down. When the snow falls, I sweep it off their heads. Yep, my wife's got me talking to them too."

Sean was doubled up in laughter, and tears were flowing down his face. "Schlomo, this is the funniest thing I've heard in years. It's a story, for a photo journalist. I'll write it, Bud Beckett will take pictures. What do you say? We'll sell it." Schlomo grew excited, then Sean remembered something, "Hey, Schlomo, I forgot to give Mary the photo."

Schlomo followed Sean back in the house. Sean gave Mary the newspaper picture and she looked at the picture for a long time. She was emotional as she saw her son and Sean together, caught in a shot resting on the rock, sipping a cup of coffee together. She asked Sean if he and Philip had had words. Sean was amazed, and asked why she would ask such a question. "There's the body language, Sean. Obviously you two were supposed to look at each other with your coffee canteens and instead, Philip is turning away from you facing the camera, you lean towards him. Did you have words?" she asked, and Sean said, "Yes, and I don't want to touch that topic, Mary, so let's not. We did part on a good note. You see, we both love his mother."

"Tesoro," she said softly, evoking memories of Sean and their brief interlude. Giovanna enjoyed watching the interaction between this beautiful man and Mary. Their eyes revealed everything they were feeling.

The phone rang. It was Marco. Grace was hungry. Sean and Mary put on their coats and ran back home.

As they came up the walk, Mary said, "Can you hear her big voice? Music to my ears, my baby girl." Marco left with a small bag. He had asked to sleep at Schlomo's, and Giovanna told him that he was a wise young man. His room was ready. Mary asked him, "Why are you sleeping at Schlomo's?" Sean blushed, but Marco was swift to smoothen the situation. "I'm teaching Rafaele chess, and I'll be late, so I might as well sleep there." As Mary took Grace to the upstairs bedroom, near her own master bedroom, Sean walked Marco to the Schwarzes.

Sean revealed to Marco how worried he was about the situation of Maggie. Maggie whipped him with words every chance she got. She was on a mission to demoralize him and she was successful at it. He minced no words about how he felt, and he told Marco that Mary had opened up his soul, and that he wouldn't rest until she consented to be his wife. Marco gave Sean a big hug, and told him, "You belong with her, Sean. You love each other, and you have an exquisite kid, an Irish kid, I might add." Sean said, "Whom I'm going to adopt." Marco realized that Sean was right. Grace was a Petracca.

As they got to Schlomo's house, Sean laughed again at the stations of the cross all around the house.

"I swear, I never saw anything like it. What was he thinking?" Sean asked. Marco answered, "How much he wanted to please the Catholic woman he had married."

"I know how he feels, Marco. You see, your mother's my life. She's sacrificed so much for our baby, Marco. She could have had an abortion, or given the baby up, but she didn't." Sean was absorbing the depths of Mary's love for him.

Marco told him that when the baby was born, his mother's prayer had been that she wanted her to look exactly like her father.

"If she never saw you again," Marco explained, "the baby would be the part of you which she could keep.

My mother told me that meeting you gave her a good feeling about herself. I saw the change, we all did, and it was because of you." Sean felt his spirits soar, because kind and heart lifting words had not nurtured this man during his lifetime.

* * *

Marco said goodnight to Sean, and Sean watched him go into the house, then walked back slowly. He had forgotten his cane at Schlomo's house, and his right leg was burning with pain. When he walked in the house, Grace was already sleeping.

Sean asked for two aspirin, and was at an impasse as to what was expected of him. Would she want to make love? Mary had been through a lot because of him, there might be a residue of resentment towards him. He wasn't sure. This woman meant the world to him, and he wasn't about to put his own desires first.

She showed Sean his bedroom. His gut feeling was right. Mary wasn't ready. He kissed her goodnight, slightly at first, then deeply, and he moaned as Mary eased out of his arms.

"Goodnight Sean," she said wistfully.

"My beloved Mary," he responded.

Mary went to bed, but she couldn't sleep. She stood on the fence of indecision. It was her call, it was her home, and he would not make a move on her. Stimulated by his touch, she walked back to Sean's room, knocked gently, opened the door and saw him reading on the bed wearing his undershirt and his underwear. "Mary?" he sat up as she walked in. She opened her arms. "Come to bed with me Sean. I don't want to sleep without you."

"Are you sure, beloved?" he looked into her eyes, and he felt himself pulled into her soul. Yes, she was ready. He followed her to the master bedroom adjacent to Grace's, and got into bed with her. Mary cried out when she saw how badly his right leg had been mutilated. *"Povero tesoro."* She caressed his leg, and prayed over it, then disrobed, and held Sean in her arms cradling him and whispered terms of Sicilian endearment to him.

They made love, and in the communion of their bodies, their sense of one-ness in their love for each other brought them to the greatest heights. "I'm home, Mary," Sean said.

Mary shut her eyes, and held him close to her, stroking his body, as Sean fell into a deep sleep. She lay awake thinking of how all of this might never have transpired, had she gone to pick up the photo herself, had Schlomo's apparent heart attack not been a case of severe indigestion after all.

The moonbeams lit up the room and she could see the handsome face of the man she loved, and she traced his fine features as though she was sculpting them herself.

In the peace which followed, Mary's thoughts slowed and sank into the sweet oblivion of her nocturnal sanctuary, nestled in the arms of the man she had dared to love.

Chapter XXIII

The Breakup And Resolution

Sean Quinn came up several weekends a month to be with his family. He had fit in to Mary's domestic scene, and had done it very well. For the first time, a household routine had become part of his life. He bathed Grace, sang to her in his drone like voice with no sense of pitch, and often sent Mary running out of the room laughing at his inability to sing.

Everything in their lives had jelled better than Mary or Sean could have anticipated. Yet, Sean was stymied because he could not get Mary to commit to a wedding date. As one month glided into the next, Sean's contentment with his situation deteriorated. Ironically after half a lifetime of avoiding this scenario with women, he was on the receiving end of rejection. It did not sit well with Sean, and Mary was extremely apprehensive of another marriage.

Sean Quinn was the love of Mary's life, a fact she would not reveal to any of her children. Mary and Sean shared a similar history in their respective childhoods of early emotional deprivation.

Mary had not seen too many good marriages in her life, except for the early years of her marriage to Vito. Her parents' marriage had been a nightmare. However, there were good marriages and Mary analyzed these. Culturally, Schlomo and Giovanna had nothing in common, yet their relationship was warm and nurturing encompassing Rafaele. There was a mutual need and respect between them.

Battista Lucca and his wife Concetta were her role models. Of similar culture and ideals, these two gave a new meaning to marriage: a real partnership, which, like wine, got better with time.

Sean suspected that Mary's reticence was due to his past with Maggie. Sean recalled when he initially revealed that his source of information on Philip's situation had been Maggie, Mary was curt and cut him off on the phone.

Sean came up to Yonkers during the week and visited his friend Father Peter Sullivan.

"Bring Mary here, Sean. Let me talk to her."

Sean gave a guffaw of sarcasm. "You think you can move her? She likes things exactly as they are."

"Your relationship can't go anywhere, unless you're serious about your love in the eyes of God. Once in a while, dear friend, trust God."

"Why would He listen to me?" Sean asked.

"Why didn't you marry her as soon as you came home?"

"I asked, and she put me off," Sean said, sweating.

"And so you resumed relations with her, without the sanctity of marriage. And this is free love right? I tell you Sean, your free love isn't free. You pay the piper, don't you? Mistrust and insecurity builds suspicion and you have nothing to gain and everything to lose."

Sean was frustrated hearing what he already knew and had ignored. Payback was a bitch, Sean thought to himself. Even Peter declined invitations to Mary's house because they were living in sin. He always found a good excuse not to come. Yet, he'd meet Sean for dinner at a restaurant just the two of them.

"Oh, God, Sean, I'm tired of seeing you bang your head against a stone wall ignoring all the values you grew up with, suffering the consequences and learning nothing. When, Sean?"

Sean was upset. "Peter, I want to marry her. I'm at an impasse, okay? I'm on the receiving end of a situation I used to cause. What irony. Now what? Spit it out. I'm open for suggestions, although I know what you're gonna say." Father Peter held the crucifix hanging around his neck on a long leather strip, as he advised his dearest friend.

"Okay, stop the intimacy. Distance yourself from her, change the status quo, not by dialogue, but by changing the dynamic. You'll see her come around. Of this I'm certain. I've never seen you as happy over a relationship in all the years of our friendship. This woman's gone through a lot, Sean, more than you know. Your usual way of dealing has to change if she's to change."

"What if I lose her?" Sean asked.

"I doubt it," Father Peter answered, "Bring in the other equation and you'll see in time how it'll change."

"The spiritual law?" Sean asked.

"Yes Sean," Father Peter responded.

They parted with their usual hug, a prayer, and Father Peter's blessing.

* * *

It was Grace's first birthday, and Mary had invited her children as well as her dear neighbors, the Luccas and the

Schwarzes. Analise came by with a gift for Grace, and Mary prepared a wonderful dinner of lasagna and a salad as well as a large baking dish of eggplant parmigiano.

Battista Lucca made a hand made wooden rocking horse pulling a miniature Sicilian cart, for Grace. Tess arrived early with beautiful outfits from Henri Bendel's in New York, Marco brought a huge stuffed teddy bear for Grace. Marco came alone because Mary didn't include Vivian until their relationship was official. Mary disapproved of her son's cohabitation with the first girl he had ever dated.

Grace was so joyful at the balloons, the gifts, and the attention, that she sang happy birthday to herself in perfect pitch with the guests, which sent everyone into gales of laughter and applause.

After the party, Mary asked Tess if she would stay to watch Grace so that she could drive Sean to the subway terminal.

"Sure mom. I'll sleep over and leave in the morning. What's going on between you two?" Tess asked, and Mary's expression changed.

"Does it show?" she asked.

"Yes, Mom. Everybody sees you ignoring him. Repeat performance, mom?" Tess admonished. Mary didn't answer.

Sean picked up his daughter and placed her in the red wooden wagon which he had bought in New York. It had wooden slats around the cart so that she wouldn't fall out, and he gave her a ride around the living room.

At 7:00 o'clock, Sean kissed his baby goodnight, and gave Tess a hug, got his coat and cane and walked out to the car. Mary had taken the Studebaker out of the garage and waited by the curb. He wanted so much to talk to her, to address the wall which had slowly but steadily grown between them. His heart was actually hurting knowing that perhaps the end of the line for them was imminent. How could Peter be so sure of the outcome? Yet he had to be decisive, because the status quo was driving him crazy.

* * *

Mary drove him to the terminal, and parked. Neither of them spoke because so much was going on in their own heads. Finally Sean broke the silence.

"Mary," he sighed, "What do you want?"

Mary was stunned. She expected them to have dialogue, not a direct question like this, almost as though he was ready to dismiss her. She was hurt.

"What do you want, Sean?" He, too, was surprised at the diversionary tactic of answering his question with another question.

"I wanted to marry you. When I bring it up, you put me off, and hey, what the hell, maybe you're right Mary. So... time to move on to another phase of my life." A chill swept through Mary's body.

"I see," she commented. She couldn't look at him.

Sean opened the door, and turned to Mary who was looking straight ahead trying to fight her hysteria.

"I'll call you, and I'll make arrangements to visit my daughter." Mary retained her stoic posture, and waited until he got out and shut the door. As soon as he did, she tore off with screeching tires down the road.

* * *

Sean was distraught as he struggled to concentrate on the newspaper business. No one got near Sean Quinn during this personal trauma. He was unapproachable. Sean started to drink heavily again. He spent hours after work at Luigi's bar and felt even lonelier surrounded by his colleagues.

* * *

They would not see each other for seven months. When Sean came to visit Grace, Giovanna would be there to dress the baby and to put her in a carriage while he walked down the road with her. These visits lasted an hour or two, and occurred only twice a month, then dwindled to once a month. Mary never made an appearance at the door again. She was mortified.

When Mary got home from dropping off Sean, she tore into the house, ran in to her bedroom and sobbed. Tess ran in after Grace fell asleep, and asked her mother what had happened.

"Tess. It's over. If he calls for his daughter, I don't want to see him, so Giovanna will be here to put Grace in her carriage so that he could see her. I'm devastated. I destroy relationships, once with your father, and now with Sean. I should have been a nun."

Tess suggested that Mary and Grace spend the next weekend with her. Maggie was coming over. They had made their peace. It was an attractive invitation. Maggie was always on her mind.

* * *

On Friday night, Mary fastened her daughter in a seat belt next to her, and drove to Bleecker Street in the village. When

Mary pulled up in front of the building Tess saw her from her window. She ran out, and directed her mother to an all night garage.

They went upstairs and Tess took Grace from Mary as she walked in. "Oh *Dio, figlia mia.*" Mary exclaimed, as they embraced.

"I missed you, Momma," Maggie admitted.

"Me too," Mary replied.

"The baby's beautiful. She's all her father, look at that," Maggie laughed, "even her blonde hair sticks up."

Mary didn't comment. She couldn't. Anything she said would come out wrong, so silence was the best response.

The next day, they dressed Grace and went out, taking turns carrying her. She was a heavy baby and each one could only carry her for about a block or less. Mary asked her daughter if she was going with anyone. Maggie shrugged and said, "A married man whose marriage is on a cliff, even though he loves his wife." Mary cringed. "Then why are you with him?"

Maggie said, "It's safe. He's married."

Mary was hesitant about pursuing the open door Maggie had given her, but she made one more comment. "Maggie, it's wrong." As soon as the words came tumbling out, Mary realized that she had made a mistake.

"Who are you to preach about what's wrong?" Maggie said, outraged. Oh yes, Mary thought, she'd never forgive her mother for Sean, never!

"Sorry Maggie," Mary whispered. "Let's not quarrel."

That afternoon, Mary cooked spaghetti with marinara sauce, and after they ate, they went out for a walk in the village looking for a place to have a cup of demi tasse coffee and dessert.

Since Mary had forgotten her stroller at home, Maggie walked into a second hand baby shop and bought a used stroller for Grace for five dollars. They put Grace in it, and strolled in East Greenwich village.

Tess spotted a coffee shop with empty tables and room for the stroller. Maggie had cappucino with Sambucca and a large *canolo*. Tess sipped her black coffee and talked about her recent visit to a gypsy card reader on Canal Street by the name of Madame Rouge.

"Philip's not dead, Momma, he's safe and" she giggled, "quite happy." Mary gasped, and grimaced painfully. "Stop it, Tess, that's cruel, don't give me false hopes."

Tess took out a small notebook. "Mom, these are my notes. You don't have to believe a thing. But hold on, this is about me. Let's see--when I'm out of law school the man I'm going to marry will come. He'd be a widower, about twenty years older than me, and a judge. She said I know him and that I had a wild crush on him once. He's trying to find me. I have no idea who she's talking about."

Maggie asked, "And Poppa?"

"Poppa was murdered by someone he trusted. I wonder if he had a premonition."

Tess continued, this was the last page of her notes. "Maggie, you self destruct," Maggie grumbled, "Damn! Even you have to nip at my ass?"

Mary looked at her lap once more, as she did when she felt at an impasse. Tess leaned towards her mom and whispered, "Do you want me to tell you about Sean?"

"No," Mary said. They paid the bill and left for home. Grace was waking up and crying. She was hungry. They walked the four blocks very rapidly.

As they walked, Mary asked Tess to tell her the rest of the reading.

Tess explained that the gypsy was perturbed over Marco's cards. "Only bad things can come of this," she had said without going into detail. Mary was chilled at the impact of such a message.

"Stop it, Tess," Maggie snapped. "I don't want to hear another word. Vivian and Marco are made for each other. This is crazy, a gypsy playing God? Come on, you know it's bullshit."

Mary's gut feelings about Vivian had never been sanguine, and her reasons for this were not even clear to her.

They were almost home. Grace called her mother in a sing-song fashion. "Right now she's singing my name, in a minute, she'll be screaming it. Hurry Maggie." Maggie forged ahead and they walked one behind the other, because of thick pedestrian traffic.

Tess ordered pizza from the downstairs pizzeria, and a six pack of cold beer. Grace liked pizza, and she managed to chew and swallow at least a half a slice.

Maggie laughed as Grace ate her pizza, "She eats like Poppa, stuffs her face before she even begins to chew."

After pizza, Maggie and Mary went for a walk. It was dark out, and getting cold, and they walked arm in arm.

"Momma, I'm glad we made our peace. It was killing me," Maggie said.

"Me too," Mary said holding her daughter around the waist as they walked.

They talked about Philip again and Mary reverted to Madame Rouge's prediction, and wished that Philip was alive.

Maggie was nostalgic, "Mom, I wish Poppa had not died. Maybe you and he could've somehow gotten together. We would have been happier."

"And life would have been less complicated, Maggie. I miss him now more than ever. I treasure those early years, and I try not to remember the rest of it. I was in prison."

"We knew mom, but dammit, Mom, he loved you." Maggie said emphatically.

"Yes, as much as a Sicilian man could. I question the word love. What is it? How can one mistreat or demoralize someone you love? Your father did that to me," Mary added. Maggie observed that her mother's candor about her life had started right after Vito's death. With Vito dead, there was no need for Mary's *omerta*. Family secrets were revealed.

Maggie commented, "It was Sicilian pride, mom. I swear to you, I shall never get involved with an Italian man, neither will Tess. Poppa's love was dispensed as long as you did what he wanted. You're not alone, mom, he didn't love me either. I used to hear him belly ache about me to you. You'd listen and say nothing. I hated you for that."

Mary was sad that Maggie didn't know that she had indeed defended her to her father. She almost said something, but she decided against it. Maggie needed to be listened to.

"Yeah, Vito Petracca was a saint to the rest of the world, and to his family he was a shit," Maggie said.

Mary and Grace returned to Yonkers. She felt pleased at the time she had spent with her two daughters. They had shared their anguish and had gotten closer.

* * *

In May, seven months after her break-up with Sean, Mary could no longer bear it and decided to contact Sean. He hadn't seen Grace in two months. Maybe he was on assignment on some foreign trouble spot of the world. She had to find out. She called the *Tribune.*

Sean wasn't at his desk, and Mary asked the young cub reporter who answered his phone, if she could speak to the editor.

The woman took Mary's phone number down, and walked across the newsroom to Patrick Mulcahey's office.

Patrick was in his office talking to Sean Quinn about editorial copy. Sean had such an edge to him, that most people stayed away from him, teasing had disappeared, and there was no point in talking to him, because he snapped like a snapping turtle.

The cub reporter knocked on the door, and gave Patrick a piece of paper with a phone number written on it.

"A Mary Petracca called, sir," she said. Sean sat up.

"What the hell is she calling you for?" he asked. Patrick said, "Maybe there's a crisis with the baby, Sean, and she doesn't know what to do. Shall I call her with you here?" Sean grew pale, Patrick might be right.

"Please, I swear to God, I'll behave." Sean's forehead beaded with perspiration. His nerves were raw, and his ready wit had all but disappeared.

Patrick dialed Mary's number.

"Mary? This is Patrick Mulcahey. How can I help you?"

Sean heard only Patrick's end of the conversation and deduced Mary's questions by Patrick's answers.

"Sure, right now, he's still in town. Is your daughter okay?" he asked, Sean stood up ready to bolt out.

"Mary, of course he's leaving again. We have the tail end of this war to report on, and I didn't wanna send him, but he's asked for it, so he'll be shipping out soon." Patrick gesticulated to Sean giving him the high sign, that Mary's reaction to his conversation was exactly what he expected.

"Look, Sean's here. Why don't you two talk to each other, I have to go to the conference room. Take care Mary. Hold on, here's Sean."

Patrick motioned for Sean to sit in his chair, and he walked out shutting the door behind him.

"Sean, you stopped coming to see Grace. Why?" Mary asked, concern quite obvious in her voice.

"I was busy, Mary." His heart was beating fast, and though she called, he realized it was only for Grace and not herself, so he feigned a control he did not feel.

"Do you have time to see her before you ship out?" she asked.

"Yes. Suppose I call you tonight. Okay with you?"

"Of course, Sean." Mary's voice was soft, and she seemed sanguine enough, and Sean was slightly encouraged.

He hung up and sighed from the bottom of his gut as he leaned back in Patrick's leather chair. Patrick walked in with a quizzical expression.

"Well?" he asked.

"She wants me to see the baby before I ship out. How the hell did you pull that off? I'm not shipping out, Patrick." Sean burst out laughing.

"Hey, buddy, ever hear of that old cliché that all's fair in love and war?" Sean said, "Amen." He went back to his desk and felt better. Walking on eggs would be easier.

The following weekend, Sean went to Yonkers on a Friday morning. Patrick told him to "get the hell out of here, you're no good to anybody in that shape, and for God's sake, get married already." Sean was lighthearted.

Mary picked him up at the station, and Sean embraced his daughter, "Hi Grace, I'm your Daddy, remember me?" Grace grabbed his face and giggled.

As Mary drove home, she asked: "Sean, are you really leaving us?"

"Looks that way, Mary there's nothing here for me."

"Isn't there, Sean?" she asked.

"Suppose you tell me what you want?" he asked.

373

"You!" she answered. Sean grinned. Father Peter was right, he thought to himself.

"So what are you going to do about it?" he asked briskly.

"Marry you!" Mary said matter of factly.

"Okay." Sean sighed deeply and looked out the window with a big grin on his face. He could hardly believe what had just happened and was pleased by the favorable turn of events.

Chapter XXIV

The Wedding: September 1952

In June, Mary and Sean resumed their relationship with a number of exclusions. One of them was intimacy. When Sean told Mary his decision, she agreed to it readily. The second exclusion was that he would not interfere with the family dynamic of Mary and her children.

Sean of course never left for Korea, and he confessed that it was Patrick's idea to break the impasse between Sean and Mary. It worked.

Mary had suffered enormously after she and Sean parted. She was mortified because the breakup had been totally precipitated by her anxieties. They were open with each other discussing their fears, their dreams and their expectations. Sean's request was that no secrets should be kept from each other. He imposed no restrictions on Mary's life except that he wanted two things, communication on a daily basis, and discussing even the most mundane events of the day. In addition Sean suggested that they should never go to sleep at night with unresolved conflicts.

Sean insisted that Mary write a will, that all monies earned by Vito Petracca in Mary's estate be divided as she saw fit among her five children leaving him out entirely. He wanted no part of Vito's money.

"Talk it over with the kids, Mary. Get that clear before we marry. We started off on the wrong foot, but not this time."

"You're incredible Sean. I had no idea." Mary was in awe.

"I have to start my life with you on a clean slate. I've learned some lessons. I'm not marrying your money, your kids have to know this."

"Yes, Sean," Mary said, "they shall, it'll be easier."

So," he laughed, as he mentioned his best friend Father Peter Sullivan, "maybe now after we get married, he'll accept an invitation to our home."

"Wonderful, Sean. Please ask him to come to the reception too."

At the end of their talk Sean mentioned that Peter had suggested one more thing.

"What's that?" Mary asked.

"You'll love this, Mary. He told me to put Christ in the equation."

"I love that, Sean," Mary said emotionally. "I used to be part of St. Ann's Altar Society, and every week I'd go in and sweep the church and wash the altar and do the linens, and I just felt so good about it." Sean could relate.

Sean took Mary to meet Father Peter at his rectory and introduced them. They took him out for a fish dinner at his favorite restaurant off the Saw Mill River Parkway.

Peter and Sean were hilariously funny, and Mary laughed at their antics. They reminded her of small boys teasing and competing with each other.

Peter asked Mary how her health was, and then he realized that Mary was surprised at his question.

"I'm fine," she answered, puzzled. Why would he inquire about her health when he hadn't met her until now? Father Peter was flustered, because for a moment, he had almost slipped information on Mary's health which he had learned about in the confessional. Mary was left wondering.

After dinner Mary asked him to come to dinner at their home, but Father Peter accepted with a qualified answer:

"Thank you, Mary, I shall, after you two are married."

Mary and Sean Quinn married the first day of September in a quiet ceremony at St. Barnabas church on Lockwood Avenue in Yonkers. The bride wore an ankle length ivory dress, starkly simple, and the groom a dark suit. Mary wore a wreath of live baby breath flowers in her hair. Maggie and Dennis were maid of honor and best man. Baby Grace wore a white lace dress, and carried the rings sewn on an ivory satin pillow while Tess held her hand and walked up the aisle with her. In order to keep Grace quiet during the ceremony, she dragged her small blanket (laundered) to the church. Everyone smiled at the antics and scene stealer of the wedding. Marco gave the bride away.

Patrick Mulcahey came with his wife, a beauty from Falkirk, Scotland, Annie Mulcahey. He beamed with pride at one of his best foreign correspondents, and whispered to Annie, "The day he walked into the newsroom holding her hand was the day we all knew, that Sean Quinn had been bitten by the love bug." Annie asked, "What was different about Mary that turned Sean around?" Patrick smiled and looked into his wife's eyes, "Chemistry, my love. Falling in love can't even be described without that word."

Fifty guests mostly from the newspaper industry were invited. The ceremony was a short mass, and a charming homily by guest priest Father Peter Sullivan a childhood friend of Sean Quinn. After the gospel, Father Peter spoke from the hip. No notes, no rehearsed speech, but just a brief and touching tribute to his friend Sean Quinn.

"I am honored to officiate at this wedding between my good friend Sean Quinn, and his lovely Sicilian bride, Mary Petracca. My earliest recollection of Sean was that he was going to grow up and see the world. No ties he told me, nobody would ever rope him in. I almost believed him. However, man proposes, and God disposes, and when he met Mary, he called me and said, Pete, I've been struck by lightning. He didn't explain, but I knew.

I've known Sean from the time we were boys growing up in Corona, Queens. We came from large poor families, and often we distracted our hunger pains by chasing a ball in the cemetery, may God forgive us." The congregation laughed. "Sometimes a meal was a bowl of soup with day old dried bread. Yet our faith was the only thing we could be sure of in those days of poverty and deprivation. We had much in common.

But at ten years old, we knew what we wanted. I wanted to be a basketball player in a cemetery and Sean a hobo." More laughter. "Yep, he said to me back then, "No roots. I never want to get married," Sean looked down and was embarrassed. Mary smiled. "Honest, I thought for sure he was a confirmed bachelor. How fitting that Sean was struck by lightning on Christ's birthday.

He called me, told me, then hung up. My missives from Sean were sporadic. Just before I'd say a mass, Sean would call, and ask me to pray for something. Yes, being best friends locked me into being his intermediary with the Lord and believe me that is a full time job. (the congregation laughed) When he was shipping out, I got a call, Pray for me Pete. I got a paragraph from Korea, I need a novena for Philip Petracca. I'd write back, asking just what he wanted me to pray for, to be specific, and he wrote a shorter note, You don't have to know. It's enough that He knows, just do it. Love Sean.

He came home, and again one of those quick terse messages, Pray for me and Mary. In fact I couldn't even forget Mary, because every time I saw Sean, he talked about her. I knew that at some point they'd bless their love with the sacrament of marriage, sooner or later, and for them it was later. I am the happiest priest in the world to have officiated at their wedding. The rest of the story we're all privy to, by being invited to the wedding.

So the end of this story of two skinny boys growing up in Corona, Queens had a different outcome than we had planned. I who couldn't hit a basket until well after the fifth try, became a priest. Sean, who traveled all over the world chasing wars, is a married man. God in His infinite wisdom rearranged our lives for the better. May the Quinns grow in love and honor the God who brought them together."

After the ceremony, Mary and Sean looked as though they had just bitten off a piece of heaven. Sheer joy was in their faces. The guests drove to the Yonkers catering restaurant the Riverview which overlooked the Hudson River. The setting on the water was peaceful. White sailboats dotted the seascape moving at a languid pace with their sails flying in the mild wind.

Music was provided by a small ensemble of three musicians, keyboard, accordion and drums, with each performer doubling vocals as well as on flute, guitar and clarinet. The music was the swing music from the late 1940's, and ballads made famous by Frank Sinatra.

Food was simple, a clear soup with egg noodles and cut up chives, and filet mignon steak and a lobster tail as one choice, and the other choice was: stuffed salmon and julienne cut carrots, small grilled potatoes, and salad. The wedding cake was a gift by Giovanna and Schlomo, a huge cassata layer cake with cannoli cream from Arthur Avenue in the Bronx, and the second tier was topped by a miniature likeness of the bride and groom.

However since the bakery had run out of white couples, they put a black couple on the cassata cake. Giovanna was upset, but Mary thought it was hilarious, as did the guests.

The newlyweds, Mr. and Mrs. Quinn danced to the song made famous by the recording artist, Tony Bennett. Sean chose the song "Because of You" because the lyrics reflected his feelings towards Mary. Sean attempted to sing the words to Mary as they danced. In his monotone voice he sang in Mary's ear: "Because of you, there's a song in my heart. Because of you our romance got its start. Because of you the sun will shine, the moon and stars will say you're mine forever, and never to part." Sean stopped singing, and repeated the last line to her, then added, "And don't you forget this, Mary Quinn, you once signed a letter Eternally yours. I'm taking you up on it." Mary tried to stifle her giggles, because Sean couldn't carry a tune, and she thought of her criticism of Vivian's weak voice when she first heard her and was displeased. You sure have a sense of humor, Lord.. He saw her giggle and covered her mouth with his, and she laughed even louder.

The M.C. called on the maid of honor and best man to join the Quinns on the dance floor then asked them to switch partners.

Mary had a brief moment of discomfort as Maggie glided into Sean's arms. I'm not going to look, she said to herself.

However, Mary took the opportunity to talk to Dennis. "Dennis, are you and Maggie serious?" she asked point blank, and he blushing, "I'm trying to survive...I can't answer that." He was taken aback by her question, and thought he'd give her a zinger right back by asking a personal question.

"Is Sean adopting Grace?" he retorted, but Mary didn't flinch. "Wouldn't you, Dennis? He's her father. Dennis, are you trying to make me uncomfortable?" he did not answer. "You don't love my Maggie," she said. "Don't use her as a distraction. I understand you have a beautiful teen age daughter. Watch out, Dennis, life pays you back."

Her argument hit him in the gut. He tried to ease out of her grip.

"The dance is not over yet, Dennis. Negotiate with your wife. My first husband and I didn't, we destroyed a beautiful marriage, and I almost shriveled up and died in it. You see, we didn't know how to fix it. Stupid Sicilian pride killed our marriage, but in America?. You stand helpless on a fence? Fences were built to separate property, not a married couple." He smiled and softened up. The woman was formidable.

Mary's honest opinion was the catalyst he needed to reconcile himself with his wife. "I needed that, Mary, thanks." He kissed her on the cheek.

"How'd you rope him in?" Dennis asked.

"I love him."

Meanwhile as Sean and Maggie danced, everyone's eyes were focused on them. She asked, "What do I call you, Dad?" and he laughed,

"You'll probably call me a son of a bitch, but whatever you do, not in front of my daughter."

Maggie snapped. "You really are an old married frump, aren't you?"

"Yep, and I love it." Sean became serious.

"Maggie, you know why your mother married me? Because you made your peace with her." She snarled, "It's not the way I wanted this to end, Sean, so don't make me Mother Cabrini, you son of a bitch. It was your choice not mine."

"Still, Maggie?" he realized her implication.

"Still, Sean. I would've turned myself inside out for you."

Sean felt badly, he whispered, "Maggie, I'm sorry I hurt you."

"Sean, after you met my mother. I just didn't put two and two together."

"Maggie for me it was love at first sight. I didn't plan it."

"When did you date my mother? Tell me," she demanded.

"Only when I was assigned to cover the Korean war." He was uncomfortable sharing even that information with her. The song was almost over, he couldn't wait for it to end.

"I thought so," Maggie answered, and Sean winked at his wife while she danced with Dennis.

After the dance they walked away from each other, and Sean socialized with his wife and friends for the rest of the evening.

The mood at the wedding was warm, and people actually mingled with guests they did not know. Schlomo danced one dance with Mary, and stepped on her feet several times, and Mary held him away. The food was wonderful, the ambiance and atmosphere of the Hudson river right outside the huge picture window was stunning as the evening progressed and boats with lights made their way through the moonlit river.

Meanwhile Marco urged Vivian to set a date for their wedding. Vivian was reticent on two counts, that both mothers did not sanction their relationship.

"Your mother doesn't like me Marco," Vivian whispered.

"When we set a date, she'll have to. Look who she married. You think we wanted this? Viv, it'll change, look around you."

Vivian said she'd think about it.

Patrick spoke to Mary Quinn. "Mary, I wish for you the kind of love and marriage that I have with my Annie. Sean's overdue. I never thought the old salt would find anyone to put up with him. He comes into my office and talks about his daughter, and I swear to God, he sounds like a mother hen. I enjoyed Father Peter's talk. Your husband, like me was hit by lightning."

Annie told Mary that after their honeymoon they should all go out for dinner. Mary agreed.

"What exotic places are you two going to for your honeymoon?" Patrick asked.

"To the Plaza for the weekend," Mary answered. "We're going to the Metropolitan Museum of Art, Rainbow room for dancing, and Birdland for jazz. Two of his favorites pianists are playing, Max Roach, and Horace Silver." Patrick and Annie listened with interest.

"Probably what we would have done too," Annie said.

At eleven, Grace fell asleep in Sean's arms. He didn't want to leave Grace. They got home, and changed, and Marco and Vivian drove them to the Plaza hotel for their honeymoon weekend.

The Quinns began their marriage, and this time when Sean registered as Mr. and Mrs. Sean Quinn, Mary commented, "Oh Sean, how beautiful that sounds, Mrs. Sean Quinn." He kissed her outside the hotel room door, and apologized for not carrying her over the threshold. "With two bum legs, if I pick you up, we'd spend our wedding night on the floor."

"As we did in the McCools bed and breakfast, remember?"

"I never forgot Mary. I played those days and nights over and over in my head when I was in Korea."

As they lay in bed for the first time as a married couple, lying side by side under the covers, Sean took Mary's hand and kissed it.

"Mrs. Mary Quinn," he whispered, Mary snuggled up to him, "I like it Sean."

Sean's mind went over the events of their journey together racing quickly like a movie in fast forward mode.

"Did you think we would ever make it?" Sean asked.

"When you and I walked away from each other with no more than two words between us, I thought it was over. I suffered Sean, oh God, how I suffered."

"Well I stopped eating and I didn't care if I lived or died, but one thing bothered the hell out of me was that nobody would ever mourn or miss me."

"How mistaken you were," Mary answered.

"So you called Patrick and it all changed. I'm one hell of a happy man." Mary sighed and reached for him and kissed him deeply. *Amure Amure mio,* she uttered, and her Sicilian terms of endearment aroused Sean's passion as he swooped his wife into his arms and made love to her.

As they became one, Sean and Mary experienced a height of perfect mutual joy. Tonight, as they entered into the first chapter of their marriage all the ingredients in their separate lives which had created anxiety before were swept away, and they entered into married life on a billowing white cloud of carnal and emotional harmony.

Chapter XXV

Murder in Bayside

Mary and Sean came home after a weekend in the city, enjoying a brief interlude of leisure doing the things they enjoyed, jazz music, dancing and dining. Marriage brought a sense of closeness they had not experienced before, and Sean shared with Mary the counseling sessions he had had with his friend Father Peter. Mary realized that changes had occurred in Sean, and now she saw why. Peter was a friend whom one had to hang on to, a treasure, who, with a spiritual flashlight, focused on the eternal truths, often lost in the quest for fulfillment. She wanted Peter as her friend too. He seemed to know things, to be intuitive in a way that Mary had not ever seen in a man. She knew it had to be his inner ear tuned in to the spiritual connection of universal law.

Mary had discovered something else about herself. When she set out to escape 107th street, to shed the old life she had three reasons to flee: the secrecy of her pregnancy, being stalked by Joe Marra, and the horrible affair of the cellar.

At the time of her midnight flight, with her household goods, she had no idea why she had purchased such a huge home, but her intuitiveness told her she needed a palace, and that's when she called it Petracca's Palace. Mary's subconscious had projected into a future which included Sean Quinn.

As she apportioned space in her very large house, the opposite side of the living room had a suite of smaller rooms for servants, beyond the foyer, kitchen and dining room. These two rooms became her focus for her husband. They had formerly been used by Giovanna and her son Rafaele. Now vacated completely, Mary went into the next gear of her master plan.

Mary loved books, and she was in awe of writers. She wanted to be part of the creative process of the literary world even in some small way. Sean Quinn was one of the elite journalists in the city and Mary felt that she could easily have put him on a pedestal, and after marriage she did. She now had her own permission to do so.

Sean had always wanted to write a book, and Mary planned to give him a place in the house which would be exclusively his, a place for him to be quiet and to pour out his thoughts on paper. Mary had taken typing courses, English grammar, and literature. No one was privy to her studious activities.

The month after their honeymoon, his intense work schedule at the newspaper kept him several nights a week in his bachelor pad. He had his bare furnishings and some clothes and books there. Every weekend, Sean carried books to the marital home. Mary piled them on the floor in her bedroom and got clean wooden crates from the vegetable store to put them in.

Her plan was to ask Battista Lucca, her next door neighbor who owned a Sicilian construction company for help. Battista's homes were top of the line, and they were expensive. A single family dwelling sold for forty to fifty thousand dollars. They were written up in the real estate section of the New York Times one Sunday, and so Battista Lucca had officially "arrived," in the real estate market place. He liked Sean and Mary. Mary went there one Friday morning with Grace, and Concetta offered her a cup of cappuccino and a home made almond and anisette biscotto. Mary loved these cookies as did Grace.

Battista strolled in, and Mary told him that she needed something from him which was going to be a major project. "You'll probably tell me no, Battista, but I'm desperate." She explained that On March 31st, Sean Quinn was going to be 38 years old, and for his birthday she wanted him to have a library, with wood panels, indirect lighting, and a balcony overlooking a small side garden with two stone benches facing a fountain of running water.

Battista complained. "Mary, I need a year for that."

She said, "I knew you would say that, but I also know that you would do it. You see, Sean wants to write a book. Writers go away to quiet places to work. I want my husband at home. I also type and I can help him in his work. Battista, you would be responsible for Sean writing his memoirs of the war in Korea, only if you get this room done without his knowledge before his birthday." Battista smacked himself on the forehead.

"Managia la miseria, Mary, you think I'm a magician? You want an extension on the house?" he asked.

"No, Battista, this is easy," Mary said, "I've got the whole thing drawn up for you. It's the last two rooms, inside work. The man who did Schlomo's stone statues can do some fancy stone work outside the library window." Battista looked disapprovingly at Mary.

"That *disgraziato* is no artisan. The statues have foundations deeper than Schlomo's house. How the hell does he build? Mary, he's a *cafone.* Let me put it this way, had he been living in the days of the construction of the coloseum, they would have looked at his work, and fed him to the lions. Don't even bring up that *disgraziato's* name. The biggest *cafone* in Yonkers, don't call him. I'll check your plans, draw some of my own, and we'll work around the clock when Sean's not here. This is going to cost you."

"I know," Mary said, "but I didn't want to ask you to do the whole thing. I mean that's an imposition."

"Mary, please don't stand on ceremony, I'm honored that you're asking me but Michaelangelo never rushed. Trust me."

Battista came over and measured, and grunted, and talked to himself while Grace remained with Concetta for a half hour.

"What do you think?" Mary asked.

"In Hyde Park in the home of Franklin Delano Roosevelt, there's a beautiful library, very large, and it has a desk on one side, books all around and seating arrangements in the rest of the space. Beautiful! I have to break walls Mary to get that spacious yet intimate feeling in a library. Leave it up to me. Give me your plans and your notes, I'll use them as a guide."

The Sean Quinn library was to begin the next morning. Sean was told that the last two rooms of the house would be storage space for Mary's belongings from 107th street, therefore, he never went into that part of the house. It would be a real surprise.

The garden outside of the library window would be started at the end of February. A mammoth job in a brief period of time. Battista wiped his brow as he walked out of the house, "Mary, I swear to God, I wouldn't agree to do this even for my own sister. But you? You've captured our imagination, both my wife and I, and I'm impressed to be living next door to one of the great journalists of this era. Some day I want to be mentioned in his memoirs." Mary thanked him and then went back for her daughter.

Maggie came home from New York University school of journalism, having entered her second year, and found Dee Dee Marra in front of her apartment door in a heap, crying. Maggie was shocked. She hadn't seen Dee Dee in months. The girl was hysterical and incoherent. Maggie unlocked the apartment door, and helped Dee Dee to her feet.

After ten minutes of sobbing in Maggie's arms, Dee Dee spoke of the tragic scene she had found in her house in Bayside. She went home to get some slacks her mother had bought her, and when she walked in, she found her mother's left arm bleeding, and her father stabbed to death on their bed.

Gina was incoherent, and babbled like a baby. Dee Dee was terrified, and she called the police and told them her mother had snapped, and her father had been murdered. Within moments they came, and Gina was taken away by the police. Dee Dee, ran away and went back to the subway to come to the city to find Maggie. "I'm here, because we don't have anybody. Joey lives with the Peluso family on 108th street, and I can't tell him this on the phone."

Maggie called Sean at the *Tribune,* and was told that he was out to lunch. She called him at Luigi's, and he was there, having lunch with Dennis and Justin Deeks, a crime reporter for the New *York Daily Mirror.*

Sean took Maggie's call. He got excited, told Justin "The victim's daughter is at Maggie's, hysterical." Justin jumped up, and said to Sean, "Let's go. We've got a story here."

Tabloid newspapers kept small apartments all around the city nicknamed "shacks" for their reporters. These shacks had desks equipped with telephones used by reporters from different newspapers who covered crime stories. They were strategically located near the police precincts with the highest crime rate in the city.

Sean bristled with anticipation as all reporters do at the smell of a story. This one could have an interesting slant given the personal relationship of Maggie to Dee Dee Marra. Sean and

Justin headed for Maggie's apartment. They took a cab so that they'd get there faster and to be privy to personal information from the victim's daughter.

Gina Marra was at the police station. She was arrested for the murder of her husband.

The next day her attorney, Gaetano Furioso, a Sicilian attorney renowned for defending difficult cases, interviewed Gina. His assistant attorney, interning with the Furioso firm, Angela Medina, was allowed into the room.

"Gina," Gaetano began, "what happened to your husband?"

"He died. I don't know who did it. They think I did it, but he got cut up so did I."

"Your wounds were superficial, Gina." Gaetano said.

"I know." She asked for a cigarette and Gaetano lit it. She sucked in the smoke and it swirled around in her mouth. As she exhaled, she pursed her mouth into a perfect 0, and blew circles of smoke. Her pudgy fingers were stained yellow from years of nicotine use.

Gina's hair was poufed up. Her face was streaked with the black smudge of eye mascara. She had cried considerably. As Gaetano questioned her about the event, it was obvious to him that her wounds had been self inflicted. Her left arm had more cuts on it. She was right handed. The right arm had one small cut.

"All of a sudden, he was dead," Gina said as she took her handkerchief out to wipe her eyes, "and I'm a widow." She feigned tears and Gaetano said, "Save it, Gina, save it for the jury."

"So who did it?" he asked.

"I went crazy when he told me he was leaving me in this Godforsaken place of Bayside. He tore me away from my home in East Harlem, brought me here, tried to screw his best friend's widow Mary Petracca, and told me he was gonna marry her. I killed him in self defense." He laughed.

"Self defense? Gina, the man was sleeping in your bed, stoned out of his head with wine, and you stabbed him ten times. How can a sleeping man be a threat to you? Let's start directing your answers to my questions."

"Mr. Furioso, before he went to sleep, we talked. I begged him not to divorce me, and he answered that I was gonna be history. So I figured that if I'm gonna be history he was gonna do a divorce Sicilian style, and that in the mind of a Sicilian man means murder! I was afraid for my life." Gina's hand quivered, as she gesticulated wildly.

Gina asked to go to the bathroom. She looked at her face in the mirror. She looked like a clown, a sad one. She took the paper towel, soaked it with hot water, and scrubbed at her face until it was red. Her hair needed combing. She was a mess.

The defense attorney had his work cut out for him. Justin and Sean worked on background facts provided by Dee Dee and Maggie together. The dynamic of the marriage, the wanderlust of Joe Marra, and the lust of Joe Marra towards Mary Petracca. Sean was shocked. His wife was involved. Justin felt Sean's discomfort as he heard him take frequent deep breaths. "What the hell do I do?" he said helplessly, Sean answered, "Go for it, buddy, it's your story."

Justin hesitated for a moment, knowing that family secrets in Sean's life would come out. Justin hated doing this. His buddy's bubble might burst with disillusionment about his bride. Sean looked shaken.

The story unfolded about the marriage of the Marras, the conflicts and other family secrets. Anything dealing with Mafia related relationships were big news in the tabloids. Stories were well read and circulation doubled in the three months of the trial of Gina Marra. Every newspaper carried the events including the *New York Times* which devoted a small amount of space to the story.

Mary Petracca was called by Gaetano Furioso to testify on Gina's behalf.

When Mary saw Gina in court sitting next to her attorney, she didn't recognize her. Her frizzy high teased hairdo was gone, her hair was cut in an attractive frame around her pretty face, heavy makeup was replaced by a touch of blush on her cheeks and light lipstick. Pearl earrings gave her a classic look. Her top heavy look was minimized by good foundation garments.

Gina's small round figure had been altered so that she gave the illusion of a slimmer body and more height even though the high heels were replaced by a simple black pump with cuban two inch heels. Gina had trouble recognizing herself. Gaetano Furioso had told her not to chew gum, not to smoke, and to smell clean. Angela, his assistant had done a thorough job of making a brassy, ostentatious looking woman who paraded her well endowed breasts in low cut garments, into a demure, sedate and genteel looking woman. A woman who could easily be believed as being a victim in an oppressive marriage.

Mary Petracca testified that Joe Marra was paid by her husband to help her to take over her real estate responsibilities in the event of his death. Joe Marra deposited the checks issued him by Schlomo Schwarz in a joint account in Joe's and Mary's name. He also deposited forty five thousand dollars in the same account. Mary's answers to the prosecuting attorney was that she immediately suspected Joe Marra of absconding with union dues. She linked Vito's death with this theft to cover up the real perpetrator.

Joe Marra withdrew forty thousand dollars, the missing union money, before he bought the house in Bayside. Motives evolved as the movement of stolen money was explored by Gaetano Furioso.

Mr. Donovan was subpoenaed to appear and to testify about the Marra/Petracca bank account. He corroborated Mary's testimony.

"Mrs. Marra, were you ever aware of any act of violence your husband might have committed?"

"Yes," she said. "I found out that he had poisoned Vito Petracca's demi tasse coffee while he sat at his office at the union headquarters." A gasp went through the court room, and Mary let out an involuntary cry. Even though she had suspected Joe

Marra's involvement in Vito's death; to hear Gina articulate that Joe had been directly responsible for Vito's murder was a shock. She thought he had fingered Vito, instead Joe murdered him.

"So, then Mrs. Marra," Gaetano Furioso continued, "you were really afraid that you'd be next." The prosecuting attorney shouted, "Objection! He's leading the witness." The judge said, "Sustained." Gaetano rephrased his question.

"Mrs. Marra, what was going on in your mind the day of the incident?"

"I was afraid that he'd kill me next."

"No more questions, your honor," Gaetano Furioso said. The prosecuting attorney then took over.

"Mrs. Marra, so you killed him before he killed you, right? You did it while he was sleeping." The judge was banging his hammer as Furioso stood up and objected that the prosecutor was putting words in her mouth.

The proceedings were lively, accusatory, and passionate. The newspapers had a field day, and with the advent of television, people hung around saloons and bars, listening to commentators report the day's proceedings.

Meanwhile, Mary had a lot of questions to answer in her own home. Her husband asked, "Will you tell me how involved you were with Joe Marra?" Mary said, "Joe was obsessed with me. Nothing happened. He tried to make moves on me, I took care of it."

After Vito's death, Mary told Sean that she was afraid for her own safety, and decided to move as soon as possible. Sean felt badly. He had suspected a relationship between Mary and Joe. He didn't exactly enjoy hearing about his wife in a courtroom. In a sense, Sean felt betrayed by Mary's *omerta.* Dynamics changed for a while between Sean and Mary.

Others were affected by the trial. Dee Dee was like a walking zombie in shock over the dark secrets the trial revealed about her father. Her revulsion over finding out that Mary Petracca had been the object of her father's lust, had probably precipitated Dee Dee's break up with Philip.

Gina received a reduced sentence than the one she feared. She was to serve two years and have five years probation. Public opinion was in her favor, and further editorials, commentaries continued in the wake of the jury's final determination.

After the trial, and verdict, Gina paid her dues to society, then left America and returned to Sicily. She had money, a new look and a new outlook which brought her a number of proposals in her old home town of Corleone.

She settled in a thousand year old house, with a *contadino* who was gone all day with the sheep in his mountain, while she gardened in the back yard facing the cemetery. Life was static in Corleone, and it finally dawned on Gina that she was in her own prison, trapped by her heinous deed.

Throughout the proceedings in court, Louie the Lip and his henchmen sat in the back of the courtroom, daily. Sean wondered why he was in the courtroom, surely it couldn't be Sicilian loyalty, he probably was worried about his own ass, Sean deduced.

Unbeknown to Gina Marra, public opinion was swayed in the creative writing skills of Justin Dirk, crime reporter, and Sean Quinn, award winning foreign correspondent. Their tale of a helpless victim, caught in a web of unsavory intrigue, by a murderer who was connected to the mafia had helped to decide the verdict.

Joey Marra, so ashamed of his family, had told his sister that now that he was seventeen years old, he was going to change the spelling of his name. He changed it to Joey Marvel, shedding any shadow of an Italian name. His father had been his hero and best friend, but no more, because the testimony and articles painted his father to be the biggest scum of the earth.

With no heroes left in his life except a cartoon character named Captain Marvel, Joey decided to name himself after a cartoon hero. At least he wouldn't be disappointed again.

The final straw for Joey was when his mother confessed that Joe Marra had poisoned his best friend Vito Petracca. Joey felt faint and had to be held up by his sister.

"Dee Dee" Joey said as they walked out of court, "now you know why I left home at fifteen. Momma called Poppa a whore master, every night, she brought up Mary Petracca, and Poppa would shrivel into a chair, cover his eyes with his hands and fucking cry. I couldn't take it. I called Jerry, and told him I was gonna jump off the pier on 107th street. Mr. Peluso was there waiting for me. He held me like a baby while I screamed my ass off. He took me home, called Poppa, and they agreed that I should stay there. But I gotta move out now. I've over stayed my welcome. We have no family." He cried.

Dee Dee held her brother's hand and wept, "I lived there too. I'd run to the Petraccas just for some peace. Momma scared the shit out of poppa. She even cut up her arms so she could claim self defense. What a set up. Poppa didn't even know what hit him, he was passed out from booze." They were the last ones in court, and they walked out arm in arm, knowing they would go their separate ways. Gina Marra looked back at her children as they took her away, but her children did not look back at her.

Dee Dee and her brother held each before parting.

"What are you gonna do?" Dee Dee asked.

"I'm joining the Army. Who knows, maybe I'll go to Korea and get killed, and it'll all be over." Dee Dee wiped a tear, "Don't Joey, make a good life for yourself. Keep in touch. You're my little brother, you're all the family I have now. Call me, okay? Take care." She waved sadly as her brother walked away slumped over as though he had been beaten.

After everyone vacated the courthouse, Louie the Lip got up and whispered to his sidekick "I thought she was gonna spill the beans that I had blackmailed Joe into murdering Vito, but Angie paid her a visit and told her to clam up, and I didn't have to whack her."

Chapter XXVI

Marco's Discovery And Aftermath

arco Petracca had just come back from his concert tour with the Longine Symphonette orchestra, after a two year stint. He had quit his position there as concert violinist to be with Vivian. Having studied composition and arranging, as well as conducting and the violin, he was trying to get contract jobs to orchestrate scores. He had studied with Vittorio Giannini for a short while, then continued with Nicolas Flagello, a leading, young composer, who had been Vittorio Giannini's star pupil.

Marco unpacked his bags, and settled his belongings in Vivian's apartment. He had called his mother and Mary's reaction was predictable. She made no secret of her dislike of the situation. She stressed that Marco had acted impulsively, with total disregard for his career.

"And," Mary said, "she's a singer, an ego centered singer. How could you throw away all that you have worked for?" Marco was not surprised. Mary had never approved of Vivian.

"Mom, I'm not going to argue with you," Marco said. "I need to chase my dream. You did. As for singers, yes, life centers around their egos. So does mine. If I had a choice of a musical career, I would have preferred to be a singer, but I can't sing, and have you listened to your husband sing lately?" Mary burst out laughing and muttered, "Spare me, Marco." And as they shared a laugh, Mary's mood changed. "I'm glad you didn't bite my head off Marco, Maggie would have."

"Maggie's issues are different...Mom, my greatest joy was practicing and performing. It was enough I thought, but when I met Vivian, my life changed. As Sean put it, something dormant in me woke up. There was another kind of joy. Mom...you of all people should understand."

"Yes I do. Son, if things don't go well, I'm here and so is your room upstairs." Mary feigned an ease she wasn't feeling.

"Thanks, Mom." He hung up and felt a sense of relief that he had been honest with Mary. She always knew anyway, and he didn't disagree with her. In fact the idea of waiting to make money was stressful. He had yet to do the work on the orchestrations of another Broadway musical. It was contractual payment, and for Marco, this was a drastic change from salary to free lance work.

Soon after their cohabitation, and living in such close quarters, with demands made on both careers, irritation corroded the fabric of their love affair. Marco was having second thoughts about continuing his relationship with Vivian. She was most unhappy about small roles and understudy assignments, and was getting moody.

Marco went up to Yonkers on weekends, and worked in his music studio on the second floor, a room which would always be his. Vivian felt insecure when Marco went to his mother's house to work, but he claimed that it was quiet there and he could concentrate better.

Stage one of romance and fantasy was over. Stage two, reality began, and with it, disillusion. Vivian was ready to ask Marco to move out, go live with his mother, and stay out of her life. She wanted him to have a great career so as to be able to help her, but when he quit the orchestra to live with her, Vivian grew disillusioned. He was unemployed.

He, on the other hand, was smitten by her, and having been nurtured to be his own person, suddenly found himself censured because he was. He too moved to the rhythm of the muse of music, and couldn't understand why she was intolerant of the pursuit of his art. In the climate of revelations in stage two, a crossroad was imminent, and it would happen sooner than not.

Marco had gone home, and Mary spent some time with him alone. Sean took care of the baby, freeing Mary to spend time with her son.

"Thank you, Sean," Mary said, "You really meant it, didn't you?" as she recalled the conversation they had had during their honeymoon on new family dynamics.

"Mary, I would have given anything to have had you as a mother."

* * *

Mary and Marco went out to lunch in Yonkers, and there they talked. He told Mary that his relationship with Vivian was strained, and he had no idea why. Mary laughed and said, "It's a man-woman thing, son, men never know what a woman is thinking, they never have a clue. Ask her why she's upset with you. Could it be that you walked away from your career to be with her, and now you're unemployed?"

Marco suspected what his mother had articulated. He still admired and loved Vivian. "You know what I suspect," he said, "and it's hurting me so much. I've fallen from her pedestal and you're right, mom, I'm sure that's what it is."

Mary was saddened to see her son falter in his career because he had fallen in love. What would he live on? Love? Ludicrous! Based on his awareness of the sinking sands of their relationship, he decided to talk to Vivian about a separation, and go to her place for his personal effects.

On Monday morning, Marco and Sean left the house, and went to the city together.

"You're a great guy," Marco said, "you've made a hell of an impact on my mother. She's blossomed. And you don't interfere in our lives, and hey, I love ya for that."

"Thanks for the accolades, Marco."

As the train got crowded, and they got into the center of the city, Sean and Marco got up and found a strap to hang on to near the exit doors. Sean's stop was next and Sean gave Marco a pep talk.

"Twice I thought your mother and I wouldn't make it," Sean said, "but we're married now, and I wouldn't have bet a plugged nickel on that last year. Don't project. A breakup is only that. Keep positive, and hey, you never know." Sean smiled and patted Marco on the back..

"Thanks for that," Marco said as he gave Sean a hug on the train with all of the New York strap hangers staring at them.

People who traveled to work in such close proximity preserved their anonymity by avoiding looking at each other, by having something to read in front of them. This morning it was different. Two men huggin on a train? Suspect, extremely suspect, they collectively thought by their questioning stares.

Marco laughed. "People are looking at us wondering what the hell's going on." Sean retorted, "Tell them we're Italian." Marco laughed. The train stopped, and Sean ran out, yelling, "*Ciao figlio mio.*" Marco laughed aloud, "*Ciao Papa,*" he responded, and everyone looked away, except one disbelieving passenger who said, "The guy's Irish; who the hell are they kidding?" Marco said "The guy's my stepfather," the man's expression looked as though a light went on in his head and gave an enlightened sigh, "Ahhhhh."

* * *

Marco's mood was lighter as he got off the train. He had a key to Vivian's apartment and walked in, surprised that she wasn't home. Theater hours were late, and most actors or singers slept until noon. Marco wrote her a note immediately telling her that he would call her. He explained that he was taking his personal belongings home. He packed his things in the duffel bag Sean had lent him, and went through his drawers in Vivian's tiny apartment.

Marco opened the wrong drawer, and was about to shut it, when he saw a beautiful publicity shot of Vivian on top of a photo album. She had a far away compelling look in her eyes. He loved her so, and couldn't bear how polarized they had grown.

But Sean's encouraging message on the train had given him hope. A separation often heals a fractured relationship. He took the album out of her drawer. It seemed to be worn and old.

Marco sat in the living room chair with the tall reading lamp turned on to his right and opened the photographic album. In it there were snapshots of Vivian as a child. He felt as though he was snooping, but he hadn't seen this book in Vivian's apartment before. She must have picked it up at her mother's house in the village. Marco looked through the album, and saw photographs of Vivian in a carriage, with her mother pushing the carriage.

Scenes of beach outings followed, probably a vacation in the borough of Staten Island. Marco smiled. One was a photograph of Vivian pouring a bucket of water inside a hole. She must have been 3 years old. Blonde curly hair framed her beautiful face.

The next photo was of her father holding her in his arms. Marco was surprised that the tall, robust man holding Vivian wasn't blonde as he had supposed, but dark haired, like his own father. The man wore a baseball hat and dark glasses. Marco lifted the album closer to the lamp. He stared at the picture of her father; an imposing figure, obviously handsome, even though the features were shadowed by the baseball hat.

As he went through a few more pages, he smiled because most of the photographs were exclusively of Vivian, an only child. Obviously, her mother was behind the camera. After ten pages of Vivian at the beach, Vivian in the water, Vivian eating and sleeping, Marco shut the book and brought it back to her bedroom on the night table. The drawer was jammed, and Marco tugged it and dropped the album to the floor. A picture of a man fell out of the book. Marco bent down to pick it up.

"Oh my God!" he cried out, "it's my father." He felt the blood drain out of him as he began to absorb the full meaning of this discovery. He could hardly focus, and he put the picture back into the album, finished getting his belongings together, and walked out very shaken.

Marco left the neighborhood. He called Sean at the *Tribune.* Sean had stepped away from his desk, and the voice on the other end asked if there was a message. Marco said he'd call back later.

Marco called Maggie. She wasn't home. He called Tess, she wasn't home and suddenly he felt the heat of panic overwhelm him. What was he to do? He didn't want to tell this to his mother, not on the phone. It would be such a shock to her. How justified Mary would be, he thought, having intuitively disliked Vivian from the moment they met.

Marco went to Luigi's where Sean hung out, and sat there for two hours, sipping soup, drinking soda and hoping his misery wasn't that conspicuous. He looked handsome in his turtle neck black shirt, and his sports clothes, and was conspicuous only because he looked like an actor, though Luigi conjectured another profession.

At noon, Sean walked in, and Luigi told him that a guy had been waiting for him at the back table.

"This guy looks mysterious, who knows, maybe he's a wise guy." Sean was puzzled. A Mafioso, here? Great, maybe there was a story, he thought.

"Luigi, order my beer and hamburger, well done. Did he say who he is?" Sean asked. Luigi groaned.

415

"Sure he did," Luigi laughed, "the guy told me he was your son, but I'm sure it's a fuckin' cover up. He's gotta be one o' those." Louie pushed his nose on the side, in a gesture which meant, Mafioso.

Sean walked to the back of the restaurant and was surprised. It was Marco! He sat down at the table. Marco looked like hell. He told Sean about his discovery.

"Sean, I've been shacking up with my half sister! I'm sick. I can't get over it, I called you at the paper first, then Maggie, she wasn't home, then Tess, she wasn't home. Mom had a sixth sense about Viv. You know, Sean, Mom used to tell us that she had an eye in the back of her head, and now I know it's true."

Sean suggested that Marco take deep breaths. He'd call the newspaper and take a half day off. Marco didn't want him to do that, but Sean said, "I've earned it...okay? There's nothing urgent pending for me. We're gonna talk, but not here. First eat something." Sean laughed. "Damn Marco, I sound like your mother." Marco smiled and told Sean about the guy who commented on the train that morning, and Sean enjoyed hearing about the passenger's reaction.

* * *

The shock waves about Marco's discovery were powerful for the whole family. The girls were devastated. Mary was numb, and contracted a fever because of the shock. As the ripple effects of this news touched each member of the family the week after Marco discovered it, the worst was yet to come.

* * *

After Vivian read Marco's note, she wept hysterically. She realized that she had been denigrating him for weeks. She was pregnant. Why would he ever marry her now, after she had treated him so horribly? Why indeed, when he had quit his job at the symphonette?

Vivian called her mother, Martha Pederson, who had taken back her maiden name, and told her about her predicament. Martha went into a tirade of anger, and Vivian cried. Martha told her daughter to take a cab and come home and Vivian did that immediately. She was desperate.

Martha got a hold of her emotions, and when Vivian collapsed into her mother's arms, crying that her life was over, her career was ended, and terrified of an abortion, Martha calmed her with a plan.

"Call up lover boy and get him to come to your place, and tell him about the baby. See what he says. He's gotta marry you." Martha said with a conviction, she was not feeling. Vivian confessed that she had whittled away at Marco's fragile ego because he had no job.

"I demoralized him, mom, he'll never come back," Vivian said dejectedly. But, her mother sounded hopeful. Vivian had to let him know. He'd forgive her, and marry her, especially after she'd tell him about the baby.

"Grovel if you have to, Vivian. Too much is at stake here."

"Oh God, how do I do this? Mom, you call him." Vivian gave her mother the phone number, and Marco Petracca's name, a name Martha knew. Martha was shaken at the revelation of Marco's last name. She asked her daughter what his mother's name was, after all Petracca was a common Italian name. Vivian said, "Mary Petracca." Martha screamed, "Vivian, your father was also his father, Marco's your brother!" Vivian passed out.

Martha called Mary for a meeting. They met at Martha's house, Mary, Marco, Martha and Vivian. Both mothers wanted it to be resolved by termination of Marco and Vivian's relationship. Marriage was out of the question

Subsequently, it was decided that Vivian would have the baby, and that it would be given up for adoption. Marco and Vivian must never see each other again. Incest of this sort could only produce abberated human beings.

Vivian did have her baby. It was a boy, and after she saw the magnificent normal, healthy child she had given birth to, she did not want to give him up, but her mother insisted upon it. Only Marco knew about his son's birth. Vivian spiraled into the quicksand of post partem depression.

Two months after the birth of her son, Vivian committed suicide in a small apartment on Canal Street. Justin Deeks was in a shack on the telephone with his informant, when he got this scoop and wrote the article.

Marco was never the same after Vivian took her life. He had received a triple blow, the death of the woman he loved, the loss of a baby boy he would never know, and the total disintegration of the love and admiration he had once had for his father.

In time, Marco's career took off as an arranger of musical scores.

Hollywood beckoned, and Marco's "stupid job" of orchestrating, and conducting movie musicals, evolved into a prominent career at Warner Brothers Studio. Eventually he wrote original scores for dance numbers.

In the aftermath of this tragedy, Sean Quinn grew in stature in the eyes of his step-children. On Father's Day, Tess presented Sean with a plaque for his new paneled F.D.R. library/office. It read: SEAN QUINN, SUPER DAD. Sean was deeply moved by her gift, which was precipitated by her admiration for his new role as father of Grace.

Maggie thought the plaque idea was wonderful, and in her slick caustic attitude, she had one made and mailed to him at the Tribune. It was a wooden piece with a brass inscription of: sean quinn, super Dick. She didn't have a return address on it, but Sean knew.

He laughed so hard when he opened it that he fell back in his chair. He called her up.

"Hey Maggie, thanks for the compliment." Maggie feigned innocence.

"I have no idea what you're talking about." After a moment she said

"Okay, I couldn't resist. Enjoy while you can, it doesn't last forever!"

He groaned as he heard her caustic comment. "Thanks Maggie." He hung up. "Damn!" he muttered: "Some things never change."

He put the plaque back in the box it had come in, went to the men's room, and flung it in the bathroom's waste bin, snarling, "Damn you!"

Chapter XXVII

Korean War Ends 7/27/53

Finally the war that nobody won was over. Objectives: Back to zero. Price of human lives: a million Korean civilians; five hundred thousand North Korean troops; fifty eight thousand South Koreans; fifty four thousand American soldiers; returning to the exact political division of North and South Korea before the war. A number of attempts at ending the war were aborted because of political posturing. However, the death of Josef Stalin eased the tension between the United States and Russia. On July 27, 1953, a cease-fire was signed.

Sean called Mary from the city and told her the good news. "Thank God, Sean. I won't rest until I find out what happened to Philip." He agreed. "I'll do what I can, Mary."

In August as the American theater of operations worked on the exodus of remaining troops to the homeland, Philip Petracca came to the base at Panmunjon with his South Korean wife. She was an English speaking nurse who had saved his life. Captain Hennessey asked him where the hell had he been hiding out all this time?

"My men and I were wounded, left for dead, and a group of people rescued us, and carried us off to the hills where they gave us medical attention." Hennessey looked at the Asian girl with disapproval, and Sean said, "This woman is my wife, sir!" Inchon bowed her head.

Captain Hennessey said he'd get them out as soon as possible, and asked Philip to come to his office.

"Young man, I don't know if you're lying, or if you abandoned your troops, or what the hell you did. But you didn't have to marry her."

Philip snapped, "She's my wife, sir!"

"So she is, buddy, so she is."

The captain dismissed Philip, and told him to wait outside his office.

Captain Hennessey called the central command office telling him that a young soldier listed: M.I.A. turned up, alive, well, and married. The Commander on the other end laughed. "Well, I'll be dipped in shit. New strategy for not getting killed: Marry the enemy! Tell the young officer I'm impressed."

Hennessey hung up laughing. Well at least there was some levity in a war. He rejoined Philip and his wife.

"Okay, you got proof of your marriage?" Philip took out his marriage certificate, and handed it to Hennessey.

"We'll do what we can."

Philip thanked him and asked if he could place a call to his mother, a widow who probably thought he was dead. Hennessey stifled a laugh, he couldn't believe the balls on this young officer, but, what the hell, why not? He had given him the best laugh he'd had in months.

The call got through. It was one o'clock in the morning in Yonkers. The phone rang, and Sean picked it up concerned that such a late call might mean a family emergency with Mary's family. The call was a stunning one.

"Sir? Captain Hennessey from Korea calling. There's an M.I.A. Philip Petracca wishing to speak to his mother. Do I have the right number?" Sean shook Mary. "Yes sir. I'll get her." Mary was startled by the phone call, "Who is it?" she asked. Sean smiled, "A call from Korea, Mary."

Mary jumped up, grabbed the phone, and held her hand to her chest to calm her rapid heart beat.

"Mom, it's me Philip." She could hardly find her voice.

"Fighiu mio, you're alive."

"I'm coming home. Are you okay?" he shouted.

425

"Yes Philip. When?" It was difficult to understand him, and Sean sat Mary on his lap on the side of the bed trying to steady her shaking body.

Because the transmission of the voice was delayed, and an echo effect followed their conversation, clear communication was not possible, and Hennessey signaled that there were transmitting problems.

"I'll call you from California," Philip bellowed into the phone,

"Wait! Philip, Wait! how are you?" Mary asked and she wondered if he had been wounded, but Philip had to end the call. "Gotta go, Mom, I love you."

Mary collapsed in Sean's arms, with a spectrum of emotions she could not hold, and Sean held her for a while, until she felt better.

"I wanted to know if he had been hurt. It was difficult to hear him, because I was almost talking at the same time. It was weird, Sean."

Sean spoke about changes in Philip which she would not see right away. War made a deep and lasting impact on returning soldiers, and sometimes they never came back to the feelings they had had before the war. Sean talked to his wife about those things, and Mary listened intently, and realized that Sean and Philip had been to the brink of hell. Her two biggest concerns were his mental health and his physical health. However, given the transmitting problems, it was impossible to know.

The next morning Mary got up early to make Sean a big breakfast. Usually Sean got up at dawn so that he could begin his day with a hearty meal which sometimes he cooked for himself, or left early and ate out.

They talked more about Philip, and then Sean said that dynamics among them would also change.

"Mary, he's going to be in shock when he finds out that you're married to me, and that we have a daughter. I'm ready to handle that, are you?" Mary was pensive.

"Yes, *amure,* I told him that 'we' were waiting for him, but he never questioned it."

Sean laughed. "Mary, before I came into your life, you had a lot of people in that 'we' word, two daughters and a son, so that's who he thinks the 'we' is."

Mary sliced up an orange and put it in a circular fashion on his plate with a grape in the middle. She was thinking about the changes her household would have, but she didn't want Sean to be uncomfortable with it.

"Will you be alright with it, Sean? He might resent you, he might give you grief." Sean held Mary by the arm, and pulled her on to his lap.

"Mary, I'm in for the long haul. Sweetheart, I didn't sell newspapers, I wrote them. By the way, I won't be going to Luigi's today. He'll have to do with one less day of aggravation from me. Damn! That'll make him happy."

"Okay. Where are you going for lunch?" she asked.

"To see the editor in chief for a well earned thank you."

Mary looked puzzled. "Patrick?" she asked.

"No, God. I'll be at St. Agnes church on 43rd street."

"Sean, you're an angel." Mary glowed with joy.

"Mary go back to bed. Battista is giving me a lift to the station." Battista was at the door. Sean kissed Mary and ran out.

* * *

Philip had to negotiate for Inchon to travel with him. If she hadn't been pregnant, she would have come three or four months later. Philip persisted in his request, and Captain Hennessey did whatever he could to expedite their trip to California.

Captain Hennessey saw Philip in the canteen and gave him his orders to ship state side, and with his wife.

"I'm indebted to you, Sir!" Philip was astounded at the expediency of his request. They saluted each other, and Hennessey felt nostalgic at seeing young Philip Petracca go. His own son would have been about his age at this time. He wondered where his son, Erin would be now. His wife had kidnapped him ten years ago. Feisty, fast, sharp and handsome, just like Lieutenant Petracca.

The day the transport plane took off, Hennessey met the Petraccas and wished them well. He watched them take off and stood there until the plane was swallowed up in the clouds.

When the plane landed in San Francisco, Philip called Marco at Warner Brothers studio. Marco had a limousine service pick them up and take them to the Warner Brothers lot. Marco would take a short leave of two days to spend time with Philip and his wife.

It was a joyful reunion. Philip was impressed with his brother's rise to such musical and influential heights. The beautiful serene Inchon was in awe. When Marco met his brother, he had not expected him to come home with a wife. That was a stunning piece of news.

After the tour of Marco's working sound studio, the limousine took them to Marco's house, a small house in Hollywood. Inchon took a shower, then remained in her room while Philip and Marco went swimming in his pool.

Marco had asked his mother just how much did she want to surprise Philip with her marriage and new baby? She agreed that Marco should tell him what he knew so that he wouldn't get off the plane and explode over his mother's new marriage to Sean Quinn. Marco realized that all the letters with the news about Grace's birth had never reached Philip. So, Mary's status in Philip's mind was exactly as he had left her.

The news was not well received, predictably, however when Marco explained the extenuating circumstances of Mary's and Sean's marriage, Philip's mindset changed. Marco spoke glowingly about Sean, and Philip could hardly believe what he was hearing. He inquired about Maggie and Tess, and Marco filled him on news about their sisters.

Marco took them to the Napa Sonoma wine valley, and Inchon was enthralled with her first sights of the grandiose country of America. After their brief vacation together, Inchon and Philip told Marco that he was going to be an uncle in six months. Marco was delighted, and he took them out to the best nightclub in Hollywood where all the movie stars fraternize. For Inchon the stop-over at Marco's was like a fairy tale.

Philip called his mother to tell her that he was bringing home a wife. He too felt that she wouldn't relish a shock about his marriage either.

"Are you going with any one?" Philip asked Marco in a private moment.

"Yep, singers, I'm always attracted to the singing stars. But, I'm small potatoes to them, so it's a date here and a date there." Philip grimaced with disapproval.

"Marco, look elsewhere for a life's companion. Singers are too involved in themselves." And so with these admonitions in place, the brothers parted sadly, because they had jammed close to two years of absence into two days. Philip would not speak of the war, and Marco expected that. Philip reminisced about his father, and Marco listened and said nothing, which seemed strange to Philip.

Finally it was time to go home, and Philip voiced concern to his brother about making a life for himself and his wife. School was out, and he had to go to work to support his family. Marco assured him that their mother had indeed bought a huge home, and that she would probably offer them the upper part of the house. With that prospect in mind, Philip's anxiety lessened. The brothers parted and promised that Philip and Inchon must come to visit at least once a year, which thrilled Inchon. She thought California was America.

The Pan American plane landed at Idlewild airport, and Sean and Mary met Philip. The reunion was passionate, and wonderful to all who saw the mother and son embrace and sob in each other's arms. Some whistled, some applauded and many others cried at the moving scene in the airport.

When they got home, Maggie and Tess waited with the latest edition in the home, Grace Quinn, Philip's two year old sister. Once more the reunion between sisters and brother was wonderful. Giovanna, Schlomo and Rafaele were there making a wonderful culinary feast for the returning hero and his wife. Inchon was enthralled with Mary. Philip looked just like her, with enormous black eyes, and a petulant mouth. She seemed so young.

Mary gave them a tour of the house and told Philip (as Marco had predicted) that he and his wife could live upstairs for as long as they wished. Philip told this to Inchon who clapped her hands and graciously accepted. She thanked Mary. Immediately this beautiful oriental girl bonded with everyone, especially her mother in law.

Weeks went by, and Philip asked his mother to speak to him about the missing years of his absence from home. He asked that Mary not leave anything out, even the awful stuff.

Three months after he got home, Mary saw how he started relaxing and feeling at ease in the house. She took him out to lunch one day while Inchon took care of Grace. At lunch she told him the story of Vivian and Marco. Philip paled in disbelief. This was a living nightmare. No wonder Marco wouldn't speak of it.

"You mean incest, Mom, don't you?"

"Yes, but they didn't know it. If that wasn't bad enough, she gave the baby up for adoption and took her own life. She suffered from post partum depression."

Philip learned how difficult Mary's life had been. He asked her why she hadn't informed Sean about the baby.

"I couldn't. Too many issues, Philip."

But they're together now, Philip thought, and his mother had blossomed. Maybe, just maybe, Sean and his mom had found a place of the communion of spirits, certainly it was so obvious. Philip was amused thinking that if his father could only

433

see his mother now, his *ngiuria* for his mother would be, "Mary, the general."

Mary filled Philip in on the gaps of family history, sparing no details about her investigation of the cellar to their house. Philip laughed at his mother's courage, was disgusted about the findings in the cellar, and realized that his father had been somehow involved in this resulting in his own murder by bucking the mob.

When she got through with an hour and a half of family events of the past, Philip smacked himself on the head in disbelief.

"Mom, I swear to you, you saw more action than I did in Korea. I can't get over it." Philip wiped his brow. "My father was a good man, but Marco won't even mention him. If the two of you had been united, none of this would have happened. You told me he confided in you in the early years, and you knew everything about him. I shudder to think of the degree of hate which existed between you, to have destroyed his life and yours too."

"Son, how wise we all are in hindsight. If I had to do it over again, I could have changed things, but my feelings were so destroyed when he left on weekends. I knew that he had to have something on the side. I could only survive that degree of hurt by shutting down, and I did. I was, to put it mildly, a walking emotional zombie."

After this tale, Philip asked his mother what she thought if he would name his son Vito. "Why not, Philip? Your father didn't set out to destroy his family, it's just that a twist of fate brought Marco and Vivian together. I agree with you that Marco can't forgive his father to this day and it worries me."

Mary and Philip grew very close due to the shared confidences. The dynamic had changed among them, and it was good, it was wholesome, and nurturing. Inchon adored her husband and his family, and Mary wished they would never move out.

* * *

Sean solicited Philip's help to give his point of view as M.I.A., for Sean's saga on the Korean war.

Philip talked openly about his experiences which served several purposes: one as a catharsis for Philip to be able to speak about the war; secondly Sean and Philip bonded in their mutuality, which changed Philip's opinion of Sean from 'son of a bitch' to 'a great guy.'

As Sean and Philip worked together in Sean's library several nights a week discussing everything about Korea, Mary hired Battista to convert the upstairs bedrooms into an apartment with a kitchen for the newlyweds. Battista tried to expedite this job as quickly as possible giving it priority over his other reconstruction contracts. He and his wife had adopted Sean, Mary and their family into their hearts.

In two months, the apartment was ready, and Inchon and Philip began their married life on the top of a high hill overlooking the Hudson River Valley.

Life for the young couple was almost perfect. Philip got a job almost immediately in a department store through Sean's connections in the city.

Philip became a buyer of women's suits at Saks Fifth Avenue. He had such a fine eye for fashion that Mary asked him to go back to school, but this was not a viable option for Philip. Instead, he studied pattern making and design with private professional people. He preferred learning his craft as it was taught during the middle ages- as an apprentice to an artisan. Within a year, Philip found himself a position in a fine women's suits division in the garment district, working for David Crystal.

Fired with creativity, Philip was one of the first to transform airline stewardesses flight outfits from the mundane to the fashionable.

Inchon gave birth to young Vito Petracca on January 31st, 1954. Father Peter Sullivan baptized the beautiful baby boy, and Maggie and Marco were the godparents. Philip affectionately called his son: The New Patriarch.

Chapter XXVIII

The Sins Of The Father

In 1955, urban renewal received federal funds to build up the City of New York in tall buildings called projects. After the city paid a minimal price for the tenement buildings, they were knocked down. In East Harlem during excavation of the buildings' foundations, a gruesome discovery was made. In the Sicilian neighborhood of 107th street, almost every building had been used to bury victims of murder underneath the cellar floor. It made the news.

Sean read the story, and he brought the Daily News home to Mary. She was mortified.

"It never ends, does it?" she commented.

"No, it doesn't Mary, but not only under your building but under quite a few of them according to this article. Were all the landlords under the thumb of the mob? How the hell did Vito get involved?"

"He couldn't have been. He was so perturbed during those last two months of his life, and I thought it was about me. Instead he probably told them they no longer could rent the cellar after he found out that they had their own private cemetery there, and they had him murdered."

Mary expressed her shock that the authorities did not investigate nor did they want to. The funeral director told Mary at the time, that he had suspected foul play when he picked up the body, and called the police, who said they'd look into it. Nothing was done about the sudden death of Vito Petracca. He was Sicilian from a block of criminals, so why bother?

Sean said "It's over now," and Mary looked up to him as they finished the dishes and retorted, "Is it Sean?"

"I think he had to play ball with the mob. He was Sicilian, and most of them looked the other way when they witnessed a crime. Your block made the front pages often according to my recollection," Sean said. "My colleague's a crime reporter, and he told me that it was a shooting gallery there for the mob. A lot of kids got killed there. Oh, yeah of course Vito played ball. He had to."

Mary served the demi tasse coffee.

"Sean, you know what *omerta* is."

"It's the Sicilian code of honor, right?" Sean said.

"Yes. I was brought up with it," Mary said.

"I know Mary. It's still a struggle for you," Sean said.

"Haven't I improved?" she asked, and Sean smiled.

"I think so. Sometimes I think you hold back information, as though you're going to be struck dead if you talk."

"You're right," Mary sighed and Sean pulled the dish towel away from her, and placed it on the edge of the sink.

"Let's go to bed, sweetheart." Mary put her arm around his waist and they went into their bedroom. Once they shut the door, they shut out all the distractions of the world and found solace and intimacy in each other's arms.

* * *

Weeks later, Justin called Sean and invited him for lunch at Luigi's. He planned on writing a book on the Petracca murder, and wanted to know if he'd lose Sean's friendship by writing this. Sean told him, "Buddy, this is our profession. Write the book. I'll break it to Mary. Do you need information from her?" Justin drank his beer, looked across the table at his colleague and said, "Damn it! Yes!"

"Justin, let me ask my wife, and if she agrees to meet you, come, stay for the weekend, and good luck with my stepson Philip."

The following weekend, Justin was invited to Yonkers, and Tess came up to baby sit so as to free her mother up for this business meeting. Justin met with Mary, Philip, Maggie and Tess. He told them about his project, and the children said, "Can you prove that our father was not connected to the mob?" Philip in particular was upset as he listened to the outline of his story. How could a Sicilian family, who's driven by secrets, *omerta,* and protection of their family's reputation agree to such an expose'?

"I'll write it, show it to you, and from what I've learned, your father was not involved with the mob. I'd like your permission. The book is about Vito Petracca, and it's also about the history of 107th street. Your father's story will probably cover only one third of the book. I'll show you the first draft, and I want your input. I'm not here to destroy your father's reputation. The man is dead. He can't defend himself. We can."

That last remark did it. Philip's attitude changed. Tess was suspicious, Maggie thrilled from the point of view of having an elite journalist write the story of her father. Mary wished it would all end, and so they agreed.

As promised, the book turned out to be a favorable portrait of Vito Petracca. Philip loved it, Maggie and Tess applauded, and Sean became Justin's best champion. Justin had gone the extra mile to write a narrative of a man who had lost his way, but had his heart in the right place. The book was a best seller, and Justin's expertise at gathering information on crime stories received literary cudos.

Mary refused to read the book, or discuss Vito Petracca any further.

* * *

The Petracca girls took different paths of life. Maggie, the free spirit, the girl who, according to Vito, invaded a man's world of journalism, remained single. She wrote many short stories, and finally hit the big time in a collection of short stories which attracted the attention of the literary world. She wrote in a frenetic style, writing in long narrative separated only by commas. Sometimes a page held only one long sentence. She wrote fiction which was mostly autobiographical.

Tess, on the other hand, pursued her profession of the law. Fascinated by murder mysteries, Tess eventually became a judge in the city of New York.

The prophecy of Madame Rouge in the village materialized almost exactly as she had predicted. During a rape case, a professor of law at Columbia came into the courtroom because of the lack of evidence in this highly publicized case. He had not forgotten Tess Petracca, bright, young and beautiful, she had made an indelible impression on him. He was not surprised that she had achieved so much in her career already. She was only a kid. He visited the courtroom where she presided over the case in question.

He sat in the back of the courthouse observing, however, Tess noticed him. She had not forgotten Professor O'Donnell. After the court adjourned, he asked to see her. What had been an ember in a classroom several years ago, now became a glowing flame. Tess blushed when he walked in. At first he addressed her as "your honor," and then, she slipped back into her former role of student. The exchange of points of law were discussed, and he asked her out for dinner.

Four weeks later after seeing her every night, he asked her to marry him. Tess tried to stall for a modicum of reticence to try to be coy. Instead she said "Yes, I'd be honored to, your honor." He laughed at the pun and took out a three karat diamond ring from his pocket. They married in Yonkers in a Catholic church, and the reception was held at her parents' palatial home.

Connor's two children, Ted 22 was best man, and Megan 20 was maid of honor. They moved to the East Side in a penthouse apartment facing the East River. The view from the window made it seem as though they lived on top of the world. From their window, they saw the East River, and a panorama of the Brooklyn Bridge, the Williamsburg Bridge and the Manhattan Bridge, a view they savored only at night as they dined in front of the window watching the lights of the city twinkling like diamonds.

Marco Petracca ran the gamut of his talent at Warner Brothers' studio. He conducted, wrote arrangements of scores for films, and composed original music. He was well liked, and he got a lot of work, including free lance orchestrations which he did for other musical groups. Marco was immersed in his music, because when he wrote he felt safe.

In 1960, Warner Brothers made a film with a brilliant talented child actor. However, the child actor couldn't sing. In the magic of the movie industry, that didn't matter. Marco suggested to the head of the studio that they audition boys of seven to dub the singing voice. Marco chose a child named Luke Crespino.

From the first moment Luke walked into the studio, Marco looked into his blue eyes and felt a chill go through him. When the boy sang, Marco got goose bumps. Something about this child seemed familiar, his mannerisms, his large blue eyes, and his mouth.

The boy had been adopted by Wanda and Christopher Crespino who lived in Pacific Palisades. They invited the 28 year old conductor to their home. As the friendship grew, they told Marco that Luke had been adopted.

Born in a New York hospital seven years earlier, his natural mother had taken her own life shortly after the child's birth. As Marco listened to the circumstances and location of the child's beginnings, he computed the birth date and everything pointed to the fact that Luke was his son.

Luke's large blue eyes were unmistakably Vivian's. When Marco fell in love with her, it was the instant he looked into her eyes. Vivian had to be Luke's mother.

Through the years, as Marco worked with Luke, he noticed other similarities between him and his mother. Before a recording session, Luke pulled nervously at his hair just as Vivian had. Another manifestation of nervousness was Vivian's habit of drumming her right hand fingers against her leg to let off anxiety. Luke did it too. Marco was enthralled that the child was not only normal but handsome and talented.

When Luke was 17, Marco invited the Crespino family to Yonkers for Easter. Unfortunately they couldn't take time off because they were expecting business guests from Israel so they offered to send Luke instead.

Marco called home, told his mother about finding his son. Mary could hardly believe what he was saying. Marco explained, "My son doesn't know that I'm his father. I don't want him to know, ever!"

"Marco, is he beautiful?" Mary's voice quivered.

Marco said, "He's all his mother. He has her quirks too. It's eerie. Momma, please don't fuss over him."

"Marco, don't tell me not to hold him, not to kiss him, I can't do that." She was deeply moved.

"Mom, I'm scared to death. Just bear with me," Marco said.

"*Figlio mio,* how long have you known about this?"

"Ten years. I met him when he was seven. I looked in his eyes, and saw Vivian's eyes staring back at me. I almost passed out." Mary had chills in her body.

"And you waited ten years to tell me? Why Marco?"

"How could I talk about this with you, or with anyone? I have so much guilt, mom." Marco was overwrought.

447

"Son, at the time it was the right decision. Vivian was emotionally ill after the baby. That happens to many women, son. I had a bout with that after Maggie was born. Marco, it was nobody's fault." Marco listened intently hanging on to his mother's words like a life-line to a drowning man. "I need you, Mom," Marco sighed, "I almost forgot that."

Mary was saddened by the sound of her son's quiet desperation. She hoped that he would find someone.

Mary informed Sean about Marco's call.

"Well, I'll be damned!" Sean said. He made no other commentary, and Mary smiled as her sometimes crude husband touched the strings of her heart with every encounter. She adored him, and despite his outrageous language, it was okay with Mary.

* * *

Two days before Easter Sunday, Marco and Luke flew in to Idlewild airport in Queens. Sean and Mary drove out to pick them up.

The flight was an hour late, and Mary grew anxious. Finally the plane arrived, and passengers got off. Marco hadn't been home in two years. He had grown a beard, and Mary didn't recognize him when he came up to her and put his arms around her. She was startled at first and then laughed.

Marco introduced Luke, who was tall, blonde and blue eyed. Only seventeen years old, he looked at least twenty. He was as tall as Marco, six feet tall. Mary couldn't get her eyes off him. Sean thought of something Mary had said a long time ago, and snickered. Mary asked him what was so funny, and he wouldn't tell her. It would be insensitive of him to do so. Sean recalled the time they met Vivian at the Willard and Mary had muttered: mayonnaise, a *ngiuria* which was better left unsaid.

When they arrived in Yonkers, Grace and Luke met. Sparks flew between them. They bonded immediately as Grace asked Luke about Hollywood. She wanted to be an actress and was enthralled with Luke who looked older than his seventeen years.

Grace, who was nineteen, whispered to Mary, "Momma, he's gorgeous, I think I'm in love." Mary's eyebrow went up, much as the back of a nervous cat curls, and she said to Grace, "Careful, stay away from movie stars." Grace laughed. "Why? I'm going to be one too," she said flippantly. Philip heard it, and he pulled his mother aside and whispered something in her ear and she answered that she'd take care of it later. The rest of the family and the guests came, and Mary and Sean served dinner. Inchon, Tess and Maggie were assigned cleaning up.

Mary made the traditional Easter lamb for the afternoon pranzo, and with it she made other meats and fish for Schlomo. The side dishes were potatoes, peas, and cold salads. After her marriage to Sean, Mary's enormous meals of the past had dwindled down to one or two courses.

Luke was asked to say grace. Mary looked at her grandson adoringly and was proud of him. He had fine table manners, but it bothered her to see that he was obviously smitten by her beautiful nineteen year old daughter, Grace. This gave her a turn in her stomach. Sean gave Mary knowing glances, and he too was aware of the mutual attraction between Grace and Luke.

Conversation was lively as Connor asked about Hollywood. Young sixteen year old Vito Petracca sat with the younger people at the lower end of the table. He was elegant, and refined with oriental mannerisms of his mother's culture, and Mary adored him. They still lived upstairs in the quarters which were meant to be temporary sixteen years earlier, a living situation which surprisingly pleased the four of them.

Three hours later, dinner was over, and the girls cleared the table and put out the fresh fruit, jello molds, and roasted nuts.

Megan helped, and the young ones retired to the parlor. Rafaelo and Vito played checkers, and Grace and Luke played chess. As they played, their concentration was interrupted by looks of admiration between them.

As Mary made a pot of tea for Schlomo and her son in law Connor, Tess made the demi tasse coffee, and Maggie put up a pot of brown coffee. Giovanna brought fried cenci alla fiorentina, biscotti with almonds, sesame seed cookies, and an Italian ricotta cake. Tess and Connor brought wine and liquores, and Maggie brought cheeses from the city, and signed copies of her book of short stories which had made the *New York Times* best seller list.

As Marco peeled his orange and cracked the roasted nuts, Philip nudged him and said "Let's go for a walk." Marco got up.

"We'll be back, Momma," Marco said, and the two brothers left.

It was a brisk, but sunny day and they walked quickly. Marco's heart was pounding out of his chest. He knew what this was about.

"Marco," Philip said curtly, "what's that saying we learned in catechism at St. Ann's church in Harlem? Remember it?"

"Spit it out, Philip!" Marco said impatiently.

"Wait a minute, I got it," Philip said, "The sins of the father are visited on his children and his children's children. Isn't that correct, Marco?" Philip feigned a gentle innocence, and Marco started to sweat.

"What am I on trial here?" Marco snapped.

"Have you lost your mind? Don't you see what's going on between Grace and Luke?" Philip was adamant.

"We leave for California tomorrow. That's three thousand miles away. I won't upset my son's life." Marco was getting angrier by the minute as Philip continued to barrage him with insults and accusations.

"Marco you're no better than Poppa, can't you learn from his mistakes?" At the mention of their father, Marco blew up shouting, "Stop it! Stop it!" and hauled off and socked Philip on the nose sending him sprawling to the ground bleeding.

Philip walked in with a handkerchief covering his bleeding nose. Inchon took Philip to the bathroom to help him. Mary grabbed her coat, and ran out to find her son Marco. Sean followed her.

Half hour later, they returned with Marco. His face was red, his eyes puffy. Philip came out of the bathroom holding a cold compress against his nose. He motioned to Marco to come inside to Sean's library. Mary followed them, but Sean intercepted Mary.

"Don't Mary, they're big boys." Mary stood in the hallway worried as she stood behind the door of the library. Sean remained with his wife.

Marco said, "Philip, at the mention of poppa, I went nuts."

"Mom said it to me, and I'll repeat it. Poppa was a good man. He loved us and mom. He never set out to hurt any of us. Marco, what career would you have had if it wasn't for him? The best violin, the best teachers, live concerts in New York every Friday. Your *vendetta* will kill you, not Poppa. He's already dead. So just give it up."

"I know," Marco said, "but he screwed up my life, Philip. You and Mom found your soul-mates, I won't until I give it up, you're right. What do you suggest I do, now?" Marco asked.

"Talk to your son. He's old enough now to know, just get ready for a lot of anger just like you have for Poppa. Brace yourself," Philip warned, "Send my son in to me." Marco said. He was drained of energy and his clothes were soaking wet with perspiration.

Philip called Luke to the library. They shut the door and were there for close to an hour. Meanwhile Philip came into the hallway, held his mother's shoulders and looking at her eyes, said, "Momma, tell Grace now!"

Mary asked Grace to come with her to her bedroom. As Mary related the family secret of Vito's double life, Grace's eyes opened wider.

"Then Luke is my nephew." She exclaimed.

"Yes Grace, and my grandson. Right now your brother is telling him the family secret in Dad's library."

"Mom," Grace commented after she was finished, "I'm glad you told me. I fell in love with Luke. I'm heartbroken." Mary tried to console her daughter who's body was shaking with shock.

Luke and Grace returned to the dining room. Luke was pale, Grace extremely quiet. In her best acting persona, Grace walked in with a big smile, as she extended her hand to Luke, he took it.

"How would you like to be beaten at chess by your aunt?" Luke stared..

"Sure, it's okay, it's all in the family, isn't it?" he quipped.

As Philip sipped his espresso coffee he said, "Marco, I'm proud of you."

The day after Easter, Sean and Mary took Marco and Luke to the airport. Grace refused to come. Luke asked if they could say good bye in private. The family stepped outside and waited.

Luke swept Grace into his arms nuzzled his face to her neck, and kissed her lips. "Forgive me Grace, I wish the script could've been different."

"Oh Luke," she cried, "me too."

Sean honked the horn.

"Go, Luke. We'll see each other again." She smiled weakly as he stood by the door.

"I know, but not the way I wanted," he answered.

"Nor I Luke," Grace said as he ran out of the house into the car.

As Sean drove away, Marco said, "It'll pass, Luke, give it time."

Luke asked, "Did it pass for you, Marco?" and Marco answered, "No. I learned to live with it." Luke looked out the window, and whispered to himself, "Then I shall too."

It was quiet in the car, and as they approached the airport, Luke asked a question.

"Do you mind if I don't call you dad?" Luke asked softly.

"No, I don't. All I ask is that you remain in my life. Can you handle that?" Marco said and swallowed hard; he couldn't look at his son.

"Sure why not? You've given me my career. I love your family, all of them, and don't be concerned about Grace. I know my place, but I won't lie and say that I wish it had been different." Luke glanced at his father, and Marco's head was bowed.

Sean and Mary heard the conversation between Marco and Luke, and communicated by a look or a squeezed hand. They were pleased to hear how this exquisite young man had handled a most difficult situation, with honor and charisma.

After they left Marco and Luke in an emotional departure, Sean and Mary drove back home. For a long while Mary was quiet. Sean couldn't tolerate the pregnant silence any more and said, "Mary, your thoughts are driving me crazy. What in hell are you thinking?" Mary laughed, adoring her husband's expressions.

"I think they'll find a way to be together," Mary said.

"I hope not," Sean answered.

"What are we doing tonight?" Sean asked.

"Philip, Maggie and Inchon are taking the kids to the movies. I'd just as soon collapse in bed and go to sleep early."

"Good, we'll be alone. Mary, how would you like to go back to Corleone?" Sean asked.

"Yes," Mary said, as Sean laughed.

"Wow, that was a quick answer. I have some brochures in my briefcase."

Mary brought Sean's hand to her mouth and kissed it.

"Have I ever told you that you are my prince, *tesoro?*"

"Yeah, but I don't mind hearing it again." Mary laughed, and then cuddled up closer to Sean on the long ride back home.

THE END

Printed in the United States
31115LVS00002B/1-30